What if Derrida was wrong about Saussure?

RUSSELL DAYLIGHT

EDINBURGH UNIVERSITY PRESS

© Russell Daylight, 2011, 2012

First published in hardback by Edinburgh University Press 2011

Edinburgh University Press Ltd
22 George Square, Edinburgh EH8 9LF

www.euppublishing.com

Typeset in 10/12 Times New Roman
by Servis Filmsetting Ltd, Stockport, Cheshire,
and printed and bound in Great Britain by
CPI Antony Rowe, Chippenham and Eastbourne

A CIP record for this book is available from the British Library

ISBN 978 0 7486 4197 0 (hardback)
ISBN 978 0 7486 4940 2 (paperback)

The right of Russell Daylight
to be identified as author of this work
has been asserted in accordance with
the Copyright, Designs and Patents Act 1988.

Grateful acknowledgement is made for permission to reproduce material previously
published elsewhere. Every effort has been made to trace the copyright holders, but
if any have been inadvertently overlooked, the publisher will be pleased to make the
necessary arrangements at the first opportunity.

What if Derrida was wrong about Saussure?

'Daylight patiently combs through the fine silk weave on which Derrida has painted his broad brushstrokes. He leads us step by step through each of Derrida's readings of Saussure, then sometimes back again through some of the same texts as we proceed to the next set of Derridean claims ... Daylight's microscopic analysis is matched with a telescopic gaze over what stands or falls on whether Derrida was right about Saussure across a broad range of intellectual fields. His study contributes at least as much to our understanding of the philosopher-historian as of the philologist-grammarian, and marks a sea change in the reception of both. That is no mean feat. To have achieved it with such clarity of exposition, elegance of expression and depth of insight makes this book a rare and indispensable tour de force.'

John Joseph, University of Edinburgh, in the *Times Higher Education*

Contents

Acknowledgements

The author and publisher would like to thank the following, who have kindly given permission for the use of copyright material: Routledge, for the extracts from *Writing and Difference*, translated by Alan Bass (1978), pp. xx, 157, 162, 166, 200, 202, 203, 209, 210, 213, 278, 279, 280, 281, 284, 292; Continuum, for the extracts from *Positions*, translated by Alan Bass (1981), by kind permission of Continuum International Publishing Group; Northwestern University Press, for the extracts from *Speech and Phenomena and Other Essays on Husserl's Theory of Signs*, translated by David B. Allison (1979), pp. xiv, xxxiv, xxxviii, 5, 15, 24, 27, 31, 42, 43, 45, 46, 47, 50, 51, 52, 61, 76, 77, 78, 80, 82, 84, 99, 130, 133; The Johns Hopkins University Press, for extracts from *Of Grammatology*, translated by Gayatri Chakravorty Spivak (1997), pp. xxxix, 4, 7, 10, 11–12, 12–13, 13–14, 17, 18, 19, 20, 33, 34, 35, 38, 40, 41, 45, 47, 49, 50, 52–3, 57, 60, 62, 72, 73, 324, 329 © 1997 The Johns Hopkins University Press, and *Glyph* I. translated by Samuel Weber and Henry Sussman (1977), pp. 172–97 © 1977 The Johns Hopkins University Press; and Duckworth, for the extracts from the *Course in General Linguistics*, translated by Roy Harris (1983), by permission of Gerald Duckworth & Co. Ltd.

This work would not have been possible without the assistance and encouragement of Professor Jonathan Culler (Cornell) and Dr John O'Carroll (Charles Sturt). My warmest thanks also to Vicki Donald, Esmé Watson, Eliza Wright, Rebecca MacKenzie and all at Edinburgh University Press.

The labour of the last eight years, and any fruit it may bear, are dedicated to my wife, Tegan, and our children, Alice and Patrick.

Abbreviations and Textual Notes

For all of Derrida's works, I have cited individual essays where they appear in translated collections, such as 'Freud and the Scene of Writing' in *Writing and Difference*, and 'Semiology and Grammatology' in *Positions*. I have cited complete books only when they were originally published as a single volume, such as *Speech and Phenomena* and *Of Grammatology*. Citations of the essay 'Différance' are denoted 'Diff' for the Bass translation which appears in *Margins of Philosophy* and 'Diff (A)' for the Allison translation which appears in *Speech and Phenomena*. The Allison translation contains a preamble by Derrida which is not included in the Bass translation.

Aft	'Afterword: towards an ethic of discussion', trans. Samuel Weber and Jeffrey Mehlman. *Limited Inc*.
Diff	'Différance', trans. Alan Bass. *Margins of Philosophy*.
Diff (A)	'Différance', trans. David Allison. *Speech and Phenomena, and Other Essays on Husserl's Theory of Signs*.
F&SW	'Freud and the Scene of Writing', trans. Alan Bass. *Writing and Difference*.
Glas	*Glas*, trans. John P. Leavey Jr. and Richard Rand.
GS&P	'"Genesis and Structure" and Phenomenology', trans. Alan Bass. *Writing and Difference*.
Imp	'Implications: interview with Henri Ronse', trans. Alan Bass. *Positions*.
Intro	*Edmund Husserl's Origin of Geometry: An Introduction*, trans. John P. Leavey.
LI	'Limited Inc a b c . . .', trans. Samuel Weber and Jeffrey Mehlman. *Limited Inc*.
OG	*Of Grammatology*, trans. Gayatri Chakravorty Spivak.
S&G	'Semiology and Grammatology: Interview with Julia Kristeva', trans. Alan Bass. *Positions*.
S&P	*Speech and Phenomena*, trans. David Allison.
SEC	'Signature Event Context', trans. Samuel Weber and Jeffrey Mehlman. *Limited Inc*.

SS&P   'Structure, Sign, and Play in the Discourse of the Human
                        Sciences', trans. Alan Bass. *Writing and Difference.*

I am using Harris's translation of the *Cours de linguistique générale* except
where indicated. The citation (*Course*: 21/40) refers to text that appears on
page 21 of Harris's translation and page 40 of the standard Payot edition of
the *Cours*. It is important to note that Harris translates *signifiant* and *signifié*
as 'signal' and 'signification', respectively. One understands Harris's gesture
here as wishing to restore specificity to Saussure's terminology in an increasingly degraded field; however, it does not serve my purpose of making the
languages of Derrida and Saussure engage, and so I have replaced these with
'signifier' and 'signified' in all citations of Harris's translation.

Cahiers   *Cahiers Ferdinand de Saussure.*
Cours   *Cours de linguistique générale.* Ed. Bally and Sechehaye.
Course   *Course in General Linguistics.* Trans. Roy Harris.
Course (B)   *Course in General Linguistics.* Trans. Wade Baskin.

For the same reason, it is important to note that I have made very little
use of recently discovered manuscripts, or of various critical editions of
the *Course*, or attempted to discover which statements in the *Course* can be
attributed to Saussure and which to his students and editors. As Derrida asks:

> Up to what point is Saussure responsible for the *Course* as it was edited
> and published after his death? It is not a new question. Need we specify
> that, here at least, we cannot consider it to be pertinent? Unless my
> project has been fundamentally misunderstood, it should be clear by
> now that, caring very little about Ferdinand de Saussure's very thought
> itself, I have interested myself in a text whose literality has played a
> well-known role since 1915, operating within a system of readings,
> influences, misunderstandings, borrowings, refutations, etc. (*OG*: 329)

Anachronism alone might be sufficient reason to reject the use of manuscripts
published in 2002 against Derrida's 1967 reading of the *Cours*. But methodo-
logically, too, if this investigation attempts to understand Derrida's engagement with 'Saussure', then it follows that it does not concern the intentions
or the very thought of Ferdinand de Saussure; it concerns only the singularly
influential text which was appropriated and transformed by Derrida.

Finally, for works where I have been unable to find an English translation, I have translated the text myself; these are indicated by 'my translation'
appearing after the citation.

Introduction

On 21 October 1966, Jacques Derrida presented 'Structure, Sign, and Play in the Discourse of the Human Sciences' to the *International Colloquium on Critical Languages and the Sciences of Man*, at Johns Hopkins University, Baltimore. According to its organisers, the conference 'sought to explore the impact of contemporary "structuralist" thought on critical methods in humanistic and social studies' (Macksey and Donato 1972a: xv), and was 'the first time in the United States that structuralist thought had been considered as a cross-disciplinary phenomenon' (xvi). The invited speakers were drawn from the fields of 'anthropology, classical studies, comparative literature, linguistics, literary criticism, history, philosophy, psychoanalysis, semiology, and sociology' (xvii); among them were Jacques Lacan, Roland Barthes, Tzvetan Todorov, and René Girard. The ambition of the conference was to identify the basic problems of the structuralist approach, such as 'the status of the subject', 'the general theory of signs and language systems', and 'synchronic (vs.) diachronic descriptions', with a view to determining 'the prospects for interdisciplinary co-operation' (xvi). In brief, the event was scripted as the launch of French structuralism in America.

By the time Richard Macksey had made his 'Concluding Remarks' to the conference, however, there was already a sense of uncertainty about structuralism's future; a future that had seemed so assured only four days before. In particular, Macksey observed that: 'The sessions have allowed us . . . to investigate contending interpretative models, and to consider such radical reappraisals of our assumptions as that advanced by M. Derrida on this final day' (Macksey 1972: 320). By 1971, with the publication of the English translations of the conference papers, the tone of engagement with structuralism had changed completely. Macksey and Donato were already able to casually assert that: 'The ancestral priority of Saussure's diacritical example and the insistent logocentricity of the initial structuralist enterprises hardly require comment' (Macksey and Donato 1972b: xi). Ironically, perhaps, Derrida's theme in his paper to the conference was the 'event' of structuralism: the moment when the 'structurality' of structure begins to be thought (SS&P: 280). The force of Derrida's 1966 paper was such that it simultaneously

announced the opening and closing of structuralism in the Anglophone
world.

Derrida on Saussure

This book is an examination of Derrida's interpretation of Saussure. Between
1907 and 1911, Ferdinand de Saussure gave three series of lectures on the
topic of general linguistics at the University of Geneva. These lectures arose
from his dissatisfaction with the state of linguistics; as he wrote, 'there is not
a single term used in linguistics which has any meaning for me' (*Cahiers* 21:
95). Although largely ignored for fifty years after its publication in 1916, the
Course in General Linguistics became one of the most influential and divisive
texts of twentieth-century humanities. And in the *Course*'s ninety-five-year
history, there was no more influential and divisive reading than that of
Jacques Derrida. If Saussure's name is now synonymous with structuralism and Derrida's with post-structuralism, then one could argue that the
movement from one to the other is the most important of twentieth-century
theory. Derrida's engagement with structural linguistics brought into being
the field of cultural studies and profoundly influenced every discipline of the
humanities from anthropology to English.

  Despite the importance of Derrida's critique of Saussure, it is not generally
well understood. There has been surprisingly little written about it, and less
still that treats the philosophies of Derrida and Saussure equally seriously.
Derrida's reading of Saussure is frequently alluded to, approved of, or dis-
missed, but has not yet been comprehensively examined.[1] Indeed, there are
considerable difficulties in trying to grasp exactly what Derrida wants from
Saussure, and whether or not his interpretation stands up to scrutiny. The
first difficulty is that the engagement is *fragmented*. In the early, linguistically
oriented, texts of Derrida, the name Saussure appears fitfully: three lines
in 'Freud and the Scene of Writing'; a footnote in *Speech and Phenomena*;
five pages in 'Différance'; and a similar length response to Julia Kristeva's
interview questions in 'Semiology and Grammatology'. Nowhere, not even
in his well-known critique of 'phonocentrism' in *Of Grammatology*, is
Derrida's reading of Saussure fully articulated. The second difficulty is that
the engagement is *tangential*. Most of Derrida's interaction with Saussure
takes place on the way towards a critique of another theorist, in essays on
Husserl, Lévi-Strauss, Freud, and Austin. The third difficulty is that much
of what is essential in the engagement between the two is *implicit*, unwritten.
In both 'Structure, Sign, and Play in the Discourse of the Human Sciences',
in which Derrida announces the 'event' of structuralism, and in *Speech and
Phenomena*, in which Derrida brings 'the difference involved in signs' to bear
against Husserl's 'essential distinctions', Saussure's name is conspicuously
absent. And so Derrida's engagement with Saussure is fragmented, tangen-

tial, and implicit, and this is what makes it such an interesting challenge to gather together what Derrida wants with or does with the *Course in General Linguistics*. This introduction attempts to characterise that engagement. As will be seen, documenting Derrida's direct engagements, tangential engagements, parenthetical engagements, and even failures of engagement with Saussurean doctrine will also lay bare the questions and chapter structure of this book. The first thing to do is to discover exactly where the name 'Saussure' appears in the early and tightly intertextual texts of Derrida, in which questions of language and signs are predominant.

Speech and Phenomena

Let us begin at the beginning, with *Speech and Phenomena*, in which Derrida's first mention of Saussure takes aim at his supposed originality. In a chapter titled 'Meaning as Soliloquy', Derrida writes that in making the signifier a mental impression, rather than a physical sound, Saussure's 'sole originality' is to make the signifier internal, 'which is only to shift the problem without resolving it' (46–7). Even here, as a brief aside to a discussion of Husserl, Derrida's engagement with Saussure is framed around the question of originality. This framing is present throughout Derrida's engagement, as we shall see more clearly in Chapter 2. This issue of Saussure's originality is the first, and most pressing, question that I am pursuing: to what degree does Saussure adhere to or break from the presuppositions of Western thought that Derrida calls logocentrism?

Derrida's ambition in *Speech and Phenomena* is to show that Husserl reproduces certain essential motifs of Western metaphysics at the very moment that he claims to break free from them. In particular, Derrida's target is the theme of the self-present voice, or the internal voice of solitary mental life, that needs nothing from the world (such as language or a community of speakers) to understand itself. To this end, the above quoted passage is footnoted with an invitation to compare Husserl's *Logical Investigations* with the following passage from the *Course in General Linguistics*:

> The linguistic sign unites, not a thing and a name, but a concept and a sound-image. The latter is not the material sound, a purely physical thing, but the psychological imprint of the sound, the impression that it makes on our senses. The sound-image is sensory, and if I happen to call it 'material', it is only in that sense, and by way of opposing it to the other term of the association, the concept, which is generally more abstract. The psychological character of our sound-images becomes apparent when we observe our own speech. *Without moving our lips or tongue, we can talk to ourselves or recite mentally a selection of verse.* (*Course (B)*: 66, qtd in *S&P*: 46n, Derrida's italics)

This footnote opens up the terrain of Derrida's most sustained engagement with Saussure: the relationship between the Saussurean privilege of speech and the solitary, self-present voice which Derrida finds in Husserl; that is, the relationship between phonocentrism and logocentrism. In this regard, Derrida likens Saussure's opposition of signifier and signified to Husserl's opposition of expression and *Bedeutung* (*S&P*: 46), and will later draw a direct similarity when he defines phonic signs as ' "acoustical images" in Saussure's sense, or the phenomenological voice' (76). An analysis of this relationship between Saussure and the phenomenological voice, or between phonocentrism and logocentrism, is one of the most important ambitions of this book.

Before leaving *Speech and Phenomena*, we ought to note that Derrida is using the words 'sign', 'signifier', and 'signified' in a way that seems more peculiarly Saussurean than his hitherto absence in Derrida's work would suggest. Roy Harris observes that:

> Before Saussure is ever mentioned by name in *De la grammatologie*, Derrida is already discussing language and writing in Saussurean terms: *signe, signifiant, signifié, langue, parole*, etc. are straight away (16ff) assumed to belong to a vocabulary with which the reader is familiar and which therefore does not call for preliminary discussion or explanation. (Harris 2001: 172)

Less immediately noticeable, but perhaps even more profound, is that the rhetorical wedge that Derrida drives into the logic of the *Logical Investigations*, into Husserl's essential distinctions, is the principle of difference involved in signs. Derrida writes that: 'the prime intention' of *Speech and Phenomena* is to reintroduce 'the difference involved in "signs" at the core of what is "primordial"' (45–6n). For this reason, the relationship between this usage of 'signs' and 'difference', and the principle of semiological difference which can be considered original to Saussure, will also need to be made clear.

Of Grammatology

The relationship between Saussure and the self-present voice that we were alerted to in *Speech and Phenomena* is taken up in *Of Grammatology*. Indeed, part one of that book is by far Derrida's most sustained *explicit* engagement with Saussure (if it is understood that I will attempt to show how a work like *Speech and Phenomena* cannot do without him). Derrida's inquiry is directed to a certain history in the philosophy of language, in which priority is given to the spoken language as that which is closest to sense, to intuitive consciousness, and to truth. Derrida explores this relationship between the voice and the Divine *logos* as he finds it in Aristotle, in medieval theology, and in Saussure:

> Between being and mind, things and feelings, there would be a relation-
> ship of translation or natural signification; between mind and logos, a
> relationship of conventional symbolization. And the *first* convention,
> which would relate immediately to the order of natural and universal
> signification, would be produced as spoken language. (*OG*: 11)

Derrida attempts to reveal, in contemporary philosophies claiming to break
from classical approaches, the ongoing desire to preserve the priority of the
voice as the most natural and intuitive relationship with truth, presence, and
the word of God. This essential proximity between voice and mind is contrasted with the inessential and external quality of writing:

> All signifiers, and first and foremost the written signifier, are derivative
> with regard to what would wed the voice indissolubly to the mind or to
> the thought of the signified sense, indeed to the thing itself (whether it
> is done in the Aristotelian manner that we have just indicated or in the
> manner of medieval theology, determining the *res* as a thing created
> from its *eidos*, from its sense thought in the logos or in the infinite
> understanding of God). The written signifier is always technical and
> representative. It has no constitutive meaning . . . This notion remains
> therefore within the heritage of that logocentrism which is also a pho-
> nocentrism: absolute proximity of voice and being, of voice and the
> meaning of being, of voice and the ideality of meaning. (*OG*: 11–12)

If *Speech and Phenomena* includes an invitation to compare Saussure with
Husserl, then *Of Grammatology* surely invites one to compare Saussure with
Aristotle and the medieval theologians. Following the close textual analysis
of *Speech and Phenomena*, the broad historical sweep of *Of Grammatology*
is as unexpected as it is penetrating. Derrida's critique of Saussure comes
at a time when the debate over Saussurean linguistics concerned only the
exact natures of *langue* and *parole*, or of the mechanisms of language change,
and produced ever-increasing abstraction and complexity in the units of
language. Derrida's situation of Saussure within the epoch of classical metaphysics radically changed the way in which Saussure is read to this day. To
contradict this reading of Saussure is to exhume a figure of Saussure which
has not been seen for forty years. Such a contradiction can be performed as a
correction of the Derridean reading, or as a *reinvigoration* of certain possibilities of thought that have been extinguished by Saussure's compression into
the logocentric framework. Some of both will be attempted here.

The second chapter from *Of Grammatology*, 'Linguistics and
Grammatology', consists of an engagement with Saussure which would
be much more recognisable to the Prague and Copenhagen Schools of
Linguistics. In contrast to the first chapter, which contains no citations of
Saussure, 'Linguistics and Grammatology' musters its argument against

the text of the *Course* itself. Here, Derrida attempts to show how Saussure's own theorisation of the arbitrariness of the sign ought to forbid him from his pervasive and insistent privileging of speech over writing. Derrida asks: 'Why does a project of general linguistics, concerning the *internal system in general of language in general*, outline the limits of its field by excluding, as *exteriority in general*, a *particular* system of writing, however important it might be, even were it to be *in fact* universal?' (39). A thorough examination of the *Course* on this point is necessary. Why would Saussure maintain this privilege if it contradicted his organising principle of arbitrariness? What is the Saussurean relationship between speech, writing, and what Derrida calls the 'self-present voice', or the silent experience of meaning?

This question – of Saussure's privileging of speech over writing – is intricately interwoven with the question of Saussure's relative originality within the Aristotelian tradition which Derrida calls 'classical semiology' (Diff: 9). Derrida's suggestion of a 'classical semiology' continues and deepens the question of Saussurean terminology that was asked of *Speech and Phenomena*. Much more than merely assuming that the reader is familiar with these terms and with their position within the contemporary debates over language, Derrida, in *Of Grammatology*, appears to posit these terms as transcending a strictly Saussurean framework. Saussure would then be responsible only for naming or marking these elements which have organised the discourse around language throughout the Western tradition. Derrida writes that:

> The idea of science and the idea of writing – therefore also of the science of writing – is meaningful for us only in terms of an origin and within a world to which a certain concept of the sign (later I shall call it *the* concept of sign) and a certain concept of the relationships between speech and writing, have *already* been assigned. (4)

Positioning Saussure within a tradition of privileging speech over writing is one thing; but believing that this tradition or epoch is governed by a particular concept of the sign in which signifier opposes signified is quite another. At the very least, Derrida's manoeuvre will allow us to recast this discussion of classical phonocentrism into the technical language of Saussurean semiology. If Saussure, in his elevation of speech over writing, reproduces the phonocentrism of classical metaphysics, then to what degree does Saussure also adopt its 'logocentrism', or the privilege of an interior, self-present voice?

'Structure, Sign, and Play'

Determining the order of reading Derrida's texts is made more complex by the almost simultaneous publication of *La Voix et le phénomène, De la grammatologie*, and the essay collection *L'Écriture et la différance* in 1967. Derrida himself has suggested that *Writing and Difference* could be stapled into the middle of *Of Grammatology*, in which Derrida's analysis of the phonocentrism inherent in the concept of the sign would act as the preface to *Writing and Difference*, to which part two of *Of Grammatology* could be appended as the twelfth essay of the collection, as an extended work concerning Rousseau. On the other hand, he believes that just as easily:

> one could insert *Of Grammatology into the middle* of *Writing and Difference*, since six of the texts in that work preceded – *de facto* and *de jure* – the publication in *Critique* (two years ago) of the articles that announced *Of Grammatology*; the last five texts, beginning with 'Freud and the Scene of Writing', are engaged in the grammatological opening. But things cannot be reconstituted so easily, as you may well imagine. (Imp: 4)

There are, however, threads of engagement with Saussure that can be followed from one text to another. The first of these threads leads from 'Structure, Sign, and Play in the Discourse of the Human Sciences' (collected in *Writing and Difference*) to the interview with Julia Kristeva titled 'Semiology and Grammatology' (collected in *Positions*).

It is not easily reconciled that in an essay on Lévi-Strauss and the nature–culture opposition the first four pages of 'Structure, Sign, and Play' should be devoted to the concepts of structure and sign. Even more surprising in these pages is the conspicuous absence of Saussure's name. Derrida begins the essay by suggesting that: 'Perhaps something has occurred in the history of the concept of structure that could be called an "event"' (278). Derrida's position is that far from being an innovation of the nineteenth and twentieth centuries, the concept of structure, and what we call 'structuralism' itself, are as old as Western philosophy. However, the 'structurality' of structures and structuralism has always been governed, organised, and made coherent by a 'centre' which is both within the structure and outside of it:

> The concept of centered structure is in fact the concept of a play based on a fundamental ground, a play constituted on the basis of a fundamental immobility and a reassuring certitude, which itself is beyond the reach of play . . . If this is so, the entire history of the concept of structure, before the rupture of which we are speaking, must be thought of as a series of substitutions of center for center, as a linked chain of determinations of the center. (279)

This is the history of Western thought; the 'event' within this history, which Derrida calls a rupture, occurs when the structurality of structure had begun to be thought. From this point, it becomes possible to at least *imagine* a structure with no centre, with no point of certitude which escapes the play of differences. Derrida phrases this as: 'a system in which the central signified, the original or transcendental signified, is never absolutely present outside a system of differences. The absence of the transcendental signified extends the domain and the play of signification infinitely' (280).

Saussure's position within this event of rupturing must be somewhat controversial, however, for when Derrida comes to answer the question of 'Where and how does this decentering, this thinking the structurality of structure, occur?' (280), he specifically names three writers and their events: the Nietzschean critique of metaphysics; the Freudian critique of self-presence; and the Heideggerian destruction of metaphysics, of onto-theology, of the determination of Being as presence (280). These three names are reprised at the conclusion to this preamble to 'Structure, Sign, and Play', and yet, when Derrida comes to illustrate his argument (that each of these attempts to think the structurality of structure falls back into the language and logic of the metaphysics they seek to contest), he chooses for his example the concept of sign:

> as I suggested a moment ago, as soon as one seeks to demonstrate in this way that there is no transcendental or privileged signified and that the domain or play of signification henceforth has no limit, one must reject even the concept and word 'sign' itself – which is precisely what cannot be done. For the signification 'sign' has always been understood and determined, in its meaning, as sign-of, a signifier referring to a signified, a signifier different from its signified. If one erases the radical difference between signifier and signified, it is the word 'signifier' itself which must be abandoned as a metaphysical concept . . . The concept of the sign, in each of its aspects, has been determined by this opposition throughout the totality of its history. It has lived only on this opposition and its system. (281)

The 'scandal' that these pages ought to represent to the Saussurean reader cannot be underestimated. Derrida's simultaneous appropriation of Saussurean terminology and distinct divergence from Saussurean doctrine is coupled to a steadfast refusal to acknowledge that Saussure is on the scene at all. The labour involved in making Derrida and Saussure engage directly here is not inconsiderable. But it must be attempted, for what 'Structure, Sign, and Play' does is to challenge the Saussurean reader to establish the opposite of what Derrida asserts: that the sign has not always been understood as a signifier referring to a signified; that the concept of the sign does not have a totalising history; and above all, that what is most essential in the Saussurean theory of the sign (in everything involved with synchronic structure) prevents one from speaking of concepts with histories at all. It is fortunate, therefore, that we have at least one piece of writing in which Derrida's provocative way of speaking about the concept of the sign is directed towards Saussure specifically: the interview with Julia Kristeva titled 'Semiology and Grammatology'.

'Semiology and Grammatology'

Kristeva opens with this question, a question that my own inquiry could not do without:

> Semiology today is constructed on the model of the sign and its corre-
> lates: *communication* and *structure*. What are the 'logocentric' and eth-
> nocentric limits of these models, and how are they incapable of serving
> as the basis for a notation attempting to escape metaphysics? (S&G: 17)

Derrida provides an extended answer on communication, and a briefer answer on structure, each of which will be quoted almost in their entirety before the conclusion of my investigation. Derrida's reply also helps to determine the structure of my own engagement with Derrida's interpretation of Saussure, which begins with questions of communication before moving on to questions of structure.

Derrida begins his reply by speaking of 'the concept of the sign', as he did in 'Structure, Sign, and Play', as an event within the history of metaphysics:

> supposing, which I do not believe, that someday it will be possible
> *simply* to escape metaphysics, the concept of the sign will have marked,
> in this sense, a simultaneous impediment and progress. For if the sign,
> by its root and its implications, is in all its aspects metaphysical, if it is
> in systematic solidarity with stoic and medieval theology, the work and
> the displacement to which it has been submitted – and of which it also,
> curiously, is the instrument – have had *delimiting* effects. For this work
> and displacement have permitted the critique of how the concept of the
> sign belongs to metaphysics, which represents a simultaneous *marking*
> and *loosening* of the limits of the system in which this concept was born
> and began to serve, and so thereby also represents, to a certain extent,
> an uprooting of the sign from its own soil. (S&G: 17)

Before moving on to consider how Derrida understands Saussure's role in this history, it is worth pausing to reflect on the curious temporality of Derrida's history of the concept of the sign. This concept appears on the scene as both the instrument of innovation and as the sediment of tradition. To follow Derrida's history at all, it is necessary to imagine how the sign-as-innovation uproots the sign-as-tradition from its own soil. Derrida acknowledges the progress of the Saussurean event which helps to loosen Western metaphysics, but at the same time, shows how this event falls back into the language it seeks to contest. We start to glimpse here what is at stake in Derrida's interpretation of Saussure. Answering the question of *whether or not* Saussure reproduces a concept of the sign which would be recognisable to classical or medieval semioticians is, no doubt, a necessary step. But any such answer risks, as Kristeva suggests, utilising a notation – an entire logic and lexicon – which is incapable of escaping metaphysics. In short, while all of the resources of the *Course* must be exhausted in answering the metaphysical charges that Derrida lays against it, it must also be recognised that it is the very limits of the semiological discourse that Derrida is questioning. For the moment, though, it is enough to understand that Derrida sees Saussurean semiology as both loosening the tradition of metaphysics and confirming it.

It remains important, as a first step, to discover exactly which elements of Saussurean semiology Derrida understands to loosen or confirm metaphysics. Derrida writes that: 'one could show that a semiology of the Saussurean type has had a double role. *On the one hand*, an absolutely decisive critical role . . .' (18). In its critical role, the Saussurean sign marks, against the tradition, that the signifier is *inseparable* from the signified; that the two are of one and the same production. Furthermore, Derrida notes that the Saussurean sign *dematerialises* the expressive substance, by removing physical sound from its system. In these two gestures, 'Saussure powerfully contributed to turning against the metaphysical tradition the concept of the sign that he borrowed from it' (18). 'And yet', Derrida continues, 'Saussure could not confirm this tradition in the extent to which he continued to use the concept of the sign' (18–19). In the lengthy critique of the Saussurean concept of the sign that follows, Derrida will argue that by continuing to use the word and the concept 'sign', Saussure reproduces certain presuppositions of classical metaphysics. Derrida's critique, in brief, and retaining his own numbering, is that:

1. The distinction between signifier and signified – which is the difference between the medieval *signans* and *signatum*, or the sensible and the intelligible – 'inherently leaves open the possibility of thinking a *concept signified in and of itself*, a concept simply present for thought, independent of a relationship to language' (19). Such a 'transcendental signified' (20) is present to the mind prior to the introduction of signifiers, and hence can be transported from one person to another, from one language to another, without loss. In making this point, Derrida interweaves various threads of his argument to date, namely: the reassuring value of the transcendental signified; the relationship between Saussurean and medieval semiology; the self-present voice; and the definition of 'communication as transport', which we will come to in a moment.
2. Although Saussure claims to dematerialise the phonic substance of language, he strictly privileges speech, and 'speaks of the "natural link" between thought and voice, meaning and sound. He even speaks of "thought-sound"' (21). This contradiction is the basis of Derrida's chapter in *Of Grammatology*.
3. What is inherent in the phonocentrism of linguistics – the intimacy of voice to consciousness, and conversely, the exteriority of the signifier –

becomes inherent, due to linguistics's privileged and organising position, to an entire epoch, in which: 'a semiology has been constituted whose concepts and fundamental presuppositions are quite precisely discernible from Plato to Husserl, passing through Aristotle, Rousseau, Hegel, etc.' (22). As he does in *Of Grammatology*, Derrida here positions the problem of signs as the foundational and organising problem of Western metaphysics.

4. Derrida's last brief point is that it is not possible to make – as Saussure does – the sign entirely mental without granting a privilege to the linguistic 'sound-image' as the most characteristic, and hence the ideal model for all sign systems – which Saussure also does.

Derrida then summarises these four points under the name of *communication*, 'which in effect implies a *transmission charged with making pass, from one subject to another*, the *identity* of a *signified* object, of a *meaning* or of a *concept* rightfully separable from the process of passage and from the signifying operation' (23). And while it would never be possible to segregate all that belongs to communication from all that belongs to structure, I will use Kristeva's question and Derrida's answer to co-ordinate, under the name and theme of *communication*, all that contributes to the transport of pure meaning from one subject to another in the manner that Derrida describes above. Hence, this theme covers the ground of the transcendental signified, or the concept independent of language, of the difference between the sensible and the intelligible, of the intuitive voice, or self-presence, of the privilege of speech over writing, and of the metaphysical tradition of the concept of the sign, to give names to just those facets of communication already identified.

'The case of the concept of structure', Derrida now continues, 'is certainly more ambiguous. Everything depends on how one sets it to work. Like the concept of the sign – and therefore semiology – it can simultaneously confirm and shake logocentric and ethnocentric assuredness' (24). The remainder of 'Semiology and Grammatology' concerns what Kristeva calls 'writing as *différance*'. She asks: 'What rupture do these concepts introduce in relation to the key concepts of semiology – the (phonetic) *sign* and *structure*?' (24). Derrida's answer summarises the work of *différance* upon the Saussurean concept of structure, and so it is to the essay 'Différance' that we will turn now.

'Différance'

Derrida, in a preamble to 'Différance', describes his essay as a 'sheaf' of his utilisations of *différance*, meaning that 'the assemblage to be proposed has the complex structure of a weaving, an interlacing which permits the different threads and different lines of meaning – or of force – to go off again in different directions, just as it is always ready to tie itself up with others' (Diff: 3). The contents of this 'sheaf' are sketched here as:

> the juncture – rather than the summation – of what has been most decisively inscribed in the thought of what is conveniently called our 'epoch': the differences of forces in Nietzsche, Saussure's principle of semiological difference, differing as the possibility of (neurone) facilitation, impression and delayed effect in Freud, difference as the irreducibility of the trace of the other in Levinas, and the ontic-ontological difference in Heidegger. (Diff (A): 130)

'Différance', therefore, is an assemblage of forces, of plural utilisations of a neological intervention. And if the weaving of these interventions is too tight, then it may not be possible to do what we were able to do with 'Semiology and Grammatology', which is to isolate the Saussurean moment in Derrida, to find what Derrida wants and does with the Saussurean sign. But it is not trivial to note that the first and longest section of 'Différance' is addressed to Saussurean difference. It is even worth considering that Saussure's premier position in the discourse of *différance* might be something that Derrida cannot do without.

Derrida's engagement with Saussure is prefigured by a surprisingly 'simple and approximate' semantic construction of *différance* (Diff: 7). According to Derrida, the *Littré* dictionary offers two meanings for the verb *différer*: to differ and to defer. Derrida notes that both senses of the word are kinds of interval – of space and of time, respectively. *Différance*, in these senses, and up to this point, can therefore be positioned in between the spatial and the temporal. It is interesting to note that the English word 'space' also contains this duality; being defined in the *Oxford English Dictionary* as both an interval of time, and of relative position. Additionally, the '-*ance*' of *différance* creates the sense of being 'undecided *between* the active and the passive . . ., announcing or rather recalling something like the middle voice' (Diff: 9). And so *différance* is more correctly that which moves not just between the spatial and the temporal, but also between the more active orientations of the becoming-spatial and the becoming-temporal. The intervention of *différance*, in this utilisation, takes aim at the opposition of the spatial and the temporal in the sign (in Saussurean terms, we might say the synchronic and the diachronic), and also contests the passive form that structure takes in Saussurean structuralism. As Derrida summarises it in 'Semiology and Grammatology':

> The activity or production connoted by the *a* of *différance* refers to the generative movement in the play of differences. The latter are neither fallen from the sky nor inscribed once and for all in a closed system, a static structure that a synchronic and taxonomic operation could exhaust. Differences are the effects of transformations, and from this

vantage the theme of *différance* is incompatible with the static, synchronic, taxonomic, ahistoric motifs in the concept of *structure*. (S&G: 27)

To schematise the engagement, we could say that semiological difference is first transformed into the *différance* of spacing through its play and its activity; then, into this *différance* of spacing is interwoven the *différance* of temporalising, in which differences are never fully present within any synchronic moment. Of course, this is to schematise too neatly, and the subtlety of the relationship between difference and *différance* cannot be glossed over. But we can say, at least, that this relationship is dominated by the question of *time*, and its role in structure and structuralising.

'Signature Event Context'

A final thread of engagement, which leads from 'Freud and the Scene of Writing' to 'Signature Event Context', contains two distinct but related arguments. The first is, again, an inquiry into the nature of *communication*: as a transport of pure signifieds; of concepts which are unaffected by their communicating form and material. This engagement with Saussure has already been identified in relation to *Of Grammatology* and 'Semiology and Grammatology'. In 'Freud and the Scene of Writing', the inquiry takes place in relation to the language of dreams, and the possibility of a fixed code of translation between 'dream-content' and 'dream-meaning':

> Translation, a system of translation, is possible only if a permanent code allows a substitution or transformation of signifiers while retaining the same signified, always present, despite the absence of any specific signifier. This fundamental possibility of substitution would thus be implied by the coupled concepts signified/signifier, and would consequently be implied by the concept of the sign itself. (210)

Freud understands that the language of dreams – as the relation between a signifier (dream-content) and a signified (dream-meaning) – is not a permanent code, but is fixed only for a single person at a single point in time. The possibility of translation between subjects or between contexts is, then, compromised in the manner described by Derrida.

The roles that are played by 'subjects' and 'contexts' in communication is then taken up in 'Signature Event Context'. The essay begins with a critique of the concept of communication, in which the desire or movement towards 'presence', or the full restoration of meanings and intentions, is undermined by a consideration of the role of 'absence'. Derrida finds that the implicit condition of communication is that it must continue to function not only in the absence of the signified object (in the classical manner), but also in the absence of the sender or of the receiver of the message, and indeed, in the absence of any consciousness whatsoever. Derrida discovers these requirements first of all in written communication, but soon extends that to all communication, which he is then able to call 'writing-in-general'. The essential predicate of such a writing 'is a mark that subsists, one which does not exhaust itself in the moment of its inscription and which can give rise to an iteration in the absence and beyond the presence of the empirically determined subject who, in a given context, has emitted or produced it' (SEC: 9). And it is this 'iteration', as a theory of linguistic identity, which is the second argument that links 'Freud and the Scene of Writing' to 'Signature Event Context'.

Derrida borrows the word 'iteration' from the Sanskrit *itara*, and states that 'everything that follows can be read as the working out of the logic that ties repetition to alterity' (SEC: 7). Elsewhere, Derrida speaks of 'the primordially repetitive structure of signs in general' (*S&P*: 51), and in 'Freud and the Scene of Writing', it is repetition that makes translatability, and even language itself, possible:

> the power of 'repetition' alone . . . institutes translatability, makes possible what we call 'language', transforms an absolute idiom into a limit which is always already transgressed: a pure idiom is not a language; it becomes so only through repetition; repetition always already divides the point of departure of the first time. (213)

All that ties repetition to alterity would also seem to be the basis for a Saussurean understanding of linguistic identity. In the chapter 'Identities, Realities, Values', Saussure considers the case of '*Messieurs!*':

> we may hear in the course of a lecture several repetitions of the word *Messieurs!*. We feel that in each case it is the same expression: and yet there are variations of delivery and intonation which give rise in the several instances to very noticeable phonic differences – differences which are as marked as those which in other cases serve to differentiate one word from another (e.g. *pomme* from *paume, goutte* from *goûte, fuir* from *fouir*, etc.). Furthermore, this feeling of identity persists in spite of the fact that from a semantic point of view too there is no absolute reduplication from one *Messieurs!* to the next . . . The link between two uses of the same word is not based upon material identity, nor upon exact similarity of meaning, but upon factors the linguist must discover, if he is to come anywhere near to revealing the true nature of linguistic units. (*Course*: 106–7/150–2)

And yet, while appearing to confirm the structure of signs as being that which is repeatable as the *same*, Saussure's view of linguistic identity is radically different when it considers *who* or *what* determines this similarity. Derrida speaks of the *self*-identity that is inherent in iteration, and of how a mark contains its own repeatability: it *subsists*, in the radical absence of any consciousness. For Saussure, on the contrary, linguistic identity resides *entirely* within consciousness – both in the individual and the collective.

As we shall see, this privilege given to language users is exactly what Derrida would wish to argue against: that the self-presence of consciousness is an essential presupposition of metaphysics; that the unity of consciousness is constructed only on the basis of a more originary repeatability. This is no doubt true, from a certain *point of view*. And yet, there may be something in Saussure's attention to the language user that is able to perform a similarly destabilising operation on Derridean linguistics. This question of linguistic identity turns, then, on the problematic of 'same' and 'different', as it is understood by Derrida and Saussure. However, in concerning the problematic of 'same' and 'different', the exploration of linguistic identity will stretch any discourse to its limit, its horizon, past which it is sometimes possible to see, but not go. That horizon, I believe, plays a forceful and divisive role between Derrida and Saussure.

Plan of engagement

Despite the many threads of engagement with Saussure identified above, and other moments of indirect engagement in the *Introduction* to Husserl's *Origin of Geometry*, 'The Original Discussion of 'Différance', and 'Afterword: Towards An Ethic of Discussion', among others, there remain great difficulties in making the two philosophies of language exert force against each other. To begin to name these difficulties: Derrida does not comment on any technical aspects of Saussurean theory, most notably the theory of linguistic value; Derrida utilises a logic and lexicon which seem to exceed or transcend the capabilities of the *Course* to respond; the *Course* exists as compiled lecture notes while Derrida's essays are tightly woven strategies of textuality; Saussure's argument is supported by empirical examples, while Derrida's is not; and more. Indeed, it may be possible that a certain failure of engagement, or an incommensurability of discourses, occupies the terrain between Derrida and Saussure. The 'debate' between Derrida and Searle is no doubt instructive.

Very often in this 'debate', a failure of engagement will occur around the meanings of words: Derrida will extend, etymologise, or make a pun of, a word, then continue to use it in that altered sense, even naming this sense the 'classical' sense when the use of the term is understood fully and properly. The problem for Derrida's critics is that insisting on the original, *common*, sense of the word makes it appear as if they have failed to understand Derrida's strategy in its entirety. For example, Searle claims that: 'Derrida in this argument confuses no less than three separate and distinct phenomena: iterability, citationality and parasitism' (206). And while *we* – more sensitive readers of Derrida – will understand that what Derrida does is no simple matter of 'confusion', we can also have some sympathy for Searle, whose entire vocabulary of engagement with the theory of speech acts has been pulled from under him. The comedy is that Searle doesn't realise this. But perhaps the tragedy – not just for Searle but for J. L. Austin and an entire tradition of language theory – is that he is expected to. Stanley Cavell, in his excellent reappraisal of this debate, writes that: 'I felt both that [Derrida] understood something in Austin that others had missed and also that he was not interested in something else in Austin which I regarded as fundamental' (67); and that in the end: 'the encounter between Derrida and Austin and then Searle has proved to have done more harm than good' (44):

> Derrida's influence within literary studies has kept the image of Austin too much tethered to his theory of performatives, and, within that theory, to the several citations Derrida found suitable to his own pur-poses for 'Signature Event Context'.
> This has helped perpetuate the thought that Austin underwrites some idea that language contains a general, unified dimension of effect that can be called one of performance, and that he advances a general contrast between ordinary language and literary language. These ideas alone are sufficient to destroy any contribution Austin's distinctiveness might lend in such discussions. (44–5)

My strategy, which I hope is more like Cavell's than Searle's, is to form a bridge between comprehension and contradiction. I will, at times, attempt to resist Derrida's interventions, his brilliant and compelling rearrangement of meanings and relations. However, I recognise that in doing so, I must make fully explicit what those interventions are, and how they work. In order to make the debate between Derrida and Saussure occur, my facilitation will involve writing some of Derrida's critique of Saussure back into the lan-guage of semiology, patiently explaining to the linguist from Geneva what Professor Derrida is suggesting. My ambition, therefore, is to *hear*, and to *write* with, a language that is open to both discourses, and capable of moving beyond the 'aggressivity' that Derrida believed marked his encounter with Searle (Aft: 113).

Conclusion

But how to organise a book where the topics of discussion are not only tightly interwoven, but often only 'nicknames' for the same intervention: the self-present voice; the transcendental signified; the metaphysics of presence; the communication of pure signifieds; phono-logocentrism; the difference between *différance* and difference? Harris has described the lectures that form the *Course in General Linguistics* as 'successive reformulations' (1987: 15) and this is true also of Derrida's engagement with semiology and structuralism. It is not surprising, then, that the chapters of this book should also proceed as successive reformulations. For how can one close off the issues raised by Derrida's reading of classical and medieval semiology when one is still to discuss the division between writing and speech? And how can one finalise Derrida's critique of the 'transcendental signified' in 'Semiology and Grammatology' when one hasn't yet introduced Derrida's discussion of 'communication' in 'Signature Event Context'? The lesson is that each question that Derrida poses to Saussurean semiology cannot stand alone, but 'must pass through the difficult deconstruction of the entire history of metaphysics' (S&G: 20).

Given that a chapter that says everything at once risks saying nothing, I will proceed with a method that could be called a *cumulative* reading. It begins from a close reading of texts, giving pertinence not just to general ideas and notions but to the words and sentences, supporting statements and citations in Derrida's reading of the *Course*. It is necessary, as a first step, to hold Derrida to account: to compare his reading of the *Course* with those of other Saussurean scholars and with the text itself. At times it will seem that Searle's summation that 'Derrida has a distressing penchant for saying things that are obviously false' (203) might also apply to his reading of Saussure. On the other hand, if Derrida's engagement with Saussure occurs at only a single point, then the entire history of metaphysics passes through it, and it becomes necessary to allow more and more of Derrida's 'radical reappraisal of our assumptions' to have force. As Derrida says:

> The step 'outside philosophy' is much more difficult to conceive than is generally imagined by those who think they made it long ago with cavalier ease, and who in general are swallowed up in metaphysics in the entire body of discourse which they claim to have disengaged from it. (SS&P: 284)

If one accepts Derrida's suggestion, then it is not enough to overturn his argument simply with literal reference to the text of the *Course*. One must follow Derrida into an understanding of how semiology and structuralism are implicated in the entire history of metaphysics. Derrida's ambition is to *solicit* philosophy from its forgotten but transcendental determinations. By the final chapter, I believe that the full force of Derrida's anti-metaphysical openings will have been turned upon the *Course*, its history, its presuppositions and its axioms.

To *conclude* is, in a sense, to decide which questions will be kept open and which questions will be closed off. Each chapter of this book offers a summation and conclusion to the questions in play; but in every case, up to the final chapter, I have erred on the side of openness. Derrida's engagement with Saussure demands this. At some point, however, this exercise must contain a positive thesis, a *position*. The thesis I am pursuing at all points, however reformulated, is that the act of resisting Derrida's reading of Saussure opens up rich possibilities in linguistic and political thought.

Note

1. Even Harris, who will otherwise be frequently cited as an astute reader of Saussure, concludes that it is 'hardly worth the tedium of pointing out how and why Derrida's interpretation of Saussure is academically worthless' (Harris 2001: 188). In the case of Harris, and in Raymond Tallis's passionate (1995) defence of Saussure against Derrida's misreading, we recognise attempts to understand the engagement that are limited by a wilful reduction of Derrida's project to what can be readily assimilated into a philosophy of common sense.

1 Classical Semiology

Derrida often uses the epithet 'classical'. It appears most often in his expression 'classical metaphysics' (*S&P*: 51; GS&P: 166), but also in 'the classical concept of writing' (SEC: 9), in 'the classical opposition' between speech and writing (SEC: 21), and in how signs can be eliminated 'in the classical manner' (*S&P*: 51). Derrida first uses the expression 'classical semiology' in 'Différance', to name the metaphysical system in which a sign takes the place of the thing in its absence:

> The sign represents the present in its absence. It takes the place of the present. When we cannot grasp or show the thing, state the present, the being-present, when the present cannot be presented, we signify, we go through the detour of the sign. . . . According to this classical semiology, the substitution of the sign for the thing itself is both *secondary* and *provisional*: secondary due to an original and lost presence from which the sign thus derives; provisional as concerns this final and missing presence toward which the sign in this sense is a movement of mediation. (Diff: 9)

Classical semiology is thus the semiology of presence, and the semiology of the epoch of classical metaphysics. Within this epoch, Derrida states, 'the original and essential link to the *phonè* has never been broken. It would be easy enough to demonstrate this and I shall attempt such a demonstration later' (*OG*: 11). At times, Saussure seems to be merely *caught up* in this demonstration, as in the chapter of *Of Grammatology* from which this quote comes, where he is mentioned only in passing by Derrida. But at other times, Saussure appears entirely central and essential to Derrida's characterisation of this epoch, as when this very same chapter opens with a definition of writing as the 'signifier of a signifier' (7), which is a definition that Derrida will attribute to Saussure. What I aim to understand in this chapter is the relationship that Derrida wants to establish between classical metaphysics and the semiology of Saussure. Let us start, since we are already there, with part one of *Of Grammatology*.

Classical sources

Derrida's interrogation of classical metaphysics and its presuppositions
begins with a quotation from the opening few lines of Aristotle's *On
Interpretation*:

> Spoken words are the symbols of mental experience and written words
> are the symbols of spoken words. Just as all men have not the same
> writing, so all men have not the same speech sounds, but the mental
> experiences, which these directly symbolize, are the same for all, as also
> are those things of which our experiences are the images. (Aristotle:
> 16a, 2–4)

On the scene of language, in the Aristotelian view, and in a certain order,
are: 'things'; 'mental experiences' (which are the *images* of things); 'speech
sounds' (which are the *symbols* of mental experiences); and lastly, 'written
words' (which are, in turn, *symbols* of spoken words). A 'thing', for example,
a tree, is the same for all people, and hence the mental impression (experience, image) of a tree is the same for all people. Speech is the first symbolisation of mental experience, and writing a symbolisation of speech. Derrida
formulates this as follows:

> Between being and mind, things and feelings, there would be a relation-
> ship of translation or natural signification; between mind and logos, a
> relationship of conventional symbolization. And the *first* convention,
> which would relate immediately to the order of natural and universal
> signification, would be produced as spoken language. (11)

The relationship between things and mind is a natural one. The relationship
between the mind and the word, however, is by convention, as not all men
have the same speech sounds. But the most intimate, most interior expression
of the feelings of the mind is spoken language. The epoch of 'logocentrism',
or the natural expression of the world in the mind, is also that of 'phonocentrism', of the relative intimacy of truth and the voice, and of the relative
externality and distance of writing. In such a classical system, the word is
indifferent but the sense is not; there exists what Derrida has elsewhere called
a ' "pre-expressive" stratum of experience' (*S&P*: 15), prior to the introduction of language. An examination of the presuppositions and consequences
of such a system and an epoch are not easily exhausted, and the breadth of
Derrida's writing attests to this. Indeed, a logocentrism of an Aristotelian
kind could be understood and critiqued without the need for 'semiology' as
such, understood as a definition of certain relationships between 'signifier',
'signified' and 'sign'. The more general philosophical categories of 'being'
and 'mind', for example, could carry the burden of Derrida's enquiry. But

precisely what part one of *Of Grammatology* does is to establish this relationship between classical metaphysics and the concept of the sign.

Characterising Derrida's demonstration is difficult, not only because it takes in so many different theorists from so many different periods and genres of writing, nor only because Saussure appears on the scene so marginally/centrally (as above), but because the discourse does not take the form of an argument, so much as a list of assertions and associations. It is important to note that I do not mean this as a smear, but rather to suggest that it would be impossible to argue, in a rigorous way but yet in only a single essay, for *any* kind of schematisation of an entire epoch in the way Derrida does in the first chapter of *Of Grammatology*. Here, Derrida's engagement with any single theorist *ought* to be considered preliminary, even if usually it is not.

Derrida's association between Aristotelian metaphysics and Saussurean semiology, in the commonality of a certain relationship between signifiers and signifieds, begins in the following manner:

> All signifiers, and first and foremost the written signifier, are derivative with regard to what would wed the voice indissolubly to the mind or to the thought of the signified sense, indeed to the thing itself (whether it is done in the Aristotelian manner that we have just indicated or in the manner of medieval theology . . .). The written signifier is always technical and representative. It has no constitutive meaning. This derivation is the very origin of the notion of the 'signifier'. The notion of the sign always implies within itself the distinction between signifier and signified, even if, as Saussure argues, they are distinguished simply as the two faces of one and the same leaf. This notion remains therefore within the heritage of that logocentrism which is also a phonocentrism: absolute proximity of voice and being, of voice and the meaning of being, of voice and the ideality of meaning. (11–12)

The breathtaking ambit of this passage warns us to proceed cautiously. Derrida's object here is not just Aristotle, Saussure, or signs in general, but also ideality, presence, and the entire history of metaphysics. But let us try to write this passage out again, as if it might stand alone as a sequence of observations, if not argumentation. First, Derrida states that the written signifier – the signifier of a signifier – is derivative in regard to sense. In other words, for Aristotle the relationship between the mental image and the thing is established *prior* to the introduction of spoken or written words. In this sense, the written word can be regarded as 'secondary' or 'derivative' in that it *follows* an original coupling, and hence also that it has no bearing or influence on that original coupling. Second, since Derrida claims that the written signifier is the model for all signifiers, then signification in general is secondary to the process of sense-making. The signifier is useful only for transporting the 'signified' – which is understood as the natural relationship between thing and mind – from one person or place to another, that is, for communication. Such a transportation by signifiers would leave the signified unaffected in its relationship with the thing itself. Third, Derrida notes that this division between the external, derivative 'signifier' (Aristotle's σύμβολον, or 'symbol') and the internal, essential 'signified' (Aristotle's παθεματα, or 'mental experience') would define the concept of the 'sign'. This much seems to follow directly from the model of *On Interpretation*, if we allow a certain translation of Aristotelian terms into Saussurean ones.[1] However, the final implication that Derrida draws from Aristotle seems to exceed what appears in the text. Derrida wants to say that because the phonic symbol is the primary symbol of mental experience, and the written symbol derived from the phonic, then the 'voice' is 'wedded indissolubly' to 'the mind or to thought of the signified sense', and is therefore in 'absolute proximity' to being. This schema would then unite a logocentrism (the self-presence of mental impressions prior to or without recourse to language) with a phonocentrism (the privileging of phonic symbols over graphic symbols). There must be a certain tension here though, for in the Aristotelian model of *On Interpretation*, *both* 'spoken words' and 'written words' are *absolutely* conventional in relation to 'mental experience', even if spoken words are the first convention and written words the second. To question the logic of Derrida's interpretation of Aristotle: how can the vocal signifier – which must have the property of being *derivative* in regard to the sense or the signified – also be *wedded indissolubly* to that sense? To make Derrida's formulation of the 'voice' work at all, we would need to reduce or efface the conventional or symbolic relationship between mental images and spoken words.

How Derrida resolves this formulation leads us to first analyse in closer detail the parenthetical statement 'whether it is done in the Aristotelian manner that we have just indicated or in the manner of medieval theology', and hence also the underlying premises of Derrida's schematisation of such a classical semiology. Having done so, we will be in a better position to bring Saussure to the scene of this encounter, and to understand how a semiology of a Saussurean kind remains within a heritage of that logocentrism which is also a phonocentrism.

Medieval theology

At this point, the role of medieval theology in phonocentrism and logocentrism has not yet been made clear by Derrida. The following two paragraphs, and their anchoring reference to Roman Jakobson, might then be quoted in full:

> The epoch of the logos thus debases writing considered as mediation of mediation and as a fall into the exteriority of meaning. To this epoch

belongs the difference between signified and signifier, or at least the strange separation of their 'parallelism', and the exteriority, however extenuated, of the one to the other. This appurtenance is organized and hierarchized in a history. The difference between signified and signifier belongs in a profound and implicit way to the totality of the great epoch covered by the history of metaphysics, and in a more explicit and more systematically articulated way to the narrower epoch of Christian creationism and infinitism when these appropriate the resources of Greek conceptuality. This appurtenance is essential and irreducible; one cannot retain the convenience or the 'scientific truth' of the Stoic and later medieval opposition between *signans* and *signatum* without also bringing with it all its metaphysico-theological roots. To these roots adheres not only the distinction between the sensible and the intelligible – already a great deal – with all that it controls, namely, metaphysics in its totality. And this distinction is generally accepted as self-evident by the most careful linguists and semiologists, even by those who believe that the scientificity of their work begins where metaphysics ends. Thus, for example:

> As modern structural thought has clearly realized, language is a system of signs and linguistics is part and parcel of the science of signs, or *semiotics* (Saussure's *sémiologie*). The medieval definition of sign – '*aliquid stat pro aliquo*' – has been resurrected and put forward as still valid and productive. Thus the constitutive mark of any sign in general and of any linguistic sign in particular is its twofold character: every linguistic unit is bipartite and involves both aspects – one sensible and the other intelligible, or in other words, both the *signans* 'signifier' (Saussure's *signifiant*) and the *signatum* 'signified' (*signifié*). These two constituents of a linguistic sign (and of sign in general) necessarily suppose and require each other.[2]

But to these metaphysico-theological roots many other hidden sediments cling. The semiological or, more specifically, linguistic 'science' cannot therefore hold on to the difference between signifier and signified – the very idea of the sign – without the difference between sensible and intelligible, certainly, but also not without retaining, more profoundly and more implicitly, and by the same token the reference to a signified able to 'take place' in its intelligibility, before its 'fall', before any expulsion into the exteriority of the sensible here below. As the face of pure intelligibility, it refers to an absolute logos to which it is immediately united. This absolute logos was an infinite creative subjectivity in medieval theology: the intelligible face of the sign remains turned toward the word and the face of God. (12–13)

To summarise what emerges from these passages, which themselves are written like summaries: the epoch of the logos excludes writing as exterior and unnecessary to meaning; to this epoch belongs the difference between the signifier and the signified, or, the concept of the sign; the sign belongs more specifically to the narrower epoch of Christian creationism governed by Greek conceptuality; the difference between the signifier and the signified is rooted in and adheres to the difference between the sensible and intelligible, or, the *signans* and *signatum*; the intelligible face of the sign (the signified/ *signatum*) must be able to be felt, to take place, to communicate with the word of God, before its fall into language and externality. To summarise this summary once again: the sign is a concept developed in ancient and medieval metaphysics, and even today it cannot do without, or simply abandon, these sediments.

I feel that Derrida's gesture here is as powerful as it is original. And yet it does not seem to me that a demonstration has so far taken place. Indeed, the absence of such a demonstration becomes very much more pointed when Derrida continues that –

> It is a question at first of demonstrating the systematic and histori-
> cal solidarity of the concepts and gestures of thought that one often
> believes can be innocently separated. The sign and divinity have the
> same place and time of birth. The age of the sign is essentially theologi-
> cal. (13–14)

– and yet immediately fails to take this first step: to demonstrate the system-atic and historical solidarity of these concepts and gestures of thought, that the sign and divinity have the same place and time of birth, that the age of the sign is essentially theological. What is required – according to Derrida – is a demonstration of how even today the concept or the word 'sign' cannot do without or simply abandon these historical and theological sediments. However, Derrida does not cite a single line of medieval writing, allowing the above characterisation of an epoch to rest solely with Jakobson's compari-son of the Stoic *signans* and *signatum* with Saussure's signifier and signified. Accordingly, this *first* demonstration ought to be examined now.

Jakobson on Saussure

Beginning from Jakobson's quoted statement in volume one of *Essais de linguistique générale*, we can note, first of all, that there are no references to medieval texts for us to immediately follow up. There is no indication, once again, of how such a demonstration of the 'systematic and historical solidar-ity' between Aristotle, the Stoics, the *modistae*, and Saussure might proceed. However, that is not to say that this reference to a *signans* and *signatum* was casual or unstudied for Jakobson. His oeuvre, for all its variation, never let go of a bipartite model of the sign in which the *signans* (the sensible) is opposed to the *signatum* (the intelligible). It is equally true, though, that Jakobson continually questioned the *relationship* between these two elements, and would have insisted that this relationship had gone through many changes, both ancient and modern. In point of fact, the paragraph that Derrida cites is part of an argument in which Jakobson contrasts the neogrammarian principle of investigating language – to consider the action of each separate factor individually – with the structuralist model, which understands the *signans* and *signatum* to be both inseparable and reciprocal. That is, a model in which the *signans* articulates the *signatum* as much as the *signatum* articulates the *signans*, and neither is complete in itself. Jakobson continues that:

> The analysis of any linguistic sign whatever can be carried out only under the condition that its sensible aspect is studied in light of its intelligible aspect (the *signifiant* in light of the *signifié*) and reciprocally. The indissoluble dualism of any linguistic sign is the starting point of present day linguistics in its stubborn combat on two fronts. (Jakobson 1949: 6)

The originality that Jakobson grants to Saussure and to twentieth-century structuralism here, and elsewhere, is not slight: it is the indissolubility of the relationship between the *signans* and *signatum*, the reciprocity of that relationship, and the arbitrariness of that relationship. What is also clear is that, for Jakobson, such developments radically changed the study of language. A properly structural linguistics no longer mediates the relationship between a word and a thing, but instead remains wholly within the relationship between the word and the concept, and within the horizon of language. After studying the Saussurean doctrine in Geneva, Jakobson reflects that:

> We learned how to feel the delicate distinction between the *signatum* and the *denotatum* (the referent), to assign to this fact an intrinsically linguistic position first of all to the *signatum* and, then, by deduction, to its counterpart, also inalienable, with the *signans*. The need for establishing phonology as a new discipline, strictly intralinguistic, became increasingly obvious. (Jakobson 1973: 132, my translation)

And so it must be clear, above all, that while Jakobson understands Saussure to have borrowed the medieval concepts of *signans* and *signatum*, he also understands the relationship between these two to have undergone a radical rethinking in modern times, principally under Saussurean structuralism. In effect, Jakobson understands the sign – aside from any other characteristics it might have, in being arbitrary or motivated, in being intralinguistic or referential – as consisting of some kind of relationship between a sensible element and an intelligible element. For Jakobson, at least, no other characteristics of the Aristotelian or Stoic or medieval or neogrammarian positions are necessarily inherited by this gesture. The epoch of the sign would be, for Jakobson, one of both essential continuity and of radical re-design:

> The varied relations existing between the *signans* and the *signatum* always offer an indispensable criterion for any classification of semiotic structures, provided that those who study them manage to escape two equally hazardous deviations: on the one hand, that which seeks to force a semiotic structure into some linguistic design without paying specific attention to the features of that structure, would be and is harmful; on the other hand, all attempts to put aside all common denominators because of some variations in their properties, can equally only harm the interests of comparative and general semiotics. (Jakobson 1973: 94, my translation)

We can therefore return to the text of *Of Grammatology*, if we have ever left it, with the question of whether or not such distinctions are pertinent in Derrida's characterisation of an epoch.

Clearly, Derrida's relationship with Jakobson is by no means uncritical. Derrida cites Jakobson principally as a supporter of a certain characterisation of an epoch in which *signans* opposes *signatum*; but he also wants us to see Jakobson's position as evidence of a certain inherited trait of linguistics which Jakobson shares and cannot see beyond. In both cases, however, we can ask: What is the relationship between the *signans* and *signatum* that Derrida wants to call '*the* concept of sign' (*OG*: 4), and which carries with it all that governs the metaphysics of an epoch? Is Derrida's position on that relationship: (1) a pre-Jakobsonian, let us say Aristotelian position, in having the *signatum* already determined prior to, and independent of, a *signans*; or (2) a post-Jakobsonian position, in being interdependent, reciprocal and differential; or (3) that such a distinction remains wholly within the system of metaphysics, and hence is uncritical? Of course, the third solution appears to be the most promising: that the reciprocity of signification does not rupture the horizon of the *signans* and *signatum*, and all its metaphysico-theological roots. However, it is worth noting that when Derrida comes to repeat this quotation of Jakobson in an essay dedicated to Saussure, he will omit the last sentence of the paragraph: 'These two constituents of a linguistic sign (and of sign in general) necessarily suppose and require each other' (S&G: 98). The pertinence of this omission will be examined in the next chapter. But for the moment, the work of interrogating Jakobson's position has at least rewarded us with an understanding that Derrida's position seems to exceed any distinction that we would care to make within the broad scope of the opposition between the *signans*/sensible/signifier and *signatum*/intelligible/signified.

The effacement of 'mental experience'

There is at least one aspect of Derrida's characterisation of classical semiology with which Jakobson would disagree, which is that the 'delicate distinction' between the concept (*signatum*, sense) and the thing (*denotatum*, referent) is also uncritical. Throughout his engagement with semiology, Derrida will insist upon what we might call the *ineffectiveness* of this distinction. Derrida posits a system of classical semiology in which a *signans* is opposed to a *signatum*, and in which the *signatum* can stand equally well for the concept or the thing:

> The sign is usually said to be put in place of the thing itself, the present thing, 'thing' here standing equally for meaning or referent. The sign represents the present in its absence. It takes the place of the present. When we cannot grasp or show the thing, state the present, the being-present, when the present cannot be presented, we signify, we go through the detour of the sign. (Diff: 9)

We could ask, though, how it is that we are not be able to take a hold of the 'thing', if 'thing' holds equally for meaning or referent? For to not be able to take hold of the meaning without a signifier makes exactly the opposite point that Derrida seems to intend: that meaning does not reside in the concept prior to the introduction of language. In *Of Grammatology*, the justification for this operation is parenthetical:

> The feelings of the mind, expressing things naturally, constitute a sort of universal language which can then efface itself. It is the stage of transparence. Aristotle can sometimes omit it without risk.* In every case, the voice is closest to the signified, whether it is determined strictly as sense (thought or lived) or more loosely as thing. All signifiers, and first and foremost the written signifier, are derivative with regard to what would wed the voice indissolubly to the mind or to the thought of the signified sense, indeed to the thing itself (whether it is done in the Aristotelian manner that we have just indicated or in the manner of medieval theology . . .). (11)

In each case – of Aristotle and of medieval semiology – there is a *manner* in which 'the feelings of the mind' can be effaced. Such an operation would therefore also efface the difference between 'the thought of the signified sense' and 'the thing itself'. What Derrida is working towards is a semiology in which the voice is in absolute proximity to 'presence', whether determined as thought or thing. Let us examine these operations of effacement now, as they appear first in Aristotle and second in medieval theology.

In the case of Aristotle, we are directed to a footnote, indicated by the

asterisk above. That footnote tells us that: 'This is shown by Pierre Aubenque
. . . In the course of a provocative analysis, to which I am here indebted,
Aubenque remarks' (*OG*: 324):

> In other texts, to be sure, Aristotle designates as symbol the relation-
> ship between language and things: 'It is not possible to bring the things
> themselves into the discussion, but, instead of things, we can use their
> names as symbols'. The intermediary constituted by the mental expe-
> rience is here suppressed or at least neglected, but this suppression is
> legitimate, since, mental experiences behaving like things, things can
> be substituted for them immediately. On the other hand, one cannot by
> any means substitute names for things. (Aubenque 1962: 107–8, qtd in
> *OG*: 324)

Aubenque here notes an occasion (*Refut. Soph.*, 1, 165 a 10) when Aristotle,
contrary to the semiological construction of *On Interpretation*, suppresses the
mental intermediary, and speaks of a direct relationship between names and
things. But it is also clear that, for Aubenque as for Aristotle, there remains
no possibility of substituting names for things. Indeed, Derrida's citation of
this passage is unusual in that Aubenque seems determined to assign a certain
originality to Aristotle's thought here, which is the absolute conventionality
of the relationship between word and concept. The independence of words
and concepts is similarly argued by Hans Arens:

> The first essential element of this theory is the word-concept-relation,
> with which Socrates operates in *Cratylus*; and as the word is only a
> symbol or sign, not a secret image of a concept, the famous question
> of the ορθότης τών ονομάτων (the rightness of names), which was the
> subject of *Cratylus*, can no longer arise. Thus Aristotle tacitly rejects
> a theory expounded by Plato and others. This is remarkable progress,
> and [section] 10 points in the same direction. And by stating (13) that
> 'no word is by nature' he decides the old controversy whether the words
> are *physei* (by nature) or *thesei* (by institution). (28)

And Manetti also notes that:

> Plato considered primitive words to be the faithful representation of the
> properties of an object, almost as though vocabulary deliberately con-
> sisted entirely of onomatopoeia . . . For Aristotle, names are *symbols*
> and they are *conventional*. For Plato names are *icons* of objects and they
> are *natural*. (123)

For Plato, the names of things may contain clues, and even be traced back,
to their natural origins. For Aristotle, on the contrary, they are absolutely

conventional. Again, the question could arise as to whether such a distinction, and such an originality, disturbs Derrida's characterisation of classical semiology. But after following Derrida's referral to Aubenque, what remains unresolved is how the effacement of the concept – if such an operation can be attributed to Aristotle – would 'wed indissolubly' the voice with the thing itself, unless such a marriage could allow for absolute conventionality.

Second, the manner in which such an effacement occurs in medieval theology not only fails to resolve this question, but deepens it. The problem for Derrida's explanation of this operation in medieval theology ('determining the *res* as a thing created from its *eidos*, from its sense thought in the logos or in the infinite understanding of God') is that the single greatest division within medieval linguistic thought – what Duns Scotus called a 'magna altercatio' (qtd in Tabarroni 1989: 196) – was between the priority of the word-concept relation and the word-thing relation. From Aristotle to Augustine, the dominant position was the former, in which names signified concepts, and were only indirectly associated with things. However:

> With Bacon the problem of the relation between words and things shifts totally. Thus the term *significatio*, which up until then had served to indicate the relation between words and definition or concepts (a purely *intensional* one), is used by Bacon to indicate the relation of reference (*extension*) between words and things or states of the world. The *vox* is *significata rei extra animam*. (Eco et al. 1989: 22)

Speaking roughly, on the side of intensionalism, in the Aristotelian tradition, we could place Boethius, Augustine and Abelard; on the side of extensionalism would principally be Roger Bacon and Ockham (cf. Arens 1984; Eco et al. 1989; Meier-Oeser 2003), and 'As for Duns Scotus and the Modistae, they represent a sort of very ambiguous hinge between the extensional and the intensional position' (Eco 1989: 62). If Derrida wants there to be a direct link between words and things, and for concepts to be effaced, there is such plentiful evidence for this in medieval theology that one has to wonder why he would strain to look for it in Aristotle. But the question remains as to how such an operation can undermine the essential conventionality of the vocal *signans* in all of these positions.

One final observation is necessary before bringing the characteristics of classical semiology to bear against Saussure. It is important to note – for Derrida makes no attempt to reveal this – that the range of medieval positions on the composition of the semiological relationship is much more diverse than has so far been examined. To only begin to grapple with these distinctions, we have, for example: all manner of postulated relationships between name, mind and thing, this relationship being named as *denotatio*, *representatio*, *appellatio*, *significatio*, and others; the division between those who privilege the individual things (*res*) and those who privilege the universal

categories of thought (*species*); and the division between those who understood semiology to exist within or without a consciousness, a distinction that
may be the most important of all:

> Contrary to Ockham's concept of sign, it is not the logical function of
> referring to a *significatum* that stands in the foreground, but rather the
> sign's relation to a cognitive power . . . In view of this it should be clear
> that the widespread opinion according to which in medieval philosophy
> the sign was characterised by the 'classical definition' or the 'famous
> formula of *aliquid stat pro aliquo*' (something that stands for some-
> thing) is mistaken. It is *suppositio*, not *significatio*, that is character-
> ized by that formula. Even in Ockham's concept of sign, which comes
> closest to such a description, the aptitude 'to stand for something' is
> just one component of the whole function of the sign. In no case has the
> sign or act of signifying been conceived as a simple two-term relation of
> 'something standing for something'. (Meier-Oeser 2003: 13)

And we note that Meier-Oeser here specifically cites Jakobson's *Essais*, page
162, as an example of this oversimplification. One could argue (as Eco does)
that the essential distinction between Peircean and Saussurean semiology
resides in this distinction between signs which are independent of, or dependent on, consciousness, and I will return to this distinction in Chapter 5.

For now though, we can note that the divisions within medieval theology extend as far as the determination of the status of writing. Meier-Oeser
notes that for Peter of Ailly, John Major, and Paul of Venice, among others,
writing: 'was no longer viewed as a secondary sign system and mere comple-
ment of speech' (15). Thus, by freeing the written sign 'from its traditional
subordination to the vocal sign by immediately subordinating it to the mental
sign' (15), the late Scholastics were undoubtedly *logocentric* but not *phonocentric*. A direct semiotic relationship between the graphic sign and meaning
was formed, and semiotics was no longer restricted to a phonocentric viewpoint. Indeed, this revision was expanded to include all sensory apparatus:
'The fact that we, in general, . . . do not communicate by means of sensible
qualities like warms or smell, but rather use vocal or written terms in the
strictest sense, is only due to their greater operability' (Paul of Venice, qtd in
Meier-Oeser 2003: 15). In summary, and above all else, as Tabarroni states:
'A history of the theory of signs in the Middle Ages has not yet been written,
nor can we say that this territory has been, if not only timidly, explored'
(195). As such, if a demonstration of systematic solidarity were to take place,
it must take place in Derrida's text, rather than be assumed as self-evident.

Conclusion

What is the implicit scheme of classical semiology to which Derrida will hold Saussure? Derrida asserts that a phonocentrism is essential to certain ancient and medieval theories of language. The only textual evidence that Derrida offers for such a classical phonocentrism is Aristotle's *On Interpretation.* However, this position is hardly disputable, if one allows dissenting positions to exist on the margin. Derrida also argues that these same theories display a logocentrism, which, in this context, is the existence of a sense or meaning prior to the derivation of linguistic signifiers. Such a universal grammar, which is the same for all men, which can be transported but not affected by signifiers, also seems to be present in most ancient and medieval theories of language, although the complexity of the question invites a more complex analysis. The brilliance of Derrida's gesture is to comprehend a general compatibility between the Aristotelian σύμβολον and σημείον, the Augustinian *signum,* and the Saussurean *signe,* that even the most rigorous semiological discourse cannot recognise. But there are certain points in Derrida's account of classical semiology which must be held open if the absorption of Saussure into this metaphysical framework is not to be considered a foregone conclusion.

What Derrida mainly fails to demonstrate in his characterisation of classical semiology is the logical or linguistic co-dependence of phonocentrism and logocentrism. For phonocentrism – as the privilege of speech over writing – and logocentrism – as the belief in mental experience without the need for language – are very different notions, even if they are often found together. The existence of the grapho-logocentric tradition – in the very medieval semiology that Derrida would use against Saussure – works to undermine this connection. Derrida's suggestion that the effacement of the concept is the means by which the vocal signifier is joined to experience, and hence how phonocentrism is joined to logocentrism, does not – at least within the vicinity of Derrida's engagement with ancient and medieval semiology – stand up to any scrutiny. Derrida's observation that Saussure shares a phonocentrism with Plato, Aristotle, and Rousseau is therefore insufficient to demonstrate that he implicitly shares their logocentrism as well. Establishing the independence of the two positions would allow Saussure to be phonocentric but not necessarily logocentric.

The question that this chapter concludes with is *whether or not* Derrida commits enough resources towards demonstrating the systematic and historical solidarity of the Saussurean sign with classical semiology. The more one looks at Derrida's construction of classical semiology, and follows up Derrida's supporting texts and argumentation, the more questions emerge about the solidarity of signs, symbols, thoughts, and things throughout the epoch of the logos. We can observe, for example, that Derrida's reading of Aristotle maps the terms σύμβολον and παθεματα onto the Saussurean *signifiant* and *signifié* without a great deal of caution, or comparative analysis of the two texts. We can also observe that Derrida cites no works of medieval texts to demonstrate his claim of systematic solidarity of the sign with the age of theology. Furthermore, his appropriation of Jakobson seems to both overstate Saussure's inheritance of the medieval *signans* and *signatum*, and overlook Jakobson's warning against the harmfulness of forcing a uniform history of the sign. As such, we can at least note, as we come back to Saussure, a certain openness in Derrida's account of 'classical semiology', and of the epoch of phono-logocentrism. What Derrida's examination of the relationship between classical metaphysics and semiology has allowed us to do, however, is to open up at least three interwoven themes, which will each be pursued over the following chapters: the originality of Saussure; the nature of the concept of the sign; and the relationships between writing, speech, and the voice.

Notes

1. Although we would already have to note that there is no Aristotelian equivalent for what Derrida wants to call 'sign'. That is, there is no term for the combination of signifier/σύμβολον and signified/παθεματα. This problem is taken up in Chapter 3.
2. Roman Jakobson, 'The phonemic and grammatical aspects of language in their interrelations', presented to the *Sixth International Congress of Linguists*, 1949. Note, however, that this passage is usually cited (by Derrida and Meier-Oeser, among others) from the French collection: *Essais de linguistique générale*, vol. 1, 162.

2 The Originality of Saussure

We have just considered the notion of 'classical semiology', and the methods and techniques by which Derrida brings semiology into the framework of classical metaphysics. The centrepiece of evidence in that effort was Roman Jakobson's testimony, cited by Derrida in *Of Grammatology* and in 'Semiology and Grammatology', that the medieval theorisation of the sign has been adopted by Saussure and the structuralist science of signs. This evidence is used by Derrida to posit a metaphysical epoch reaching from Aristotle to Augustine to Saussure, governed by the conceptuality of the sign. Within such an epoch, the more homogeneous the concept of the sign becomes, the less originality can be granted to Saussure. This chapter attempts to establish the originality which Derrida grants to Saussure within the epoch of the sign. As we shall see, such originality stands or falls on the status of Saussure's theory of linguistic *value*. While Derrida never explicitly addresses this theory, his comments on Saussure's maintenance of 'a transcendental signified' would seem to neutralise the possibility of such a theory, as Saussure describes it.

Evidence for Derrida's view of Saussurean originality

What is the evidence for determining Derrida's position on the originality of Saussure? From the very first time that Saussure is mentioned in *Speech and Phenomena*, in which Derrida suggests that the only innovation of the Saussurean signifier is to make it mental, Derrida's engagement with Saussure is frequently punctuated with the question of Saussure's originality, as this sample might indicate:

> Saussure makes the sound-image, the signifier as 'mental impression', into a reality whose sole originality is to be internal, which is only to shift the problem without resolving it. (*S&P*: 46–7)

> Plato, who said basically the same thing about the relationship between writing, speech and being (or idea), had at least a more subtle, more

critical, and less complacent theory of image, painting, and imitation than the one that presides over the birth of Saussurean linguistics. (*OG*: 33)

this theme ['the thesis of *difference* as the source of linguistic value'] that is now so well known (and upon which Plato had already reflected in the Sophist). (*OG*: 52–3)

One finds exactly the same gesture and the same concepts in Hegel. (S&G: 21)

the play of difference, which, as Saussure *reminded* us, is the condition for the possibility and functioning of every sign, is in itself a silent play. (Diff: 5, my italics)

Now if we refer, once again, to semiological difference, of what does Saussure, in particular, *remind* us? That 'language (which consists only of differences) is not a function of the speaking subject'. (Diff: 15, my italics)

Saussure is the theorist who reminds us of the play of difference fundamental to every sign, and presides over a theory of language which is less cautious than Husserl and less subtle than Plato. Saussure's sole originality is to make the signifier mental, which shifts the problem without resolving it. This is not an especially complimentary description of the founder of structuralism, although it must be acknowledged that Derrida is often deeply critical, even of theorists such as Heidegger and Nietzsche, whom he obviously admires. But what is unusual in Derrida's engagement with Saussure is the attention paid to *originality*, an issue that does not play a significant role in any other of Derrida's engagements with major figures. And given that Saussure appears so infrequently in Derrida's linguistic writings, an explanation of this concern over originality is required.

The question of Saussure's originality only deepens when we pause to consider the meaning and timing of the first citation, above, from *Speech and Phenomena*. At the same time that Derrida makes this statement against Saussure's originality, he appears to be applying a very Saussurean argument against the text of Husserl's *Logical Investigations*. The most noticeable debt to Saussure comes in Derrida's decision to frequently transpose, without explanatory note, Husserl's terminology (such as 'indication' and 'expression', 'meaning-intention', and 'object') into the Saussurean terms of 'signifier' and 'signified'. These terms do not appear in the *Logical Investigations* and it is difficult to imagine of whom Derrida could be thinking, if not Saussure. Certainly, Newton Garver's preface to the English edition of *Speech and Phenomena* notes that 'Derrida assumes familiarity with Saussure's terminology and its implications' (xiv), and Roy Harris has said that:

> Before Saussure is ever mentioned by name in *De la grammatologie*, Derrida is already discussing language and writing in Saussurean terms: *signe, signifiant, signifié, langue, parole*, etc. are straight away . . . assumed to belong to a vocabulary with which the reader is familiar and which therefore does not call for preliminary discussion or explanation. (Harris 1987: 172)

But more than merely assuming Saussure's terminology, it is clear that Derrida's entire argument against Husserl's essential distinctions, his intervention in the logic of the *Logical Investigations*, rests upon what Derrida calls 'the difference involved in signs'. Throughout *Speech and Phenomena*, Derrida undermines the primordiality of phenomenological experience and intuition with a more-primordial semiological difference. In Derrida's words: 'by reintroducing the difference involved in "signs" at the core of what is "primordial", . . . we are here indicating the prime intention – and the ultimate scope – of the present essay' (*S&P*: 45–6n). Such a debt to semiological difference is not credited to any theorist in Derrida's text, and yet for David Allison, in the translator's introduction to *Speech and Phenomena*, the identity of the theorist is beyond question:

> Following Saussure, Derrida maintains that linguistic meaning is not so much the product of an explicit meaning-intention as it is the arbitrary configuration of differences between signs. Meaning derives from the distance that extends between one particular sign and the system of other signs in linguistic use. It is this differential character of signs which must first be reckoned with, and this results from conventions existing within language; it is not a matter of meaning-intentions that supervene from without. There is no meaning, no signified content, that stands above and is free from this play of differences. (xxxviii)

For Husserl, there is no 'signification' or 'communication' within interior mental life, for there is nothing to communicate. Meaning is immediately self-present to itself, prior to the need for signification. For Derrida, on the contrary, what is presented to consciousness is already a re-presentation, drawing upon signification and the differences involved in signs. And so, certainly up to a point, *Speech and Phenomena* brings to bear the pressure of semiological difference upon phenomenology, and it is quite odd that Saussure's contribution to this is not anywhere acknowledged.

The next text in which the issue of Saussurean originality is featured, and also the work of Derrida's that is usually cited as being the most direct engagement with Saussure, is *Of Grammatology*. The first chapter of that book mentions Saussure only once, and yet its whole effort is to establish an epoch of the metaphysics of presence, which would lead from Aristotle through the medieval theologians to Hegel and to Saussure and to the present. The centrepiece of evidence in this effort is the citation of Roman Jakobson, in which the structuralist era of semiology has borrowed the medieval terms of *signans* and *signatum*, and that the medieval definition of the sign – *aliquid stat pro aliquo*, something that stands for something else – continues to describe the operation of semiology today. We also remember that a caution needs to be attached to this citation, which is hinted at in the final sentence, that the *signans* and *signatum* 'necessarily suppose and require each other' (Jakobson 1963: 162, qtd in *OG*: 13). Jakobson's position on the matter is absolutely clear: that whoever deals with signs must deal with one aspect sensible and one aspect intelligible. But just as clearly, Jakobson understands that the relationship between the sensible and intelligible aspects of the sign has undergone great changes, and none greater than under Saussure, who is responsible for the structuralist revolution in the study of language. In *Of Grammatology*, Derrida cites this paragraph as his single item of evidence of contemporary semiology's complicity with medieval semiology in order to establish a certain epoch. But we've also learned that, taken alone, the citation appears to unduly indicate that Jakobson felt that Saussure borrowed everything from classical and medieval semiology, from Aristotle and the Stoics. A closer examination of Jakobson's writing, however, reveals the very great originality that he attributes to Saussure. Specifically, while Aristotle understood 'the thing itself' to present itself in the mind as an image, Jakobson credits Saussure with making semiology 'strictly intralinguistic', in which there is no named element which could act as a 'thing' or referent. Furthermore, that for Aristotle, our mental experiences are a natural and universal symbolisation of our common experience of the world, formed independently of language; whereas for Saussure, our mental experience is formed in the language itself, the sensible and intelligible being interdependent and reciprocal, in that they equally define and create the other.[1] Whether or not we take Jakobson as a reliable speaker on the issue will shortly be examined, but the fact will remain that the only similitude between the classical and structuralist systems, according to Jakobson at least, is the duality of the sign in being sensible and intelligible: a similitude which is enough for Jakobson to confer upon these elements the names *signans* and *signatum*. And so the very first response that must be made to Derrida's use of Jakobson in *Of Grammatology* is to clarify the degrees of tradition and of originality that Jakobson bestows upon Saussure. The next step is to ask how much of this acknowledgement of originality is shared by Derrida. Would Derrida wholly adopt Jakobson's position on the originality of Saussure?

   An answer to this question appears to come in a footnote to the citation of Jakobson in *Of Grammatology*, in which Derrida offers this: 'On this problem, on the tradition of the concept of the sign, and on the originality of Saussure's contribution within this continuity, cf. Ortigues' (*OG*: 324). Once again, following up Derrida's reference produces indefinite results, for Ortigues appears to credit Saussure with all the originality we might expect. He writes that: 'the distinction between the *signans* and the *signatum* is ancient. And to appreciate on this point the contribution of Saussure, some words about its history are necessary' (Ortigues 1962: 56, my translation). Ortigues's history begins with Aristotle's 'tripartite' model of the sign, taking in things, mental concepts and words. This tripartition was continued by the Stoics and in the middle ages, although the terminology undergoes several changes.[2] The formula then changes to 'bipartite' in the twelfth century in the Logic of Port-Royal, in which 'The sign contains two ideas: the one of the thing which represents, the other of the thing represented'.[3] At this point, Ortigues asks: 'Which is, on this point, the most significant contribution of Saussure? It is, I believe, his theory of value' (Ortigues 1962: 59, my translation). Ortigues then goes on to give a brief and typical account of Saussure's theory of value, as laid out in the *Course*, pages 112/158 and following, where Saussure contrasts 'meaning' (as mere correspondence between signifier and signified) with 'value' (which is differential with other signs in the language). Can we therefore state that Derrida saw Saussure's originality in such terms, that the theory of value is his contribution to the tradition of the sign?

For Harris, and for myself, the question of value is the central question in relation to the Derridean engagement with Saussurean linguistics. In short, we can ask if the following statement can still be said to be valid in light of Derrida's engagement:

> Saussurean linguistics stands or falls by the Saussurean concept of linguistic values. This is made eminently clear in the *Cours*, where that concept is presented – rightly – as Saussure's most original contribution to modern thinking about language, and indeed to linguistic thought of any era. For no thinker in the entire Western tradition before Saussure ever proposed a view which could be encapsulated in what is perhaps the most famous and contentious of all the Saussurean dicta: *la langue est un système de pures valeurs* (*Cours*: 116). Whether we accept that view or not, it is one which extends the scope of Western thinking on the subject in unprecedented and challenging ways. (Harris 1987: 231)

This position – that linguistic value is the central and defining originality of Saussure – is developed in greatest force in an essay by Samuel Weber (the editor of *Glyph* during the time of the encounter between Derrida and Searle) in his 1976 essay 'Saussure and the apparition of language'. As with Derrida's reading of Saussure, Weber's essay begins from the question of Saussure's relation to Aristotle, and of Saussure's originality within the history of the sign. Weber writes that: 'to get at the specific originality of his conception it is first necessary to clear away some dead wood, which, despite its being dead –

or perhaps because of it – has proved to be a persistent obstacle in obscuring the nature of that originality' (918). And as we shall see, this 'dead wood' is the unadventurous reading of Saussure's theory of the arbitrariness of the sign.

Weber on Saussure's theory of value

Weber opens his analysis with a refutation that the conception of the *arbitraire du signe* was ever original to Saussure. He argues, instead, that it is a notion as old as Western philosophy:

> One of the best known and most quoted features of Saussure's semiotic theory is doubtless the one in which he is also the least innovative: that of the *'arbitraire du signe'*. For inasmuch as this notion is simply held to state that the signifying material of the sign bears no intrinsic or natural resemblance to what it signifies, it subscribes to the most venerable traditions of Western thought concerning the nature of the sign. Already implicit in the writings of Plato, the notion of the arbitrary relation between sign [sic] and signified becomes quite explicit in Aristotle. (918)

Weber then quotes Aristotle, *On Interpretation*, identically to Derrida. Weber's interpretation of this passage is that Aristotle's conception of the sign clearly implies the arbitrariness of linguistic signs:

> As opposed to the mental image of the things themselves, the linguistic sign, whether spoken or written, is thus non-natural and 'arbitrary', and it is Aristotle who can thus be regarded as the first theoretician of the *'arbitraire du signe'*. Moreover, as though to make matters worse, the Aristotelian model seems already to anticipate the Saussurian division of the sign into signifier (i.e. the spoken or written sign) and signified (the mental image). Saussure's terminology, as Jakobson has pointed out, goes back to that of the Stoics, but the conception itself is virtually as old as Western philosophy. (919)

We might briefly note that Jakobson only 'pointed this out' as much as he asserted it without references. And also that it is a questionable claim that Saussure's *terminology* goes back to the Stoics, unless one is prepared to argue that *signum* is essentially the same word as either *signe* or *signifié*. But to continue, Weber makes matters worse still for Saussure, by agreeing with Derrida's critique of Saussure in *Speech and Phenomena* (46), that to make the sign internal merely shifts the problem without resolving it:

> For if he is only concerned with replacing the extralinguistic referent by a mental representation – the 'concept' or 'signified' – this would by no

means radically call into question the underlying category of denomi-
nation as the basic structure of the linguistic sign, no more than had the
mainstream of Western philosophy from Aristotle to Hegel. (919)

Aside from this willingness to fall into Derrida's way of speaking, Weber has
so far argued only for the essential similarity of Saussure and Aristotle. But
as Weber suggests at this point: 'If there is something distinctly innovative
in Saussurian semiotics, it will have to be sought somewhere else than in the
notion of the arbitrariness of the sign, at least interpreted in the conventional
manner' (919).

Weber then comes to the central argument of his essay, that to understand
the true originality, even radicality, of Saussure's theory of the arbitrariness
of the sign, it must be read in light of his theory of linguistic value. He writes
that:

> In the chapters which follow Saussure's initial rejection of the concep-
> tion of language as nomenclature, the traditional model of language as
> representation remains unshaken . . . Indeed, it is only when Saussure
> proceeds from his description of what the sign is – a concrete linguistic
> *entity* – to how it *works*, that this representational-denominational con-
> ception of language is put into question. And this step coincides with
> his introduction of the notion of 'linguistic value'. (920)

This is because the notion of linguistic value puts into doubt all previous
assurances of meaning, as found in its relationship with reality. Saussure calls
language 'a system of pure values', in which meanings only have solidity, or
reality, in relation with other meanings, and in a relationship with sound.
Weber cites Saussure –

> Psychologically our thought – apart from its expression in words – is
> only an amorphous and indistinct mass. Philosophers and linguists have
> always agreed in recognizing that without the help of signs we would be
> unable to distinguish two ideas in a clear and consistent fashion. Taken
> in itself, thought is like a nebula in which nothing is necessarily delim-
> ited. There are no preestablished ideas and nothing is distinct before the
> apparition of the language-system. (*Course (B)*: 111–12)

– and responds that even if 'philosophers and linguists' always agreed that
language is necessary to *distinguish* ideas, they have still excluded language
from the process by which ideas are *constituted*, which has always been
understood to exclude or transcend language:

> What Saussure is asserting here, by contrast, is not simply that lan-
> guage is indispensable for the distinction of ideas, but for their very

constitution. For if 'thought is like a nebula', apart from its articulation
in language, and if there are no 'preestablished ideas' antedating such
articulation, then the traditional conception of language as the representation or expression of thought is undermined, at least implicitly.
(922)

And so, 'Meaning is therefore not constituted by the reference to extralinguistic entities, Aristotle's *prágmata*, but rather in and through the semiotic
process itself' (922–3).

Weber has more to say about the Saussurean sign, particularly about the
status of the sign as representation, which I will discuss in Chapter 5, but it is
already possible to assess his opinion of Saussure's originality. For Aristotle,
linguistic meanings are constituted in the first instance as 'images' of the
things themselves. Such images would be 'the same for all men'. However,
'not all men have the same speech sounds', indicating that different languages
attach different words to these images. Unlike Plato, who believes that words
might point towards an originary and natural language, Aristotle believes
that such designations are arbitrary, or by social convention only. But despite
his belief in an arbitrary relationship between these 'signifieds' and their 'signifiers', there is nothing in Aristotle to indicate that the signifieds themselves
are constituted in a system of differential relations. Saussure's originality,
then, is to make the constitution of signifieds a product, an effect, of articulation and the differential system of language. No meanings are assured or
solid prior to the introduction of linguistic structure. Weber concludes that,
after Saussure: 'Arbitrariness is no longer a notion governed by that of
representation: it no longer designates the fact that the sign is composed of
two dissimilar, heterogeneous elements – the signifier and the signified – but
instead, points to something far more radical' (927). Reaching the end of this
line of thought, Weber believes that if it were not for the concept of value,
Saussurean linguistics would reproduce the Aristotelian notion of the sign.
Does this suggest that what Derrida fails to accept (let us not say comprehend) in Saussurean linguistics are the full implications of the theory of *value*?

The impediment and progress of Saussurean linguistics

The position of Jakobson, Ortigues, Harris and Weber is that Saussure's
originality is to be found in his theory of value. Derrida's opinion seems to
be that the theory of value – 'the thesis of *difference* as the source of linguistic
value' – remains primarily a classical conception, one that Saussure reminds
us of. This must be either because the theory of value was already extant by
the time Saussure reminded us of it, or because any such innovation falls so
firmly within a logocentric framework as to be merely a modification on a
general theme. There is some promise of a resolution to these questions in the

interview with Julia Kristeva, translated as 'Semiology and Grammatology', in which Derrida makes explicit what he sees as the advances and failures of Saussurean semiology. Kristeva asks:

> Semiology today is constructed on the model of the sign and its corre-lates: *communication* and *structure*. What are the 'logocentric' and eth-nocentric limits of these models, and how are they incapable of serving as the basis for a notation attempting to escape metaphysics? (17)

In response, Derrida states that:

> the concept of the sign will have marked, in this sense, a simultaneous impediment and progress. For the sign, by its root and its implications, is in all its aspects metaphysical, if it is in systematic solidarity with stoic and medieval theology, the work and the displacement to which it has been submitted – and of which it also, curiously, is the instrument – have had *delimiting* effects. (17)

As such, as Derrida states, 'a semiology of the Saussurean type has had a double role. *On the one hand*, an absolutely decisive critical role' (S&G: 18). In favour of Saussurean originality, Derrida makes these two points:

1. It has marked, against the tradition, that the signified is inseparable from the signifier, that the signified and signifier are the two sides of one and the same production. Saussure even purposely refused to have this opposition or this 'two-sided unity' conform to the rela-tionship between soul and body, as had always been done. . . .
2. By emphasizing the *differential* and *formal* characteristics of semi-ological functioning, by showing that it 'is impossible for sound, the material element, itself to belong to language' and that 'in its essence (the linguistic signifier) is not at all phonic' (*Cours*: 164); by desub-stantializing both the signified content and the 'expressive substance' – which therefore is no longer in a privileged or exclusive way phonic – by making linguistics a division of general semiology (*Cours*: 33), Saussure powerfully contributed to turning against the metaphysical tradition the concept of sign that he borrowed from it. (S&G: 18)

Some comments on these two advances of Saussurean linguistics are neces-sary, for each point is curious for its own reasons. A detailed review of each will help us to more precisely understand the nature of the innovation being granted to Saussure.

Derrida's first point in support of Saussure's advancement of semiology would, at face value, appear to confirm Jakobson's statement that Saussure's originality lies in making the signified reciprocal with signifier. Unlike the

Aristotelian model, the signified is not constituted prior to its definition in signifieds, but instead, the two are inseparable and part of one production. That is, in Jakobson's words, that they 'require and suppose each another', and in Saussure's words, they comprise the 'mutually complementary delimitation of units' (*Course*: 110/156). The curiosity of this point lies in its complete retraction on the following page of 'Semiology and Grammatology'. For in his first point against the advance of Saussure, Derrida states that:

> The maintenance of the rigorous distinction – an essential and juridical distinction – between the *signans* and the *signatum*, the equation of the *signatum* and the concept (*Cours*: 99), inherently leaves open the possibility of thinking a *concept signified in and of itself*, a concept simply present for thought, independent of a relationship to language, that is of a relationship to a system of signifiers. By leaving open this possibility – and it is inherent even in the opposition signifier/signified, that is in the sign – Saussure contradicts the critical acquisitions of which we were just speaking. He accedes to the classical exigency of what I have proposed to call a 'transcendental signified', which in and of itself, in its essence, would refer to no signifier, would exceed the chain of signs, and would no longer itself function as a signifier. (19–20)

Within this passage, the word 'concept' and its reference to the *Cours* (99), is footnoted with, once again, the Jakobson citation. Except that when Derrida comes to repeat this citation, only a year after the publication of *Of Grammatology*, he omits the final sentence, Jakobson's statement that: 'These two constituents of a linguistic sign (and of sign in general) necessarily suppose and require each other'. It is difficult to believe that the omission of this sentence (which is, in the original, the entire point of Jakobson's paragraph) was accidental or due to a lack of space, given that this citation appears in a passage where Derrida is attempting to establish the exact opposite: that Saussurean semiology maintains a signified which is simply present to thought, prior to and independent of a relationship with a signifier. Given that it is, for Derrida, the maintenance of such a signified which contradicts the critical acquisitions of Saussurean semiology, a full examination of Saussure's relationship with a 'transcendental signified' needs to take place in its own right. Such an examination will be attempted shortly. But it is enough for the moment to note that the first point of originality that Derrida grants to Saussure is immediately revoked upon the truncated testimony of Jakobson.

The second point that Derrida makes for Saussure's originality has its own curiosities. To begin with, Derrida uses three technical terms of Saussurean semiology – being the differential, formal, and material aspects of the sign – as if they were synonymous. Derrida's discussion of the *Course* in this passage is, however, limited to the dematerialisation of the sign. And if Saussure's contribution to linguistics was only to make the signifier and signified mental, rather than physical, it would be a minor advance indeed. To claim that such a gesture 'powerfully contributed to turning against the metaphysical tradition' would seem to contradict Derrida's own observation, in *Speech and Phenomena*, that to simply make the sign mental 'is only to shift the problem without resolving it' (47). Weber's argument that Saussurean linguistics goes much further than merely 'replacing the extralinguistic referent by a mental representation' would certainly seem to be relevant here. The second curiosity to arise from this point is in Derrida's choice of words when he writes that Saussure 'emphasised' the differential and formal characteristics of the sign. This is consistent with Derrida's view in 'Différance' that it was Saussure who 'reminded' us of the principle of difference involved in signs. It suggests that Derrida's view is that Saussure's contribution to semiological difference is minimal or non-existent, and certainly falls far short of the prevailing view of Saussure as the founder of the principle of difference as a radically original basis for studying language. In a point that is supposed to be marking Saussure's contribution to linguistics it is question-begging to make such an oblique remark against the generally held belief that Saussure is rightly the founder of the principle of difference. If it was Derrida's ambition to write a counter-argument to this belief, he has chosen a particularly tangential and enigmatic way of going about it. But such a view, that Saussure only 'emphasised' the differential and formal aspects of the sign, would perhaps help to explain how Derrida can acknowledge the advancement of 'the difference involved in signs' while at the same time undermining Saussure's own contribution to such a theory. What complicates such a view is that Derrida declines to ever discuss the notion of 'value', perhaps the only term in the semiological lexicon that can be unequivocally attributed to Saussure.

The question being posed in this chapter concerns the originality that Derrida grants to Saussure within the tradition of the sign. Throughout his engagement with Saussure, Derrida presents 'the difference involved in signs' as a classical conception, already in the writing of Plato and the Stoics. In this way, Derrida consistently, but implicitly, challenges the prevailing view that Saussure's theory of linguistic value represents a radical reappraisal of signs, language and semantics. When Derrida argues *for* Saussure's originality, it falls far short of that even granted by Jakobson. Answering the question of this chapter is frustrated by Derrida's failure, or refusal, to directly critique Saussure's theory of linguistic value. In order to make Derrida's commentary engage with Saussure's theory it is necessary, and not unreasonable, to imagine his critique of 'the transcendental signified' as his closest refutation of Saussurean value. And so, before bringing this question to a close, a critical examination of the role of the transcendental signified in Derrida's engagement with Saussure is essential.

The transcendental signified

In 'Semiology and Grammatology', Derrida states that the concept of the sign is divided between a *signans* and a *signatum*, which then allows 'thinking a *concept signified in and of itself*, a concept simply present for thought, independent of a relationship to language, that is of a relationship to a system of signifiers' (19). In maintaining such a conception of the sign, Saussure confirms the classical commitment to 'a "transcendental signified", which in and of itself, in its essence, would refer to no signifier, would exceed the chain of signs, and would no longer itself function as a signifier' (19–20). If such a transcendental signified can exist independently of signifiers, that is, of language, then it can remain a pure mental essence, ready to be transported through some medium of communication to another. To rephrase, as he does in 'Semiology and Grammatology', what Derrida objects to so forcefully is:

> absolutely pure, transparent, and unequivocal translatability . . . We will never have, and in fact have never had, to do with some 'transport' of pure signifieds from one language to another, or within one and the same language, that the signifying instrument would leave virgin and untouched. (20)

The question that 'Semiology and Grammatology' provokes is *whether or not* Saussure leaves open this possibility of a transcendental signified. Within Saussurean linguistics, is it possible to think a concept independently of a system of signifiers?

The first, and possibly weakest, argument against Derrida's position is that Saussure does not seem to present signifieds as independent of signifiers in the text of the *Course*. I say weakest, because to some extent this defence relies on reconstituting Saussure's intentions within the often contradictory arrangement of the *Course*. But we will use what we have, and quote Saussure, as so many others have done, from the first section of the first chapter, titled 'The Nature of the Linguistic Sign':

> For some people a language, reduced to its essentials, is a nomenclature: a list of terms corresponding to a list of things . . . This conception is open to a number of objections. It assumes that ideas exist independently of words. (*Course*: 65/97)

The frequency of citation of this paragraph suggests that it is one of the strongest in the *Course*. It announces the theme of the entire book, with almost arrogant certainty, that thought is dependent upon language. In the same vein, Saussure asserts that:

Languages are not mechanisms created and organised with a view to the concepts to be expressed, although people are mistakenly inclined to think so. (*Course*: 85/121–2)

And similarly that:

Any linguistic entity exists only in virtue of the association between signifier and signified. It disappears the moment we concentrate exclusively on just one or the other. (*Course*: 101/144)

As the *Course* progresses, and each orthodoxy is challenged in turn, Saussure's conceptualisation of the sign gains in complexity and robustness. The most complete statement on the mutual dependence of signifiers and signifieds appears in the chapter 'Linguistic Value', a passage that Samuel Weber has already cited in support of Saussurean originality:

Psychologically, setting aside its expression in words, our thought is simply a vague, shapeless mass. Philosophers and linguists have always agreed that were it not for signs, we should be incapable of differentiating any two ideas in a clear and constant way. In itself, thought is like a swirling cloud, where no shape is intrinsically determinate. No ideas are established in advance, and nothing is distinct, before the introduction of linguistic structure. (*Course*: 110/155)

Saussure continues:

But do sounds, which lie outside this nebulous world of thought, in themselves constitute entities established in advance? No more than ideas do. . . .
    The characteristic role of a language in relation to thought is not to supply the material phonetic means by which ideas may be expressed. It is to act as intermediary between thought and sound, in such a way that the combination of both necessarily produces a mutually complementary delimitation of units. Thought, chaotic by nature, is made precise by this process of segmentation. But what happens is neither a transformation of thoughts into matter, nor a transformation of sounds into ideas. What takes place, is a somewhat mysterious process by which 'thought-sound' evolves divisions, and a language takes shape with its linguistic units in between those two amorphous masses. (*Course*: 110–11/155–6)

Saussure follows these observations with the categorical conclusion that: 'it is impossible in a language to isolate sound from thought, or thought from sound' (*Course*: 111/157). For many readers, although evidently not

Derrida, these quotes support the view that, for Saussure, signifieds cannot exist independently of signifiers, or before the introduction of linguistic structure. To conclude, therefore, this recourse to the *Course*: the evidence against Derrida's position, at least at the level of semiological discourse, is overwhelming.

One could counter at this point that Derrida's engagement with Saussure exceeds the language and logic of semiology to respond, and hence that attention to individual sentences in the *Course* is insufficient to apprehend the logocentric drive in the whole. This is no doubt true, and further consideration will be given to this possibility in the next chapter. But it needs to be observed, if we are to give pertinence to the *Course* at all, that none of the above anti-logocentric passages is cited by Derrida in his commentary on Saussure, except for the single composite word 'thought-sound' (S&G: 21).[4] At no point does Derrida address any contradiction or errors in logic or procedure in these passages from the *Course* which outline his theory of linguistic value. There is, in fact, only *one* passage in the *Course* concerning linguistic value, and the reciprocality of signifiers and signifieds, that Derrida addresses. Derrida's analysis of this passage, however, raises more questions than it answers about his commitment to exploring the subtlety of the theory of value as it appears in the *Course*.

Language as a sheet of paper

Along with the analogy of the chess game (which illustrates the synchronic structure of *la langue*), Saussure's most famous analogy compares the language system to a sheet of paper. Immediately following his definition of linguistic value, cited above, Saussure provides this analogy to illustrate the interdependence of signifiers and signifieds:

> A language might also be compared to a sheet of paper. Thought is one side of the sheet and sound the reverse side. Just as it is impossible to take a pair of scissors and cut one side of the paper without at the same time cutting the other, so it is impossible in a language to isolate sound from thought, or thought from sound. (111/157)

Derrida refers to this analogy twice in his writings on Saussure. First, in 'Freud and the Scene of Writing', he writes that:

> Even if, along with Saussure, we envisage the distinction between signified and signifier only as the two sides of a sheet of paper, nothing is changed. Originary writing, if there is one, must produce the space and the materiality of the sheet itself. (210)

And then again in *Of Grammatology*:

> The notion of the sign always implies within itself the distinction
> between signifier and signified, even if, as Saussure argues, they are dis-
> tinguished simply as the two faces of one and the same leaf. This notion
> remains therefore within the heritage of that logocentrism which is also
> a phonocentrism. (11)

The objection to Derrida's use of the analogy is immediately obvious to a
close reader of Saussure. Harris grasps the problem when he points out that
Derrida's interpretation of Saussure's analogy misleadingly suggests that the
sheet of paper represents the sign, with the signifier on one side and the signified on the other: 'Derrida fails to mention that the sheet is not the sign. The
sheet itself is *la langue*' (Harris 2001: 174). Similarly, Roland Barthes writes,
under the title of 'The Articulation', that:

> In order to account for the double phenomenon of signification and
> value, Saussure used the analogy of a sheet of paper ... This com-
> parison is useful because it leads us to an original conception of the
> production of meaning: no longer as the mere correlation of a signifier
> and a signified, but perhaps more essentially *as an act of simultaneously
> cutting out* two amorphous masses. (Barthes 1969: 56)

It is impossible, in other words, to cut one side without cutting the other,
hence it is impossible to partition, or 'articulate', either element without
simultaneously and reciprocally articulating the other. The analogy is for
articulation, and the analogy rests in the action of the scissors. Until contradictory evidence can be produced, it is necessary to conclude that Derrida
has either misunderstood or misrepresented Saussure's analogy of the sheet
of paper: as a single sign, rather than *la langue*; as signification, rather than
articulation; and as a simple bilateral entity, rather than the mutual and differential articulation of units.

The possibility that Derrida fails to fully engage with the implications of
Saussurean value is also supported by Derrida's comment that, following
Nietzsche's work to liberate 'the signifier from its dependence or derivation
with respect to the logos and the related concept of truth or the primary signified' (*OG*: 19):

> This does not, by simple inversion, mean that signifier is fundamental
> or primary. The 'primacy' or 'priority' of the signifier would be an
> expression untenable and absurd to formulate illogically within the
> very logic that it would legitimately destroy. The signifier will never
> by rights precede the signified, in which case it would no longer be a
> signifier and the 'signifying' signifier would no longer have a possible
> signified. (*OG*: 324)

One would ask how Derrida can so easily admit that a signifier which is prior to and independent of a signified ceases to be a signifier, without taking the exactly opposite precaution.

Conclusion

It is therefore my conclusion that Derrida's stated belief that Saussure reproduces a transcendental signified – a belief which is seldom argued for but very often implied – is untenable in a literal reading of the *Course*. The division of the sign into two related elements is not inherently logocentric; it is only so if the division allows 'a concept simply present for thought, independent of a relationship to language, that is of a relationship to a system of signifiers' (S&G: 19). In Saussure's case, his semiological system determines otherwise. As we shall see in the following chapters, there are a number of important consequences to be drawn from Derrida's failure to support his claim, particularly given the place, not just within semiology but within Western metaphysics in its totality, that Derrida gives to 'this fundamental quest for a "transcendental signified" and a concept independent of language' (S&G: 20).

It would be possible, of course, to continue with the textual pursuit attempted in this chapter, but perhaps it is not possible to exhaust a totalising discussion of *whether or not* the *Course* maintains the metaphysical quest for the transcendental signified. For this question cannot stand alone, but as Derrida says, 'it must pass through the difficult deconstruction of the entire history of metaphysics' (S&G: 20). If one accepts Derrida's suggestion, then it is not enough to overturn his argument by literal reference to the text of the *Course*; one must follow Derrida into an understanding of how the sign is implicated in the entire history of metaphysics. As Derrida puts it in 'Structure, Sign, and Play':

> we can pronounce not a single destructive proposition which has not already had to slip into the form, the logic, and the implicit postulations of precisely what it seeks to contest. To take one example from many: the metaphysics of presence is shaken with the help of the concept of *sign*. But as I suggested a moment ago, as soon as one seeks to demonstrate in this way that there is no transcendental or privileged signified and that the domain or play of signification henceforth has no limit, one must reject even the concept and word 'sign' itself – which is precisely what cannot be done. (280–1)

According to this proposition, it is impossible to continue to use the concept of the sign 'without also bringing with it all its metaphysico-theological roots. To these roots adheres not only the distinction between the sensible and the intelligible – already a great deal – with all that it controls, namely, metaphysics in its totality' (*OG*: 13). The critical acquisitions of the *Course* in: (1) making the signifier reciprocal with the signified, and (2) dematerialising and formalising the sign, are essentially neutralised, or made *ineffective*, by Saussure's continued use of the word and concept 'sign', and maintenance of a classical and logocentric relationship with presence.

But what the *Course* does, in its complex and rigorous formulations of the theory of value, is to force Derrida into showing exactly *how* the Saussurean sign follows certain metaphysical presuppositions. Too often, for Derrida, 'it would be easy enough to show' (SS&P: 278), or 'it could be shown' (S&G: 32; SS&P: 279), or 'it would be easy to demonstrate' (*OG*: 11; SEC: 6), or 'we ought to demonstrate' (Diff: 12). And yet Derrida fails to prosecute his case on *each* of these occasions. In relation to the demonstration that Saussure maintains a transcendental signified, Derrida does not cite any of the passages in the *Course* in which Saussure announces the impossibility of separating thought from sound, and of a signified independent of signifiers. Nor does Derrida ever critique the theory of linguistic value. At the same time, in demonstrating that Saussure's paper analogy allows an independent signified, he appears to underestimate the originality in Saussure's theory of *articulation*. The question of this chapter concerns the originality granted to Saussure within the tradition of the sign. Alternatively, we could ask how Saussure's metaphysics intervene to prevent him from claiming the critical acquisitions of the theory of value as the source of semiological difference. Even after considering Derrida's discussion of the 'transcendental signified', such a question must still be open.

Notes

1. In Saussure's words, the 'mutually complementary delimitation of units' (*Course*: 110/156).
2. '[The Stoics] distinguished three terms: the signifier (*semaïnon*), which is the voice (*phonē*); the signified (*semaïnomenon*), which is the concept, or that which it is shown (*pragma*, *deloumenon*); and finally the reality of the event (*tunchanon*), which supplies us with the subject (*hypokeimenon*). This tripartite division was preserved in the Middle Ages: the signans becomes the *vox* or the *nomen* (the *consignificantia* are the grammatical forms or morphemes); the *signatum* is the concept, which is distinguished from the *res*' (Ortigues 1962: 56, my translation).
3. Ortigues cites this as: '*La logique*, par MM. De Port-Royal, p. 1, chap. 4'.
4. A discussion of this citation of 'thought-sound' takes place in Chapter 4.

3 The Concept of the Sign

I have just spent some time working through what Derrida calls 'the tradition of the concept of the sign, and . . . the originality of Saussure's contribution within this continuity' (*OG*: 324). This analysis of Saussure's contribution to this tradition was undertaken in the faith that we can speak coherently of 'the tradition of the concept of the sign'. It is curious, however, given his efforts to identify logocentric operations in the metaphysics of philosophy, that Derrida should be so willing to speak of 'the concept of the sign' as if it had an identity and a history independent from the names one might assign to it. Such a commitment also seems to override everything in Saussure's own theory of semiology that rejects the very possibility of concepts with histories. Exactly how does this concept exist through time: as a signified without a signifier, or as a signified which is passed from one signifier to another, from σύμβολον to *signum* to *signe*? In Saussurean terms, we would have to ask how this concept survives the linguistic rigours of the passing of time.

And so, *if*, in the previous chapter we finally came to understand that what holds Saussure back from all the loosening implications of his work, all that marks him as maintaining a relationship with presence, is carried by his continued use of 'the concept of the sign', then what is this concept, and what is its history? What enables its coherence and unity, even when Derrida himself allows that certain conceptual changes have occurred under the name of the sign? There is a pivotal moment in Derrida's engagement with Saussure, in 'Semiology and Grammatology', immediately after Derrida has granted certain innovations to the Saussurean version of the sign, when he writes that: 'There is at least one moment at which Saussure must renounce drawing all the conclusions from the critical work he has undertaken, and that is the not fortuitous moment when he resigns himself to using the word "sign", lacking anything better' (19). Derrida states that Saussure's continued use of the concept of the sign necessitates a certain adherence to its traditional values: 'One necessarily assumes, in a non-critical way, at least some of the implications inscribed in its system' (19). But how is this continuity achieved, given that Derrida immediately prior to this statement acknowledges at least two Saussurean innovations in the conceptualisation of the sign, in the *reciprocity* of the signifier-signified relation, and the *dematerialisation* of the signifier? At what point, for Derrida, could the features of the sign change so much that the concept would be no longer the same? In relation specifically to 'the concept of the sign', this question is particularly pertinent; for prior to Saussure, there was, *in fact*, no name for this concept as Derrida intends it. As we shall see, Derrida repeatedly states that 'the concept of the sign' is defined as the combination of a signifier and signified. And yet before Saussure, no name existed for this entity, this concept. As Saussure states in the passage that Derrida cites above, the word 'sign' has only ever been applied to 'the sound pattern alone' (*Course*: 99). And so, if such a concept of sign did exist, then it did so without a name, which is a theoretical complication for Derrida as much as it is for Saussure. In this chapter I will explore Derrida's paradoxical treatment of the identity and history of the concept of the sign.

Derrida's definition of the sign

We can begin by examining what evidence exists for a unified definition of 'the concept of the sign', as it is understood by Derrida. Earliest of all, in 'Freud and the Scene of Writing', the name 'Saussure' appears in connection with this description:

> Translation, a system of translation, is possible only if a permanent code allows a substitution or transformation of signifiers while retaining the same significd, always present, despite the absence of any specific signifier. This fundamental possibility of substitution would thus be implied by the coupled concepts signified/signifier, and would consequently be implied by the concept of the sign itself. (210)

Derrida here defines the concept of the sign as the coupled concepts signified and signifier, which implies a signified which exists independently of the signifier, which is then a transcendental signified. Such a transcendental signified can be transported by signifiers without affecting the transported concept. As we shall see, this is the fundamental way in which Derrida will speak of the concept of the sign throughout his early, linguistically oriented essays.

In 'Structure, Sign, and Play', for example, Derrida has already begun to move away from the close textual analysis of his earliest essays towards the grander scale of *Of Grammatology*, and yet a certain conceptualisation of the sign is retained:

> the signification 'sign' has always been understood and determined, in its meaning, as sign-of, as signifier referring to a signified, a signifier different to its signified. If one erases the radical difference between signifier and signified, it is the word 'signifier' itself which must be abandoned

as a metaphysical concept. . . . [T]he concept of the sign cannot in itself surpass this opposition between the sensible and the intelligible. The concept of the sign, in each of its aspects, has been determined by this opposition throughout the totality of its history. (SS&P: 281)

The first issue that needs to be raised about this passage is that Derrida's statement: 'the signification "sign" has always been understood and determined, in its meaning, as sign-of, as signifier referring to a signified, a signifier different to its signified', is difficult to accept in its current form. On the contrary, what is correct is Saussure's statement, partially quoted by Derrida, above, that the word 'sign' has always referred to the sound pattern alone:

> In our terminology a *sign* is the combination of a concept and a sound pattern. But in current usage the term *sign* generally refers to the sound pattern alone, e.g. the word form *arbor*. It is forgotten that if *arbor* is called a sign, it is only because it carries within it the concept 'tree', so that the sensory part of the term implies reference to the whole.
>   The ambiguity would be removed if the three notions in question were designated by terms which are related but contrast. We propose to keep the term *sign* to designate the whole, but to replace *concept* and *sound pattern* respectively by *signified* and *signifier*. The latter terms have the advantage of indicating the distinction which separates each from the other and both from the whole of which they are part. We retain the term *sign*, because current usage suggests no alternative by which it might be replaced. (*Course*: 67/99–100)

As I have already stated, prior to this proposal of Saussure's, there was no word for the relation between the signifier and signified, and in Saussurean terms at least, this implies that no such concept existed either.

Derrida's characterisation of 'the concept of the sign' rouses deeper concerns in the Saussurean reader. For if, in 'Freud and the Scene of Writing', Derrida wrote only of concepts – of the sign and of signifiers and signifieds – as having a certain historical existence, then in 'Structure, Sign, and Play' *both* the concepts *and* the words of sign, signifier and signified are implicated in this characterisation of an epoch. Derrida claims that it is 'the word signifier itself' which must be abandoned in order to loosen the metaphysics of presence. And again in this passage, Derrida writes that both the concept and the word sign must be rejected:

> as soon as one seeks to demonstrate in this way that there is no transcendental or privileged signified and that the domain or play of signification henceforth has no limit, one must reject even the concept and word 'sign' itself – which is precisely what cannot be done. (SS&P: 280–1)

This gesture confirms what Derrida seems to be suggesting in the first citation of this chapter, that Saussure continues to use the concept of the sign in that moment when he uses the word 'sign', lacking anything better. What is difficult to understand about Derrida's gesture is the extent to which such a word could have unity, or identity. It is not ever clear whether 'the word "sign" itself' would apply as much to the Aristotelian σύμβολον, Augustine's *signum*, or even to Saussure's *signifiant*. Perhaps this 'word' can survive lexical variation to the same degree that 'the concept of the sign' can survive the conceptual variations of Aristotle, Augustine, Bacon, Locke and Saussure. A close reading of Derrida's statements here begins to provoke the anxiety that one can never be completely sure whether Derrida is talking about signs, signifiers or signifieds at any particular point. Indeed, in that very sentence when Derrida is defining the meaning of 'sign' ('the signification *sign* has always been understood and determined in its meaning, as sign of, as signifier referring to a signified, a signifier different to its signified'), he is content to use 'sign, 'signifier', and even 'signification' as synonyms.

On this issue, Roy Harris makes a rather acute point. He believes that Derrida's engagement with the terminology of Saussure is not an application of argument, but merely of lexical association. He says:

> We are not dealing here with accidental infelicities of style but with a calculated rhetorical technique of which there are many other examples in Derrida's writing. In political journalism it is known as the 'smear'. Rather than actually demonstrate a connexion between person *A* and person *B*, the journalist implies connexion by means of lexical association. The technique is all the more effective when the lexical association can be based on terms that either *A* or *B* actually uses. This dispenses with any need to argue a case; or, if any case is argued, its conclusion is already tacitly anticipated in the terms used to present it. (Harris 2001: 173)

Of course, we know that following 'Structure, Sign, and Play', Derrida only expanded his use of what Harris calls 'lexical association' in a clearly strategic way. Puns and homophones and other plays on language became, for Derrida, a powerful tool in his effort to deconstruct the historical privilege of meaning over signification. Derrida's linguistic strategies draw our attention back to signifiers, which we might otherwise want to discard as quickly as possible in order to get to the thing that matters – the signified sense. As such, there is nothing illegitimate about Derrida's use of lexical association in general. However, what Derrida does with *this particular* lexical association almost definitely exceeds the profundity of his observation. That is, the implications and extensions of classical semiology that Derrida draws from, in all aspects of his rhetoric, far exceeds the source – the fund in the rhetorical bank – which he has established with the lexical association of the word 'sign'. To say that Aristotle's σύμβολον has conceptual similarities to Saussure's *signifi-ant* is one thing, but to claim that both the word and the concept of *signe* have a continuous history as a signifier divided from a signified is excessive.

Harris, as I have, questions Derrida's approach to the conceptual continu-ity of the sign as a signifier opposed to a signified:

> Derrida wedges his foot in the semiological door with the claim that 'la notion de signe implique toujours en elle-même la distinction du signifié et du signifiant'. But does it? And where does this 'notion de signe . . . en elle-même' come from? Saussure, for one, would have been among the first to contest its validity . . . For while there are various grounds on which Saussurean semiology might be criticized, it is question-begging to attack it by invoking an *a priori* 'notion of the sign itself'. (Harris 2001: 174–5)

What never actually becomes clear is whether it is the *concept* of the sign, or the *name* of the sign, or *both* elements which have continuity. In the single paragraph from 'Structure, Sign, and Play' being examined here, there is evidence for all positions. On the side of it being the concept which has conti-nuity, Derrida writes that 'the concept of the sign cannot in itself surpass this opposition between the sensible and the intelligible. The concept of the sign, in each of its aspects, has been determined by this opposition throughout the totality of its history' (281). However, on the side of it being the signifier of sign which has continuity, Derrida writes that 'the signification sign' and 'the word signifier itself' must be abandoned. Such a gesture relates to Derrida's belief that Saussure's unfortunate use of the *word* sign means that he must renounce the advances that his novel *conceptualisation* of the sign could offer. Perhaps it is as Harris suggests, that something far less technical than the language of Saussure's semiology – something like a 'notion' of the sign – is the element with unity and continuity. Although, having brought attention to this issue of words and concepts in the epoch of the sign, we could alterna-tively argue that a phrase such as: 'it is the *word* "signifier" itself which must be abandoned as a metaphysical *concept*' (SS&P: 281, my italics) reveals the not always rigorous way in which the *Course*, and Saussure's terminology, is appropriated by Derrida. Critically, when Derrida writes that: 'No more than any other, this concept cannot be employed in both an absolutely novel and an absolutely conventional way' (S&G: 18–19), we begin to genuinely wonder whether Derrida might have meant to say 'this word' instead of 'this concept'. Derrida's slippage from signs to signifiers, and from concepts to words and back again, can be interpreted as either a lack of care with the ele-ments of the theory he is critiquing, or as simply another instance of how the epoch of the metaphysics of presence subsumes all such distinctions within its operant conditions. However, it is precisely these moments of terminological laissez-faire that confuse and aggrieve linguists such as Harris. For myself, I

feel that the lack of direct and consistent engagement with Saussurean terminology begins to reveal a more comprehensive incommensurability between
the critical languages of Derrida and Saussure. But this is an incommensurability that can only be revealed slowly. For the moment, it is enough to note
that Derrida's definition of 'the concept of the sign' is of a provisional and
secondary signifier divided from its transcendental and permanent signified.
This is the concept of the sign which has defined and controlled that history
of metaphysics, and which has as its goal the reunification of thought and
matter, and hence also the reassurance of the possibility of truth. Despite all
this, Derrida's own engagement with the sign is marked by an 'equivocality'.
For Derrida, the sign both confirms and shakes logocentric assumptions. But
what does Derrida want with this concept of the sign? In what ways does he
wish to continue to use the concept of the sign, and in what ways must the
sign be reformed or restored, or abandoned?

The difference involved in signs

Returning again to 'Structure, Sign, and Play', we see that Derrida's belief in
the potential of the sign to loosen metaphysics is as powerful as it is short-
lived. Derrida writes of the moment in which 'the structurality of structure
had to begin to be thought':

> This was the moment when language invaded the universal problem-
> atic, the moment when, in the absence of a center or origin, everything
> became discourse – provided we can agree on this word – that is to say,
> a system in which the central signified, the original or transcendental
> signified, is never absolutely present outside a system of differences. The
> absence of the transcendental signified extends the domain and the play
> of signification infinitely. (280)

If only momentarily, Derrida allows the differences involved in signs to
rupture that bond between thought and the material world which is essential
to the epoch of the metaphysics of presence. And even if Derrida immediately
moves to show how the sign restores this bond, we can at least in this moment
understand the emancipatory advance of the concept of the sign as the *possibility* of the unlimited play of difference, and of the absence of a centring,
reassuring, transcendental signified.

This possibility is most forcefully applied by Derrida when he brings
'the difference involved in signs' to bear against Husserl's phenomenology
in *Speech and Phenomena*. The semiological nature of Derrida's critique is
acknowledged here, where he writes that: 'by reintroducing the difference
involved in "signs" at the core of what is "primordial", . . . we are here indicating the prime intention – and the ultimate scope – of the present essay'

(45–6n). Derrida's critique of Husserl's phenomenology is of a philosophical system which aims to restore an intuitive relationship with truth without the need for language and signs, as this selection from *Speech and Phenomena* indicates:

> Husserl no doubt did want to maintain . . . an originally silent, 'pre-expressive' stratum of experience. (15)

> Husserl, who never wanted to assimilate experience in general (empirical or transcendental) with language, will ceaselessly strive to keep signification outside the self-presence of transcendental life. (31)

> Husserl believes in the existence of a pre-expressive and prelinguistic stratum of sense. (31)

> the certitude of inner existence, Husserl thinks, has no need to be signified. It is immediately present to itself. It is living consciousness. (43)

In short, Husserl's phenomenological method proceeds by:

> repressing difference by assigning it to the exteriority of the signifiers. (82)

Derrida's intervention in the logic of the *Logical Investigations* is to bring the outside of semiological difference to the inside of phenomenological experience. Derrida's semiological argument builds to the point where he can state that:

> the whole theory of signification introduced in this first chapter devoted to essential distinctions would collapse if . . . the ideal or absolute solitude of subjectivity 'proper' still needed indications to constitute its own relation to itself. We see unmistakably that in the end the need for indications simply means the need for signs. (42)

In other words, Derrida understands Husserl as wanting to exclude signs from the interiority of solitary mental life. For Derrida's purposes – for his critique of Husserl, for his undermining of Husserl's essential distinctions – all that he requires is the restoration of the primordiality of semiological difference. Derrida goes beyond this elsewhere, and even in *Speech and Phenomena* to some degree, but this intervention could rest on Saussurean notions exclusively.

But if *Speech and Phenomena* shows how the concept of the sign helps to shake logocentric assuredness, then at the same time, Derrida claims that the sign falls back into the language of the metaphysics it seeks to escape. The simultaneity of these arguments makes it possible, or even necessary, to begin to imagine two different manifestations of the 'notion' of the sign: one carrying the differentiating potential to uproot the relationship with presence; and the other falling back into the language and logic of logocentrism through the sign's unbreakable commitment to a transcendental signified. Derrida writes of these two ways in which semiological difference can operate; first of all in 'Structure, Sign, and Play':

> there are two heterogenous ways of erasing the difference between the signifier and the signified: one, the classic way, consists in reducing or deriving the signifier, that is to say, ultimately in *submitting* the sign to thought; the other, the one we are using here against the first one, consists in putting into question the system in which the preceding reduction functioned: first and foremost, the opposition between the sensible and the intelligible. (281)

And then in *Speech and Phenomena*:

> there are two ways of eliminating the primordiality of the sign . . . Signs can be eliminated in the classical manner in a philosophy of intuition and presence. Such a philosophy eliminates signs by making them derivative; it annuls reproduction and representation by making signs a modification of a simple presence. But because it is just such a philosophy – which is, in fact, *the* philosophy and history of the West – which has so constituted and established the very concept of signs, the sign is from its origin and to the core of its sense marked by this will to derivation or effacement. Thus, to restore the original and nonderivative character of signs, in opposition to classical metaphysics, is, by an apparent paradox, at the same time to eliminate a concept of signs whose whole history and meaning belong to the adventure of the metaphysics of presence. (51)

To paraphrase: the sign is defined by the opposition between the signifier and the signified, or equivalently, by the sensible and the intelligible; classical metaphysics reduces or derives or eliminates signifiers by making them exterior to meaning; the signified can then remain untouched by the influence of signs; signs are then understood as modifications, or transportations, of an originary presence. Against these operations of classical metaphysics, Derrida offers an alternative treatment of the sign: to restore the original and non-derivative character of the sign by putting into question the sign's very essence – the opposition between the sensible and the intelligible.

58 *What if Derrida was wrong about Saussure?*

The paradox of the concept of the sign

At this point, we begin to sense a certain tension between Derrida's simultaneous uses of the concept of the sign as both confirming and shaking the metaphysics of presence. Derrida writes that the 'primordiality' of the sign can be eliminated by Western metaphysics, which would imply that the primordial and differential sign, the sign-as-play, predates Western metaphysics, which then eliminates it by making it derivative. Such a primordial sign can be 'restored' to its 'original' character by putting into question the division between signifier and signified. Given that Derrida explicitly refers to metaphysics as an 'epoch' and an 'adventure', with real historical actors, it is reasonable to suppose that Derrida means that a historical time existed prior to the advent of Western metaphysics in which the difference involved in signs was primordial. However, as Derrida acknowledges, it is apparently paradoxical that such a metaphysics should also have 'constituted' and 'established' the concept of the sign. It is particularly difficult to understand why Derrida's intervention should be understood as a 'restoration' of the 'original' character of the sign, when Derrida will at other times state that 'when one submits the sign to the question of essence, to the "ti esti" . . . the formal essence of the sign can only be determined in terms of presence' (*OG*: 18). Or again, that the function of 'grammatology' is to transform the concept of the sign by 'uprooting it from its congenital expressivism' (S&G: 34).

Gathering together all these epochal statements from Derrida's early, linguistically oriented texts reveals that he believes the sign to be – from its birth and in its essence – logocentric. But at the same time, Derrida claims to want to restore the original and primordial characteristic of the sign as difference and play. Such an 'apparent paradox' is not isolated to one or two instances, but is, we could say, congenital to Derrida's approach to the sign. For example, this tension between the sign-as-play and sign-as-presence is evident here:

> the concept of the sign will have marked, in this sense, a simultaneous impediment and progress. For if the sign, by its root and its implications, is in all its aspects metaphysical, if it is in systematic solidarity with stoic and medieval theology, the work and the displacement to which it has been submitted – and of which it also, curiously, is the instrument – have had *delimiting* effects. For this work and displacement have permitted the critique of how the concept of the sign belongs to metaphysics, which represents simultaneous *marking* and *loosening* of the limits of the system in which this concept was born and began to serve, and thereby also represents, to a certain extent, an uprooting of the sign from its own soil. (S&G: 17)

We can see once again the two simultaneous manifestations of the sign: as progress and impediment, or as marking and loosening. But what is indeed 'curious' is that the sign can function as both the instrument of uprooting and as the material uprooted. Accordingly, there exists in this passage, and in those above, two manifestations of the *temporality* of the sign: one which appears at the time of Saussure, which loosens metaphysics, which uproots metaphysics; and another which is born with metaphysics, is Stoic and medieval, is the metaphysics which is uprooted by the thinking of the sign. At no point does Derrida elaborate on, or back away from, the paradox of a sign which is the instrument which delimits and loosens itself. In 'Structure, Sign, and Play', the 'event' of the sign occurs when the structurality of structure begins to be thought, which undermines a 'history' and 'epoch' of the metaphysical sign. And in *Of Grammatology*, the 'moment' of the sign's emergence is simultaneous with its demise:

> From the moment that there is meaning there are nothing but signs. We *think only in signs*. Which amounts to ruining the notion of the sign at the very moment when . . . its exigency is recognized in the absoluteness of its right. (*OG*: 50)

That is, the emergence of the sign-as-play ruins the notion of the sign-as-presence because it reveals that the sign-as-presence has nothing to refer to. From the moment there is meaning there is nothing but signs-as-play; we think only in signs-as-play which amounts to ruining the notion of the sign-as-presence simultaneously with our recognition of the absoluteness of its right.

In all of the passages cited above, Derrida is working towards an insight into Western metaphysics which exceeds the logic and language of the semiology that he has taken as a privileged example. But whatever coherence pertains to Derrida's multiplicitous appropriations of the notion of the sign, it is this very multiplicity which threatens the unity of the sign that is the basis of Derrida's inquiry. Working our way through Derrida's doubled or equivocal handling of the sign, it becomes necessary to divide the sign from itself, to think of the sign-as-play and the sign-as-presence, or of the sign-as-innovation and the sign-as-tradition, or else of primordial signs and derived signs. The coherence of this multiplicity, and the resolution of the paradox of Derrida's equivocal handling of the epoch and adventure of the concept of the sign, can only occur when it is understood exactly how Derrida is able to speak of a concept with a history *at all*. The paradox can only be resolved when it is understood that the two manifestations of the sign in question are the *de jure* and the *de facto*. The notion of the sign which Derrida wishes to recover from the historical, de facto adventure of metaphysics exists only in a non-empirical, logically necessary, de jure primordiality.[1] For Derrida, the de facto history of metaphysics is of a structure of differences thought on the basis of presence: 'A' is 'A' and 'B' is 'B' and so they are different. Derrida's deconstruction of this hierarchy begins from the proposal that presence must instead be thought of on the basis of difference, and not the other way around. It is primordial difference which allows us, *by rights*, to perceive conceptual or material distinctions necessary to establish 'A' and 'B'. Such a reversal makes 'the difference involved in signs' not a derived element in the structure, but the primordially necessary condition for meaning, for communication, and for truth.

Exactly how such a deconstruction is both similar and different to Saussure's proposal for the sign is the subject of the final chapter of this book. But for now, we can at least understand the coherence of Derrida's appropriation of the Saussurean sign, which simultaneously confirms and loosens the metaphysical opposition between presence and difference. At the same time, we can immediately recognise a proposal which would be untenable within the language and logic of semiology. And so before bringing this chapter to a close, it is useful to remind ourselves of the Saussurean position, and the Saussurean way of speaking about signs.

Conclusion

I want to begin by suggesting that there are two things wrong with the following sentence from 'Structure, Sign, and Play':

> It would be easy enough to show that the concept of structure and even the word 'structure' itself are as old as the *epistēmē* – that is to say, as old as Western science and Western philosophy. (278)

First, if it was easy enough to show then Derrida ought to do that: he ought to show us the longevity of the concept and of the word structure. On occasions such as this, Derrida is less careful about his historical gestures than, say, Husserl is about his essential distinctions. Second, in the phrase 'the concept of structure and even the word "structure" itself', Derrida clearly allows the *concept* of structure independence from the *word* structure; independence, also, from time and from any specific language community. The concept of structure may not have been associated with a *word*, in a particular *language*, but it was always the same concept nonetheless. This operation, however, is contested by the Saussurean view of words and meanings. The concept of 'structure' would come into being simultaneously and reciprocally with the word 'structure', and could not exist outside of such an association. As Saussure says:

> Any linguistic entity exists only in virtue of the association between signifier and signified. It disappears the moment we concentrate exclusively on just one or the other. (*Course*: 101/144)

The word and the concept of 'structure' are the products of a particular language community at a particular moment in time. Because of this, neither can have a continuous existence in time or history:

For in order to be able to say that a given unit has remained the same over time, or that, while remaining a distinct unit, it has changed in form or meaning – any of which is possible – I must know on what I base the claim that an element taken from one period – e.g. the French word *chaud* ('hot') – is the same as an element taken from another period – e.g. the Latin *calidum*. (*Course*: 180/249)

In other words, it is impossible to compare a sign from one language and time with a sign from another language and time, for we wouldn't know where to begin: with the continuity of the word or of the concept. This social-synchronic system of language, and Derrida's critique or deconstruction of it, are examined in greater detail in Chapter 7.

It is for these reasons that Derrida's historical construction of 'the concept of the sign' is incommensurable with the Saussurean view of language. First, Derrida fails to provide sufficient textual evidence for the existence of either a word or a concept more than ephemerally similar to the Saussurean *signe*, *signifiant*, and *signifié*. Second, Derrida wishes to restore a de jure, logically necessary, notion of the sign, from its historical, de facto adventure of metaphysics, and it is this de jure sense of the sign which he uses against Husserl's phenomenology. However, such a de jure sense of the sign would be, from a Saussurean point of view, nomenclaturist, and hence from a Derridean perspective, transcendental and logocentric.

What does Derrida want to do with the concept of the sign: how does he want to reform it or abandon it as a word or concept? He writes:

It is not a question of junking these concepts, nor do we have the means to do so. Doubtless it is more necessary, from within semiology, to transform concepts, to displace them, to turn them against their presuppositions, to reinscribe them in other chains, and little by little to modify the terrain of our work and thereby produce new configurations. (S&G: 24)

Derrida is here asking semiology to do exactly what he has condemned Saussure for, some five pages prior, in continuing to use the word sign. Indeed the notion of transforming concepts, displacing them, turning them against their presuppositions, should be a very good description of what Saussure does in chapter 1 of the *Course*, in his relational definitions of the terms sign, signifier and signified, and his rejection of nomenclaturism. The genuinely radical advance of Derrida's observations and methodology – to bring close attention to the classical presuppositions within philosophies that claim to break free from these – does not, in this case, excuse Derrida from his unjustifiable and untenable unification of Saussure with the writings of Aristotle, Augustine, Rousseau, and Husserl, under the name of 'sign'.

Note

1. Bennington phrases it as 'logically prior', as in: 'Logically prior to the distinction between speech and writing is the differential system and the trace-structure' (2004: 195).

4 Writing, Speech, and the Voice

In many of his early works, particularly *Of Grammatology*, 'Structure, Sign, and Play' and 'Semiology and Grammatology', Derrida presents the concept of the sign as essentially produced by, and limited by, a certain metaphysical tradition. That claim produces, for us, three interwoven themes of inquiry. The first assessed the originality that Derrida would grant to Saussure within the tradition of the sign; the second explored the identity and history of what Derrida calls *the* concept of the sign. The third, and probably best-known theme of inquiry in Derrida's engagement with Saussure, concerns the relationship between writing, speech, and the voice.

For Derrida, it is the exclusion of writing which enables classical metaphysics to mark the division between the exterior and interior of meaning. Outside of meaning is writing, empty marks which facilitate the transport of meaning from person to person; inside of meaning is the mental voice, and the guarantee of the possibility of an immediate relationship with referents and hence with truth. To take one example, the 'Exergue' from *Of Grammatology* announces the field of its inquiry as follows:

> The idea of science and the idea of writing – therefore also of the science of writing – is meaningful for us only in terms of an origin and within a world to which a certain concept of the sign (later I shall call it *the* concept of sign) and a certain concept of the relationships between speech and writing, have *already* been assigned. (4)

This chapter will review Derrida's analysis of the relationship between writing, speech and the logocentric voice, and attempt to bring this assessment to bear against Saussure's well-known privileging of speech over writing as the proper basis of linguistics. The question at stake in this chapter is: How well does Derrida gather Saussure into the framework of the logocentric voice?

Defining the logocentric voice

As we have already seen, Derrida begins his assessment of classical meta-physics, and of the classical relationship between speech and writing, with Aristotle's epoch-defining hypothesis that:

> Spoken words are the symbols of mental experience and written words are the symbols of spoken words. Just as all men have not the same writing, so all men have not the same speech sounds, but the mental experiences, which these directly symbolize, are the same for all, as also are those things of which our experiences are the images. (16a, 2–4)

Derrida, in response, observes that the vocal signifier is closest to the signi-fied sense, while the written sign is derivative of this first relationship, and contributes nothing to that relationship. It follows that:

> This notion remains therefore within the heritage of that logocentrism which is also a phonocentrism: absolute proximity of voice and being, of voice and the meaning of being, of voice and the ideality of meaning. (*OG*: 11–12)

The exclusion of writing is not an accident of history, but rather a neces-sary preliminary condition for metaphysics if it is to allow the self-present voice – or the mental, unspoken, experiential, internal voice – an immediate and pre-linguistic relationship with nature, truth and the *logos*. Without this possibility, metaphysics is forever cut off from the possibility of truth; and it is this threat which has driven metaphysics to regain a relationship with pre-linguistic presence throughout this epoch of the sign. *Of Grammatology* is the pursuit of the logocentric voice as it variously appears in Aristotle, Saussure, Rousseau, and others.

The logocentric voice appears in some form in most of Derrida's early, lin-guistically oriented works. 'Signature Event Context', for example, develops this theme by explaining how the division between speech and writing, and the interiorisation of the former and exteriorisation of the latter, is necessary for the communication of pure signifieds. Communication is revealed as the transport of meanings (signifieds) unaffected by the medium of transport (signifiers). To support this view Derrida cites just one example – indeed, just one paragraph – from Condillac's *Essay on the Origin of Human Knowledge*, but writes that: 'I do not believe that a single counterexample can be found in the entire history of philosophy' (3). The paragraph cited is this:

> Men in a state of communicating their thoughts by means of sounds, felt the necessity of imagining new signs capable of perpetuating those thoughts and of making them *known* to persons who are *absent*. Thus,

the imagination will represent to them only the very *same* images that they had already expressed through actions and words, and which had, from the very beginning, rendered language figural and metaphorical. *The most natural means* was thus to depict images of things. *To express the idea* of a man or of a horse, one represented the form of the one or of the other, and the first attempt at writing was nothing but a simple painting. (Condillac, qtd in SEC: 4–5, Derrida's italics)[1]

Condillac's viewpoint, in the classical manner, according to Derrida, is that thought existed prior to language: oral communication came about as a response to the desire to communicate one's thoughts to others; writing in particular was created to extend oral communication to receivers who are not present. Derrida writes that:

If men write it is: (1) because they have to communicate; (2) because what they have to communicate is their 'thought', their 'ideas', their representations. Thought, as representation, precedes and governs communication, which transports the 'idea', the signified content; (3) because men are *already* in a state that allows them to communicate their thought to themselves and to each other when, in a continuous manner, they invent the particular means of communication, writing. (SEC: 4)

Men are already in a state to communicate their thoughts at the time of the invention of writing, and thus: 'writing will never have the slightest effect on either the structure or the contents of the meaning (the ideas) that it is supposed to transmit' (SEC: 4). Whether or not this is a reasonable interpretation of Condillac's chapter,[2] we recognise that Derrida's work in 'Signature Event Context' is to demonstrate that the exteriorisation of writing is the exteriorisation of signification in general. The pure and pre-linguistic 'thought' or 'idea' can then be transported from person to person, or within one and the same person, without loss. Condillac describes the progressive modification of presence that enables philosophy, by a reverse process, to regain pure intuitions from even the most formal and codified representations.

If *Of Grammatology* critiques an epoch of the sign in which the relationship between speech and writing had already been assigned, then 'Signature Event Context' elaborates how such phonocentrism is necessary to facilitate the full communication of intended meanings. But the most thorough reading of this drive to expel language from what is essential in the human experience of the world is found in *Speech and Phenomena*. This reading, this first and most substantial argumentation against the internalisation of the voice, is made in relation to Husserl's *Logical Investigations*. Derrida's engagement with Husserl is aimed at how phenomenology conceals its metaphysics, which:

would be done precisely in what soon comes to become recognized as the source and guarantee of all value, the 'principle of principles': i.e., the original self-giving evidence, the *present* or *presence* of sense to a full and primordial intuition. (*S&P*: 5)

A full and primordial intuition, the guarantee of all value, is the internal, pre-linguistic, logocentric voice. Derrida will insist on this point throughout his engagement with Husserl, that he 'believes in the existence of a pre-expressive and prelinguistic stratum of sense' (*S&P*: 31), and 'will ceaselessly strive to keep signification outside the self-presence of transcendental life' (*S&P*: 31). The method by which Husserl achieves this is, according to Derrida, the exteriorisation of what Husserl calls 'indication' – which is the use of signs in communication – and the interiorisation of what Husserl calls 'expression', which functions 'even in *isolated mental life, where they no longer serve to indicate anything*' (Husserl 1970: 183). In doing so, Husserl is able to maintain an experiential and pre-linguistic relationship between the subject and an ideal object, by making language posterior to an originary intuition. Derrida writes this as 'the extrinsic relation of the indicative sign to expression' (*S&P*: 27). The exteriorisation of indicative signs and signification allows Husserl to reduce and efface the signifier without loss, leaving the pure signified sense, or the logocentric voice, available for communication and transportation. As Derrida concludes, it is only on the condition of the: 'absolute proximity of the signifier to the signified, and its effacement in immediate presence, . . . that he will be able to reduce it without loss and assert that there exists a pre-expressive stratum of sense' (*S&P*: 80).

Derrida's view of Husserlian phenomenology, and by inference all of Western metaphysics, is thoroughly and consistently argued in *Speech and Phenomena*, and this is not the place to intervene in or resist Derrida's interpretation of Husserl. However, this last citation from *Speech and Phenomena* also serves to reveal that the terminology of Husserl's expressive and indicative signs, can also, for Derrida, be transported to the language of Saussurean signifiers and signifieds. Derrida's only remark on this is puzzling, for he writes: 'The equivalencies signifier/expression and signified/*Bedeutung* could be posited were not the *bedeuten/Bedeutung*/sense/object structure much more complex for Husserl than for Saussure' (*S&P*: 46n), and yet will make this equivalence in the previous citation above, and indeed throughout *Speech and Phenomena*. Derrida utilises the terms signifier and signified in relation to Husserl's text freely and without any need for critique or acknowledgment of any source of the terms. Such a correlation, or even synonym, is taken to be self-evident. Whether such an equivalence can be made between Husserlian and Saussurean signification is the point which will be examined here.

Comparing Saussure with Husserl

Saussure is mentioned, in passing, only twice in *Speech and Phenomena*. He first appears in a footnote in which Derrida invites us to compare the *Logical Investigations* with the *Course in General Linguistics*: 'The operation by which Husserl proceeds in the First Investigation would also have to be systematically compared with Saussure's delimitation of the "internal system" of language' (46–7n). Derrida exhorts us to compare the *Logical Investigations* with the following passage from the *Course*:

> the linguistic sign unites, not a thing and a name, but a concept and a sound-image. The latter is not the material sound, a purely physical thing, but the psychological imprint of the sound, the impression that it makes on our senses. The sound-image is sensory, and if I happen to call it 'material', it is only in that sense, and by way of opposing it to the other term of the association, the concept, which is generally more abstract. The psychological character of our sound-images becomes apparent when we observe our own speech. *Without moving our lips or tongue*, we can talk to ourselves or recite mentally a selection of verse. (*Course (B)*: 66, qtd in *S&P*: 46, Derrida's italics)

Derrida cites Saussure's description of the *image-acoustique*, literally the sound-image, or the sound-pattern, as a way of incorporating Saussure into the history of the logocentric voice. Certainly, this passage indicates that we need to proceed with such a comparison only on the basis that Saussure *does* intend that mental speech is possible, and that it is mental, rather than physical, articulation that is his primary object of study. However, while the sound-pattern can function 'without moving our lips or tongue', it is not clear whether this mental speech is, for Saussure, pre-linguistic or intuitive in the way that Derrida suggests it is for Husserl. Such a defence against the equivalence between Husserl and Saussure would seem necessary, given that Derrida's only other reference to Saussure in *Speech and Phenomena* is the following:

> The ideality of the object, which is only its being-for a nonempirical consciousness, can only be expressed in an element whose phenomenality does not have worldly form. *The name of this element is the voice. The voice is heard.* Phonic signs ('acoustical images' in Saussure's sense, or the phenomenological voice) are heard by the subject who proffers them in the absolute proximity of the present. The subject does not have to pass forth beyond himself to be immediately affected by his expressive activity. (76)

Saussure's signifier is directly compared to the phenomenological voice, in which the subject silently expresses his inner thoughts to himself. As a first step, as Derrida suggests, the resources of the *Course* must be exhausted in beginning to make this comparison between Saussurean speech and the logocentric voice that Derrida finds first in Husserl.

Among the many citations from the *Logical Investigations* that Derrida makes use of in *Speech and Phenomena*, there is one that strikes me as being particularly rich in the logocentric drive towards pure signifieds, and more precisely written in the logocentric language that Derrida wishes to arrest. Husserl suggests that if we:

> reflect on the relation of expression to meaning, and to this end break up our complex, intimately unified experience of the sense-filled expression, into the two factors of word and sense, the word comes before us as intrinsically indifferent, whereas the sense seems the thing aimed at by the verbal sign and meant by its means: the expression seems to direct interest away from itself towards its sense, and to point to the latter. But this pointing is not an indication in the sense previously discussed. The existence of the sign neither 'motivates' the existence of the meaning, nor, properly expressed, our belief in the meaning's existence. (Husserl 1970: 190–1)

Against all its drives to exclude the traditions of Western metaphysics, the Aristotelian conception of language seems to emerge from out of the deepest commitment of phenomenology, in the process of reduction to intuitive sense. Husserl suggests that if we reflect on the relation of the word and sense, the word is indifferent, intrinsically indifferent, whereas the sense is not. Or as Aristotle phrases it, all men do not have the same speech sounds, and hence they are immaterial to what they signify; but mental experiences are natural and non-arbitrary images of the things themselves. For Husserl, as for Aristotle, the existence of the sign follows an originary intuition, an intuition that signification can neither 'motivate' nor alter our experience or belief in. The critique of such a relation of word to sense is continued in *Of Grammatology* and 'Signature Event Context', among others. We can also read in this passage the phenomenological drive towards the effacement of the signifier in the voice. Husserl's 'verbal sign' – what Derrida will also refer to as 'the signifier' – is a mere token which expends itself in the moment of signification. The critique of such an effacement is continued in both 'Structure, Sign, and Play' and 'Semiology and Grammatology'.

But can these critiques be made equally well for the Saussurean sign? Rephrasing the above arguments in the terminology of the Saussurean rather than Husserlian sign, Derrida tells us that:

> The 'apparent transcendence' of the voice thus results from the fact that the signified, which is always ideal by essence, the 'expressed' *Bedeutung*, is immediately present in the act of expression. This imme-

diate presence results from the fact that the phenomenological 'body'
of the signifier seems to fade away at the very moment it is produced; it
seems already to belong to the element of ideality . . . This effacement
of the sensible body and its exteriority is *for consciousness* the very form
of the immediate presence of the signified. (*S&P*: 77)

And that the logocentric voice:

> does not risk death in the body of a signifier that is given over to the
> world and the visibility of space. It can *show* the ideal object or ideal
> *Bedeutung* connected to it without venturing outside ideality, outside
> the interiority of self-present life. (*S&P*: 77–8)

Can we say – for this is what *Speech and Phenomena* implies – that the
Saussurean sign consists of a signifier which effaces itself in the moment of
signification, allowing the signified to merge with intuition? Can we say that
the Saussurean signifier contributes nothing to the thought of the signified
sense, or inversely, that communication with oneself takes nothing from the
world? For this is exactly the view of Saussure today within the Derridean
tradition. Robert Young's gloss is typical: 'Saussure's theories remain
clearly within the logocentric tradition. . . . For Saussure, as for Aristotle
and Plato, speech is privileged because it seems closest to the self-presence
of consciousness' (16). But does such a view follow from the text of the
Course?

Evidence from the *Course*

Derrida's opinion of this matter is not to be found in *Speech and Phenomena*,
but in his most direct engagement with the Saussurean sign, the interview
with Julia Kristeva called 'Semiology and Grammatology'. I would argue,
though, that Derrida's critique of the Saussurean sign, and his assertion of
the Saussurean sign's classical and logocentric roots, is indistinguishable
from his critique of Husserl:

> When I speak, not only am I conscious of being present for what I
> think, but I am conscious also of keeping as close as possible to my
> thought, or to the 'concept', a signifier that does not fall into the world,
> a signifier that I hear as soon as I emit it, that seems to depend upon
> my pure and free spontaneity, requiring the use of no instrument, no
> accessory, no force taken from the world. Not only do the signifier and
> signified seem to unite, but also, in this confusion, the signifier seems to
> erase itself or to become transparent, in order to allow the concept to

present itself as what it is, referring to nothing other than its presence. (S&G: 22)

There is nothing in this description to suggest that the Saussurean sign might contain some development or contradiction of the Aristotelian or Husserlian 'sign'. Despite this, there is in fact much in the *Course* which suggests not only a revision of this particular aspect of the sign, but its opposite. First, we can note that Saussure seems intent on establishing the impossibility of thinking a concept prior to, or without, signifiers:

> Psychologically, setting aside its expression in words, our thought is simply a vague, shapeless mass ... were it not for signs, we should be incapable of differentiating any two ideas in a clear and constant way. In itself, thought is like a swirling cloud, where no shape is intrinsically determinate. No ideas are established in advance, and nothing is distinct, before the introduction of linguistic structure. (110/155)

And continuing this theme:

> The characteristic role of a language in relation to thought is not to supply the material phonetic means by which ideas may be expressed. It is to act as intermediary between thought and sound, in such a way that the combination of both produces a mutually complementary delimitation of units. Thought, chaotic by nature, is made precise by this process of segmentation. (110/156)

And furthermore, directly challenging the possibility of signifiers effacing themselves, leaving behind a pure signified:

> Any linguistic entity exists only in virtue of the association between signifier and signified. It disappears the moment we concentrate exclusively on just one or the other. (101/144)

Derrida's characterisation of thought as a self-present intuition, able to dispense with its signifying material, would seem to be compromised by Saussure's statements here, at least superficially.

Second, Derrida's characterisation of expression as depending only 'upon my pure and free spontaneity, requiring the use of no instruments, no accessory, no force taken from the world' would seem to be challenged by what Saussure says about the passivity of the individual in relation to the social communality of *la langue*.

> A community is necessary in order to establish values. Values have no other rationale than usage and general agreement. An individual, acting alone, is incapable of establishing a value. (112/157)

And that:

> in order to have a language, there must be a *community of speakers*.
> Contrary to what might appear to be the case, a language never exists
> even for a moment except as a social fact, for it is a semiological phe-
> nomenon. Its social nature is one of its internal characteristics. (77/112)

In Saussure's sign system *everything* is taken from the world. The individual
is unable to have clear and constant thoughts prior to the introduction of
linguistic structure. What's more, this structure is not produced from within,
but passively accepted from without, so that one's most intimate thoughts are
made possible by and *structured by* the collection of social agreements called
la langue.

The difference between Saussurean and Husserlian semiology is perhaps
most evident in Husserl's consideration of soliloquy:

> Shall one say that in soliloquy one speaks to oneself, and employs
> words as signs, i.e., as indications of one's own inner experiences? I
> cannot think such a view acceptable. (Husserl 1970: 190)

For Husserl, one's inner thoughts and experiences can be articulated without
the need for language and signs. There exists a stratum of sense prior to the
introduction of language. For Saussure, however, one's very *experience* of
the world is dependent on one's particular language system. Here, he offers
the example of how verb tenses in Slavic languages allow one to differentiate
between a single-moment future action and a developing-action taking place
over time. For Saussure:

> These categories are difficult for a Frenchman, because his language
> does not recognise them. If they were predetermined categories, there
> would be no such difficulty. In all these cases what we find, instead of
> *ideas* given in advance, are *values* emanating from a linguistic system.
> (*Course*: 115/162)

In other words, it is difficult or even impossible to think certain thoughts if
one's language does not suggest or allow it. All of these citations above, and
many other examples and argumentation in the *Course*, strongly suggest that
Saussure explicitly attempted to overturn those characteristics of classical
signification that Derrida critiques in *Speech and Phenomena*. And whether
or not this attempt was ultimately successful, Derrida perhaps ought to
have spent more time with, and made a more cautious and careful example
of, Saussure's efforts here. When the *Course* is compared with the *Logical
Investigations* in the manner suggested by Derrida, it is quite impossible to
say that Saussure would 'want to maintain' or to 'assert' that there exists a

'pre-expressive substratum of sense', or that speech depends only upon 'my pure and free spontaneity' and 'takes nothing from the world'.

Internal and external elements of a language

However, that is not to say that Saussure never pronounced on what is 'internal' or 'external' to a language. Chapter five of the *Course* is, in fact, titled 'Internal and External Elements of a Language', and lists ethnology, political history, cultural institutions such as school and church, and geography as external elements. It is important to note, however, the definitions of 'external' and 'internal' which appear in the chapter's opening and closing sentences. Saussure begins with:

> Our definition of a language assumes that we disregard everything which does not belong to its structure as a system; in short everything that is designated by the term 'external linguistics'. (21/40)

And ends with:

> Everything is internal which alters the system in any degree whatsoever. (23/43)

These are important definitions, for they allow Saussure to acknowledge the great influence that ethnology ('a nation's way of life has an effect upon the language'), political history ('major historical events such as the Roman Conquest are of incalculable linguistic importance'), cultural institutions ('a language has connexions with institutions of every sort'), and geography ('every language in existence has its own geographical area') have on a language (*Course*: 21–2/40–1). But what Saussure is attempting here is a delineation between language-as-a-system and language-in-its-totality. For Saussure, systematicity and internality are synonymous, as his example illustrates well:

> It is sometimes claimed that it is absolutely impossible to separate all these questions from the study of the language itself. That is a view which is associated especially with the insistence that science should study 'Realia'. Just as a plant has its internal structure modified by outside factors, such as soil, climate, etc., in the same way does not grammatical structure depend constantly upon external factors of linguistic change? Is it not difficult to explain technical terms and borrowings, which commonly appear in a language, if we give no consideration to their provenance? (22/41–2)

Saussure responds that:

> The main point here is that a borrowed word no longer counts as bor-
> rowed as soon as it is studied in the context of a system. Then it exists
> only in virtue of its relation and opposition to words associated with it,
> just like any indigenous word. (22–3/42)

In essence, what Saussure is naming as 'internal' to a language is its systematicity, that is, its operation as a differential structure.[3]

Having established this definition, Saussure then turns to the most contentious division between what is internal and external to a language, that
is, the division between speech and writing. In chapter six of the *Course* –
'Representation of a Language by Writing' – Saussure states that: 'although
writing is in itself not part of the internal system of the language, it is impossible to ignore this way in which the language is constantly represented'
(24/44). Saussure elaborates this relationship as follows:

> A language and its written form constitute two separate systems of
> signs. The sole reason for the existence of the latter is to represent
> the former. The object of study in linguistics is not a combination of
> the written word and the spoken word. The spoken word alone consti-
> tutes that object. But the written word is so intimately connected with
> the spoken word it represents that it manages to usurp the principal
> role. As much or even more importance is given to this representation
> of the vocal sign as to the vocal sign itself. It is as if people believed
> that in order to find out what a person looks like it is better to study his
> photograph than his face. (24–5/45)

The remainder of chapter six documents the many instances when ortho-
graphic priority has led to pronunciation changes; in other words, where
writing has affected speech.[4] Of course, as we have seen above, the ability of
writing to *affect* speech is no reason at all to include it as an *internal* element
of language. However, it must also be acknowledged that Saussure does not
expend much effort justifying his claim that the sole reason for the existence
of writing is to represent speech. There is something of the 'self-evident' in
Saussure's claim to the priority of speech, and as such, Derrida's critique
enters at exactly the right point. He asks:

> Why does a project of *general* linguistics, concerning the *internal system
> in general of language in general*, outline the limits of its field by exclud-
> ing, as *exteriority in general*, a *particular* system of writing, however
> important it might be, even if it were to be *in fact* universal? (*OG*: 39)

This is, *in general*, an excellent question. However, in wondering *why*
Saussure would exclude writing from linguistics, Derrida's question could

lead one down the difficult path of trying to reconstruct Saussure's intentions and motives from the collective production of the *Course*. And despite his claim, elsewhere, of 'caring very little about Ferdinand de Saussure's *very* thought *itself*' (*OG*: 329), this is exactly what Derrida does. It becomes necessary, then, to enter this discussion of Saussure's motives, before we can consider in closer textual detail the arguments for and against Saussure's justification for the priority of speech over writing.

The passion of Saussure

Across Derrida's diffuse engagement with Saussurean linguistics, the particularity of *Of Grammatology* rests upon its extensive critique of the division between speech and writing. Derrida's approach to the *Course* here is, however, from the outset, personal and psychological. He claims that Saussure's exclusion of writing is not by chance, but is instead a response to the exigency of expelling the impurities and risks of writing from the natural and safe bond between voice and mind:

> Writing would thus have the exteriority that one attributes to utensils; to what is even an imperfect tool and a dangerous, almost maleficent, technique. One understands better why, instead of treating this exterior figuration in an appendix or marginally, Saussure devotes so laborious a chapter to it almost at the beginning of the *Course*. It is less a question of outlining than of protecting, and even of restoring the internal system of the language in the purity of its concept against the gravest, most perfidious, most permanent contamination which has not ceased to menace, even to corrupt that system, in the course of what Saussure strongly wishes, in spite of all opposition, to consider as an external history, as a series of accidents affecting the language and befalling it *from without*, at the moment of 'notation' (45), as if writing began and ended with notation. Already in the *Phaedrus*, Plato says that the evil of writing comes from without (275a). The contamination by writing, the fact or the threat of it, are denounced in the accents of the moralist or preacher by the linguist from Geneva. The tone counts; it is as if, at the moment when the modern science of the logos would come into its autonomy and its scientificity, it became necessary again to attack a heresy . . . Thus incensed, Saussure's vehement argumentation aims at more than a theoretical error, more than a moral fault: at a sort of stain and primarily at a sin. (*OG*: 34)

In keeping with my overall ambition here I will not speculate on *why* Derrida finds chapter six 'laborious'. But I can at least provide the data that the chapter occupies pages 45 to 54 of the 317 pages of the *Cours*. Such data might serve to warn the reader that Derrida's indignant language should not be confused with evidence. Derrida's ambition is to arrest Saussure's 'tone' in the chapter 'Representation of a Language by Writing' and to reveal it to be in alliance with Plato's view of writing as the 'mere image' of the 'living, ensouled speech of a man of knowledge' (Plato: 276a).[5] Derrida will also say that:

> has it ever been doubted that writing was the clothing of speech? For Saussure it is even a garment of perversion and debauchery, a dress of corruption and disguise, a festival mask that must be exorcised. (*OG*: 35)

And that:

> For Saussure, to give in to the 'prestige of the written form' is, as I have just said, to give in to *passion*. It is passion – and I weigh my word – that Saussure analyzes and criticizes here, as a moralist and a psychologist of a very old tradition. As one knows, passion is tyrannical and enslaving . . . That tyranny is at bottom the mastery of the body over the soul, and passion is a passivity and sickness of the soul, the moral perversion is *pathological*. (*OG*: 38)

Saussure, as a moralist of a very old tradition, seeks to protect the purity of the living, ensouled voice from corruption, contamination and the fall into the world by exorcising the sinful and *bodily* excesses of writing.

A brief but serious response to this must be that Derrida ought to have weighed the word *passion* and found it too heavy by far. A longer response would be necessary if Roy Harris hadn't already allowed himself a passionate response:

> Of all the artful misrepresentations displayed in Derrida's interpretation of Saussure, none is more insidious than the attempt to portray the *Cours* as the fire-and-brimstone tract of a puritanical doctrinaire. (Harris 2001: 186)

Against Derrida's interpretation of Saussure's 'tone' in 'Representation of a Language by Writing', Harris counters with:

> Writing as sin. Saussure as the Calvin of linguistics. (For *Geneva*, read 'centre of reformed Protestantism, hotbed of Calvinism' . . .) Sin, heresy, redemption: Derrida, as self-appointed Grand Inquisitor of Western culture, is well qualified in the art of extracting self-condemnatory confessions. (Harris 2001: 186–7)

In the section which Derrida cites, Saussure is attempting to address 'the prestige of writing' in the linguistics of his time. That is, he is attempting to reproach linguists who have interpreted the literary evidence of a language without first taking the precaution of checking for changes in the ortho-graphic relationship with the spoken language. The full paragraph reads as follows:

> A language, then, has an oral tradition independent of writing, and much more stable; but the prestige of the written form prevents us from seeing this. The first linguists were misled in this way, as the humanists had been before them. Even Bopp does not distinguish clearly between letters and sounds. Reading Bopp, we might think that a language is inseparable from its alphabet. His immediate successors fell into the same trap. The spelling *th* for the fricative *þ* misled Grimm into believing not only that this was a double consonant, but also that it was an aspirant stop. Hence the place he assigns to it in his Law of Consonantal Mutation. (*Course*: 26/46)

Saussure's passion, to the degree that it exists, is directed against fellow lin-guists who make simple errors of analysis because of their failure to compare literary and phonetic evidence. The *Course* is filled with such examples of erroneous scholarship and Saussure's tone is similar throughout. Contrast, for example, the mildness of Saussure's tone on writing with his comments on folk etymology: 'There is something in it which may be regarded as perverted, pathological' (qtd in Gadet, 1989: 101). Unless contradictory evidence can be found, Harris would appear to be justified in feeling that Derrida's interroga-tion of Saussure's character and motives recklessly exaggerates anything that can be found in the *Course*.

The effect that Derrida's psychological profile of Saussure has had can only be guessed at, but the frequency of its citation would indicate that it is the dominant view of Saussure today. Christopher Norris, for example, writes that: 'Saussure's metaphors suggest all manner of evil, degenerate effects brought about by this exposure of language to the dangers of writing' (87). Geoffrey Bennington goes further:

> If writing were indeed merely the kind of external representation that Saussure claims (*Cours*: 44–7), how could it bring with it what Saussure calls 'dangers' (*Cours*: 44) which need to be pointed out and even denounced in a tone which is more one of moralistic indignation than of scientific description? (2004: 189)

Bennington has well learned the art of the one-word citation. From the single word 'dangers', he will mount an increasingly hysterical attack on Saussure, rising from 'Saussure's tone of indignation' (190) to 'Saussure's angry complaint' (190) and finally to 'Saussure's manifest outrage' (190). The ease of Bennington's procedure shows how comfortably Derrida's speculation has been naturalised and entrenched as fact.

Writing as crisis

Having staged this exchange of views, which has at least allowed us to scrutinise the received knowledge of Saussure's motivations for privileging speech, there remain at least two arguments in *Of Grammatology* against the division between speech and writing that are due careful consideration. The first, which reprises Derrida's work in *Speech and Phenomena*, suggests that Saussure's exclusion is made in order to maintain a pre-linguistic intuition, and hence to maintain the possibility of truth.

> What Saussure does not question here is the essential possibility of nonintuition. Like Husserl, Saussure determines this nonintuition tele-ologically as *crisis*. The *empty* symbolism of the written notation . . . is also for Husserlian intuitionism that which exiles us far from the *clear* evidence of the sense, that is to say from the full presence of the signified in its truth, and thus opens the possibility of crisis. This is indeed a crisis of the logos. (*OG*: 40)

What we know about Saussure is that he *does* treat writing as external to linguistics proper, and that writing is 'empty' in the sense that it does not form part of the double articulation of sound-pattern and sense. Written signs *follow* an originary production of linguistic semiology, and do not add anything to meaning. At least, if they *do* add something to a linguistic sign, they do so as part of language-in-its-totality, not as an element of the language-as-a-system. However, the remainder of Derrida's assertions here are more contentious: that Saussure determines 'nonintuition' as a crisis of truth, that writing obscures the clear evidence of the sense. What drives Derrida's approach to the division between speech and writing, and the privi-lege accorded to the former, is the apparently 'natural' relationship between sense and sound that Saussure takes for granted in the *Course*.

To be sure, it is possible to question many of Derrida's interpreta-tions of specific passages in the *Course*. For example, in 'Semiology and Grammatology', Derrida writes:

> Saussure, for essential, and essentially metaphysical, reasons had to privilege speech, everything that links the sign to *phonē*. He also speaks of the 'natural link' between thought and voice, meaning and sound (*Cours*: 46). He even speaks of 'thought-sound' (*Cours*: 156). (S&G: 21)

Here we would counter that this usage of 'thought-sound' appears in the *Course* as the process in which the mutual articulation of sound units and concepts occurs. In its usage here, the term 'thought-sound' undermines the prevailing nomenclaturist or logocentric view that sounds are simply allocated to pre-existing concepts. Similarly, in *Of Grammatology*, Derrida cites the *Course* as: '"Languages are independent of writing" (*Cours:* 45). Such is the truth of nature' (*OG:* 41), when in fact Saussure is here making the claim that the available empirical evidence suggests that 'linguistic stability is in no way undermined by the absence of a written form' (*Course:* 25/45), and makes no claim of this as a 'truth of nature' anywhere in the vicinity of Derrida's citation. Harris makes the point that:

> the feature of interest once again is how Derrida has both decontextualised and truncated a quotation in order to make Saussure testify against himself. When we turn to *Cours* 45 we find that this is not the generalization Derrida pretends it is . . . In other words, the comparison shows that *the pace of linguistic change does not correlate directly with the presence or absence of a writing system.* Which is quite a different proposition from Derrida's version, according to which Saussure is claiming that the independence of *la langue* is a 'vérité de la nature'. (Harris 2001: 185)

And so it is certainly possible to argue that the citations that Derrida takes from the *Course* in order to demonstrate Saussure's phono-logocentrism are excessively brief and open to contrary interpretation. However, I believe that reading the *Course* in its entirety does not alter the conclusion that Saussure felt that the primary object of linguistics was the mutual articulation of the sense and the sound-pattern, and that on each occasion when writing affects speech, it does so, like political history, as an external element affecting an internal one. The question of whether or not it might be quite reasonable for an empirical linguist to make this observation will be examined below. But for now, the question remains whether such a phonocentrism either promotes, or is driven by, a belief in 'the effacement of the signifier in the voice' (*OG:* 20), or of 'the signified producing itself spontaneously, from within the self' (*OG:* 20), or by determining 'nonintuition teleologically as *crisis*' (*OG:* 40).

In assessing Derrida's reasoning for the similarity of the Husserlian voice and Saussurean speech, we have already considered a few items of evidence. On Saussure's side, we have read the many citations from the *Course* which indicate his rejection of 'pre-linguistic intuition'. On Derrida's side, we have been alerted to the tone of Saussure's chapter on writing, and observed the apparently self-evident priority of spoken language over written language for Saussure. The question at stake is whether or not Saussure's privilege of the spoken language brings with it those elements of Husserlian phenomenology described here. The alternative conclusion is that it is possible for Saussure to be phonocentric but not logocentric. If any kind of comparison between the *Logical Investigations* and the *Course* has been made, then the first finding would be the disparity of evidence that each text provides for a linguistics of exterior representation. Husserl writes that 'the word comes before us as intrinsically indifferent, whereas the sense seems the thing aimed at by the verbal sign and meant by its means', and that 'the existence of the sign neither "motivates" the existence of the meaning, nor, properly expressed, our belief in the meaning's existence' (Husserl 1970: 191). The passage of the *Course* that Derrida exhorts us to compare with this states that 'without moving our lips or tongue, we can talk to ourselves or recite mentally a selection of verse' (*Course (B)*: 66). The core of Derrida's observations, therefore, is that Saussure excludes writing from his study of language-as-a-system, and treats it as an external element which can affect the language. Writing is empty notation in the sense that it does not participate in the double articulation of sound-image and sense. This much is undeniable. However, the remainder of Derrida's observations – of the self-presence of signifieds, of the crisis of non-intuition, of the effacement of signifiers – are a reflection of how much of Derrida's interrogation of Saussure relies on a pathological profile of the linguist from Geneva, rather than on any evidence from the *Course*.

The symbolic relation of writing to speech

The second and final point of Derrida's to consider, which he makes in the second half of the chapter 'Linguistics and Grammatology' from *Of Grammatology*, is that Saussure's own theory of the arbitrariness of the sign should prevent him from posing a natural hierarchy between writing and speech. Derrida's reasoning here requires a lengthy quote:

> The thesis of the arbitrariness of the sign thus indirectly but irrevocably contests Saussure's declared proposition when he chases writing to the outer darkness of language. This thesis successfully accounts for a conventional relationship between the phoneme and the grapheme (in phonetic writing, between the phoneme, signifier-signified, and the grapheme, pure signifier), but by the same token it forbids that the latter be an 'image' of the former. Now it was indispensable to the exclusion of writing as 'external system', that it come to impose an 'image', a 'representation', or a 'figuration', an exterior reflection of the reality of language.
> . . . What matters here is that in the synchronic structure and systematic principle of alphabetic writing – and phonetic writing in general – no relationship of 'natural' representation, none of resemblance or participation, no 'symbolic' relationship in the Hegelian-Saussurean sense, no 'iconographic' relationship in the Peircian sense, be implied.

One must therefore challenge, in the very name of the arbitrariness of the sign, the Saussurean definition of writing as 'image' – hence as natural symbol – of language. Not to mention the fact that the phoneme is the *unimaginable* itself, and no visibility can *resemble* it, it suffices to take into account what Saussure says about the difference between the symbol and the sign (*Cours:* 101) in order to be completely baffled as to how he can at the same time say of writing that it is an 'image' or 'figuration' of language and define language and writing elsewhere as 'two distinct systems of signs' (*Cours:* 45). For the property of the sign is to not be an image. (45)

To summarise: Saussure's theory of the arbitrariness of the sign demands that the relationship between phonemes and graphemes be arbitrary, and yet Saussure will at the same time define writing as an 'image' of speech; this is contradictory because the property of the sign is to not be a symbol. In this passage, Derrida *appears* to cite Saussure describing writing as an 'image', a 'representation', or a 'figuration' of speech. Hence that relationship is a 'natural' representation, a 'resemblance', a 'symbolic' relationship in the Saussurean sense; the 'image' is a 'natural symbol'. If so, then this is quite a collection of synonyms. It is necessary then to go back to chapter six of the *Course* one last time, in an attempt to determine exactly what was the postulated semiological relationship between writing and speech. We begin with the title to the chapter in question:

Representation of a Language by Writing. (24/44)

although writing is in itself not part of the internal system of the language, it is impossible to ignore this way in which the language is constantly represented. (24/44)

A language and its written form constitute two separate systems of signs. The sole reason for the existence of the latter is to represent the former. (24/45)

As much or even more importance is given to this representation of the vocal sign as to the vocal sign itself. (25/45)

Certain very subtle linguistic features can long survive without the assistance of written notation. (25/45)

For most people, visual impressions are clearer and more lasting than auditory impressions. So for preference people cling to the former. The written image in the end takes over from the sound. (26/46)

In the end, the fact that we speak before learning to write is forgotten, and the natural relation between the two is reversed. (26/47)

Two letters, for example, will be used to designate a single sound. (28/49)

Thus when people say that a certain letter should be pronounced in this way or that, it is the visual image which is mistaken for the model. (30/52)

Saussure repeatedly describes writing as the 'representation' of speech. He *never* uses the word 'symbol' – a word which Derrida uses three times in the passage above. On the two occasions that he uses the word 'image' – a word which Derrida uses five times in the passage above – it is clear that Saussure is merely distinguishing something which can be seen from something which can be heard. Despite its widespread and uncritical acceptance (cf. Gasché, 1994: 44), Derrida's reading of a 'symbolic' or 'iconic' relationship between the grapheme and phoneme is an invention.

Having said that, there remains much that is ambiguous about this relationship. If writing is the 'representation', or the 'notation', or 'designation' of speech, does that relationship form a 'sign' in the Saussurean sense? Saussure writes that writing and speech are 'two separate systems of signs', but what would form the signifier and signified of a written sign? We know from the *Course* that: 'The signs used in writing are arbitrary. The letter *t*, for instance, has no connexion with the sound it denotes . . . The values of the letters are purely negative and differential' (117–18/165). And so the graphic *signifier* would be the negative and differential mental impression of the graphic pattern. However, would the *signified* of such a sign be the phonic sign in its entirety – that is, the combination of sound-image and concept – or the phonic signifier only? The very phrase 'The Representation of a Language by Writing' suggests that it is the phonic sign in its entirety which is 'represented by writing', and Saussure's statement that: 'as much or even more importance is given to this representation of the vocal sign as to the vocal sign itself' would seem to support this. In Derrida's reading, certainly, it is the phonic sign as a whole which acts as the graphic signified. The insoluble problem for interpretation here is that this chapter on writing appears in the *Course* before Saussure's distinction between sign, signifier and signified.

Resolving this problem is not necessary, however, for what is essential is this: the written sign described in the *Course cannot* be a sign in the Saussurean sense. Certainly, the relationship between the grapheme and the phoneme (in either case) is not 'natural' or 'symbolic' in the Saussurean sense, or 'iconic' in the Peircean sense, as Derrida suggests. Rather, the relationship is 'arbitrary' in the pre-Saussurean sense that Weber has previously identified. That is, the graphic signifier chosen for any particular signified is not natural in any way – any kind of graphism would do as long as it can be distinguished from the other elements in the system. But in such a system, the graphic signified – as either the phonic signifier or the phonic sign in its entirety – is established *in advance* of the graphic signifier, and is not altered by it in any way. In other words, the graphic signified is not mutually articulated by the graphic signifier. We can take the example of Braille. If we accept that Braille is an alphabetic language with a one-to-one relationship between Braille characters and written characters, then we can say that Braille follows and is subordinate to the written alphabet. Saussure would describe this as a 'natural' hierarchy of writing over Braille. And yet at the same time, the relationships within the individual Braille-signs are arbitrary or conventional in the pre-Saussurean sense. Braille cannot be considered a sign system in the Saussurean sense unless the written alphabet is articulated by Braille as much as Braille is articulated by writing.

Of course, Saussure might be wrong. There is clearly a contradiction between Saussure's statements that: (1) writing exists only to represent speech, and that (2) writing and speech are two different sign systems, as I have explained. At least one of these statements is wrong, and quite possibly both.[6] It is possible that writing has a direct and independent relationship with thought, and hence is a sign system in its own right. It is also possible that writing is partially dependent on and partially independent of speech. Perhaps Saussure's statement that: 'The essence of a language, as we shall see, has nothing to do with the phonic nature of the linguistic sign' (*Course*: 7/21) indicates that no such division within language needs to be made. Harris makes some interesting observations on the semiological relationship between writing and speech that is assumed in the *Course*. His view is that all the historical arguments for the primacy of speech from nineteenth-century linguistics – for example, learning priority in children, and the existence of non-literate oral societies – are irrelevant for Saussure because they are external to what is essential in linguistics. What Saussure needs, Harris argues, is evidence that writing is dependent on speech:

> No semiological principle is posited in the *Cours* which rules out *a priori* the existence of 'mixed' semiological systems. In fact, the section on semiology (*Cours:* 32–5) nowhere lays down any specific criteria for the identification of a sign system.
>
> What Saussure needs, ideally, is a semiological principle which will allow him to demonstrate, deductively, the dependence of writing on speech . . . But all that, for Saussure, lies in the domain of the future science of semiology. He is simply forced to assume in advance the availability of the result which the *Cours* will take for granted. (Harris 2001: 18)

And so the relationship between writing and speech is a semiological rather than a linguistic problem, and in that sense is an as yet unsolved problem, certainly as yet by Saussure. Harris concludes that we ought to focus on articulation as the most fundamental aspect of language, and that semiology is the most fundamental science that Saussure is working towards. Linguistics is a part of semiology, and the relationship between speech and writing is the same as the relationship between linguistics and semiology, but the nature of that relationship would only be revealed in the laws of general semiology. Some of the consequences of this lacuna – in the failure of coherence of Saussure's proposed discipline of general semiology, and in the misreadings of the *Course* that are commonplace in contemporary studies of representation – will be considered in the next chapter.

Conclusion

To conclude, I want to return to Derrida's question of why a project of general linguistics excludes writing on an a priori basis. For all the reasons given above, I do not accept Derrida's explanation that Saussure does this in order to maintain a pre-linguistic relationship with experience, the truth, or logos, or that Saussure would see the alienation of the natural evidence of the senses as a crisis. Without wishing to become a Saussure apologist, it appears to me that Saussure's reasons for excluding writing are more mundane than Husserl's, more disciplinary than philosophical, and more about maintaining the possibility of his science than maintaining the proximity to an intuitive consciousness. We can accuse Saussure of scientism, among other things, but conflating his intentions and motivations with Husserl's or Plato's is excessive.

For myself, I am prepared to follow Saussure – at least some of the way – in his privileging of speech over writing. After all, the statement 'writing exists only to represent speech' is more plausible – from empirical evidence – than the statement 'speech exists only to represent writing'. As Harris observes, the priority of speech can be justified 'by the simple fact that only a very small proportion of the world's languages had ever been written down' (Harris 2001: 177). And in fact, Saussure *does* make reference to the learning priority of speech in children as evidence for the natural priority of speech: 'the fact that we learn to speak before learning to write is forgotten, and the natural relation between the two is reversed' (*Course*: 26/47). That Saussure, as a practising linguist, was interested in evidence that pointed to the priority of speech in human communication should not be surprising. And whether or not such a clear-cut phonocentrism was an appropriate foundation for the science of general linguistics is a question that must remain open. Such questions are important. But the issue at stake in Derrida's interpretation is *not* whether Saussure was right or wrong to distinguish speech from writing and to give priority to studying the former. The issue is whether this choice is a result of the desire to allow the voice intimate access to the transcendental sense.

In chapter six of the *Course*, 'Representation of a Language by Writing', Saussure attacks what he calls 'the prestige of writing' on the grounds of poor scholarship: that Bopp's errors in his analysis of the evolution of language are caused by a failure to distinguish between the spoken and written language. The chapter is presented as a defence of spoken language against what Saussure believes to be the ascendency of the written form. But it still falls to Derrida to show how this chapter reveals that Saussure felt that the voice was closer to some kind of transcendental intuition. Derrida wants Saussure to see writing as a crisis, to see the rupture of the natural bond between speech and thought as a crisis, but cannot demonstrate this from the text of the *Course*, except by assigning to Saussure the phenomenological voice, and Husserl's motivation for dividing indication from expression. On the contrary, Husserl's phenomenological voice is self-contained, whereas Saussure's speech is social, external, and differential. Saussure privileges a linguistics of speech over writing but would not ever believe in 'the effacement of the signifier in the voice' (*OG*: 20), nor of 'the signified producing itself spontaneously, from within the self' (*OG*: 20). In short, Saussurean speech is not the phenomenological voice.

Notes

1. I have cited the original English translation which appears in 'Signature Event Context'.
2. However, when Condillac's section is read in full, the main feature that emerges is a demonstration of the increasing complexity of articulation that is associated with each linguistic development, from cries to speech or from paintings to writing. When gestures or cries are all that is possible, only very gross articulation of thought is possible. When finer language is invented, then articulation and thought is also more complex. That is, the resolution of the medium determines the specificity of ideas and representations (cf. 178–81). Condillac even proposes the impossibility of 'good' translation: 'for the reasons that prove that two languages cannot have the same character also prove that the same thoughts can rarely be expressed in both with the same beauties' (194). Already Derrida's interpretation that 'writing will never have the slightest effect on either the structure or the contents of the meaning (the ideas) that it is supposed to transmit' (SEC: 4) seems excessive.
3. In a similar way, Derrida argues in *Glas* (89ff.) that Saussure tries to make onomatopoeia external to the essential arbitrariness of the internal system of *la langue*. Saussure would then perceive the naturalness of onomatopoeia a 'threat' or 'contamination' of arbitrariness (93). However, Jonathan Culler's brilliant essay 'L'essential de l'arbitraire' (2003) powerfully demonstrates Saussure's interest in the non-arbitrary. Any per-

ceived expulsion of onomatopoeia should therefore rest with the *Course*'s editors.

4. Such as Saussure's dismay at the surname Lefebure (*Course*: 31/53–4), which Derrida also comments on (*OG*: 41).
5. Even here it is worth noting that Robin Waterfield's introduction to his new translation of *Phaedrus* makes the compelling argument that the relevant opposition is not between writing and speech, but between dialogue-form and speech-form (whether written or spoken) (xxxvii–xlii). This helps to explain why Plato would *write* his philosophical system in *dialogue* form.
6. See Harris (1995: 58–63), for a discussion of Saussure's problematic definition of writing and speech as separate sign systems.

5 The Sign as Representation

We have so far considered Derrida's engagement with Saussure only in relation to *linguistic* signs, even if we have had to deliberate the inclusion or exclusion of writing. But the sign is more commonly understood as the basic unit of general semiology, or semiotics, rather than as a strictly linguistic object. Even Saussure, as a linguist, indicates that the linguistic sign is merely part, albeit the most important part, of a more inclusive science (*Course*: 68/101). And within this field of semiotics, or the science of signs, it is almost universally agreed that the sign conforms to the medieval maxim identified by Jakobson: *aliquid stat pro aliquo*, or, something that stands for something else. Steven Maras, for example, recently surveyed the semiotic landscape and found that:

> From a basic starting point, semiotics can be described as the study of signs, and the sign described as an entity that 'stands for' something else. As Umberto Eco writes, 'when – on the basis of an underlying rule – something actually presented to the perception of the addressee *stands for* something else, there is signification' (Eco 1976: 8). Peirce defines the sign as 'something which stands to somebody for something in some respect or capacity' (Peirce 1965: 2.228). Articulated in this way, semiotics cannot be restricted to natural communication or systems of representation like speech or writing. As Chandler notes, 'semiotics involves the study not only of what we refer to as 'signs' in everyday speech, but of anything which 'stands for' anything else' (Chandler 2001: 1). Sless refers to the 'stand-for' relation as 'ubiquitous', and from a semiotic point of view 'the basis of existence' (Sless 1986: 3). (Maras 2002: 115)

Given the place of Jakobson's testimony within Derrida's conception of the sign, a thorough exploration of the 'stand-for' relation is necessary. To what degree does the 'stand-for' relation hold true for Saussure, and to what degree for Derrida? If it has previously been necessary to survey classical and medieval semiology in order to find Saussure's place within or against that tradition, it is now necessary to survey the field of semiotics to the same end. As before, this work is done to prepare the ground for staging an engagement between Derrida and Saussure. Here, the debate takes place around the 'stand-for' relation, and on the function of the sign as 'representation'.

Something that stands for something else

At first glance, every semiotic definition of the sign appears to be some variation on the theme of *aliquid stat pro aliquo*. As much as this is true, the subtle differences are worth noting. In many cases, those subtle differences can be traced to the semiotic work of Charles Sanders Peirce. For example, Thomas Sebeok writes that:

> To clarify what a sign is, it is useful to begin with the medieval formula *aliquid stat pro aliquo*, broadened by Peirce, about 1897, to something which stands to somebody for something in some respect or capacity. To the classic notion of *substitution* featured in this famous phrase – Roman Jakobson called it *renvoi*, translatable as 'referral' – Peirce here added the criterion of *interpretation*. (33)

To the medieval definition of the sign, Peirce adds the human subject to whom the sign stands for something, and in doing so, introduces the notion of interpretation to the sign. In Peirce's own words, the formula is as follows:

> A sign, or *representamen*, is something which stands to somebody for something in some respect or capacity. It addresses somebody, that is, creates in the mind of that person an equivalent sign, or perhaps a more developed sign. That sign which it creates I call the *interpretant* of the first sign. The sign stands for something, its *object*. (2.228)

Peirce's definition of the sign is tripartite, consisting of *representamen*, *interpretant*, and *object*. The most obvious translation of these terms into Saussurean terminology would have the sign consisting of signifier, signified, and 'thing' (*Course*: 65/97). However, Peirce's writings on the subject are extremely complex, and even within the sources cited by Maras, above, there are many possible variations and unresolved issues in play.

Sless, for example, provides a usefully explicit account of Peircean semiotics, and it is worth reading some fairly long passages in order to grasp all of the essential features. Sless calls the basic unit of experience and action the '*stand-for* relation':

> This stand-for relation is ubiquitous. The circuit diagram *stands for* the electronic device, money *stands for* products and labour, flags *stand for*

nations, flowers *stand for* love, and even though there seem to be wide
differences in the way each of these things *stand for*, I shall argue that
they do indeed share a common underlying process; for in these and a
myriad of other circumstances is to be found our social and biological
existence – societies, organisms and indeed the fabric of the universe
itself are structured by a complex web of *stand-for* relations – and from
a semiotic point of view the *stand-for* relation is the basis of existence.
(3)

The 'sign' is something that stands for something else, its 'referent'. But as
Sless immediately moves to show, these two terms alone are insufficient for
semiosis to occur. Peircean semiotics is irreducibly tripartite:

> These two ingredients are not sufficient to describe semiosis though as
> we shall see some thinkers have thought to the contrary. We need to
> ask *how* a particular sign *stands for* a particular referent, and in more
> general terms how it is that anything *stands for* anything. This missing
> ingredient is the community, individual or organism which invokes
> the *stand-for* relation, which uses an object (sign) to *stand for* another
> object (referent). This most important feature is often forgotten or
> taken for granted, but without the active agent, the user of signs, there
> would be no semiotics to study.
>   These three features – sign, referent and user – are minimal ingredi-
> ents. The user invokes the *stand-for* relation between sign and referent,
> and to do so the user must be able to distinguish between sign and refer-
> ent. This is so important that it needs to be emphasised and repeated,
> even at the risk of pointing out the obvious. If I, as a user of signs,
> want to make one thing *stand for* another it is essential that I am able
> to distinguish between them. If the sign and the referent are indistin-
> guishable, then it is meaningless even to talk about one standing for the
> other, for they are the same. The *stand-for* relation can only be invoked
> between things which are taken to be different from each other by the
> user. (5–6)

At least three points are worth noting on these passages. The first is that Sless
acknowledges the wide differences in the *way* signs can 'stand for' things and
yet still be part of the unified science of semiotics. Peirce's semiotic would
seem to support this, with a myriad of different relationships proposed
between different types of representamen, interpretants, and objects. At one
point Peirce counts over fifty-nine thousand different kinds of sign before
economising that to sixty-six essential categories (Ogden and Richards 1927:
290). While such abundance might follow from the principles of Peircean
semiotics, it might not necessarily adhere to Saussure's proposed discipline
of general semiology. The second point to note is Sless's insistence upon the

tripartite nature of the semiotic event. With any fewer than three elements, you do not have semiosis. Deely also points to the 'irreducible triadicity' of the sign, and writes that:

> The sign not only stands for something other than itself, it does so for some third; and though these two relations – sign to signified, sign to interpretant – may be taken separately, when they are so taken, there is no longer a question of sign but of cause to effect on one hand and object to knowing subject on the other. (33–4)

Just as Saussure insists on the meaninglessness of a signifier taken without its signified, and vice versa, a Peircean semiotic would insist on these three minimal units. Although we also need to note that unlike Sless's *sign, user,* and *referent,* Deely's semiotic takes in the three elements *sign, interpretant,* and *signified,* a system which probably comes closer to the intentions of Peirce's original text, but only by naming the object for which the sign stands as the signified. Already we can see that any translation of Peircean semiotics into Saussurean terminology will be disputed. The third point to note from Sless's explanation is the possibility of non-semiosis, which occurs when the sign and the object are self-same. Deely, again, remarks on this possibility:

> So a sign is a representative, but not every representative is a sign. Things can represent themselves within experience. To the extent that they do so, they are objects and nothing more, even though in their becoming objects signs and semiosis are already invisibly at work. To be a sign, it is necessary to represent something other than the self. (35)

That is, when the sign and the referent-signified are the same object, as perhaps when an individual tree is not asked to stand for anything – not even the general category of 'tree', but only for itself – then semiosis has not occurred. Instead, another form of 'representation', which is an 'experience' without signs, has taken place. Such a representation is no doubt aligned with the pre-linguistic type of experience that Derrida finds in Husserl.

It is not yet time to bring Derrida's view of the 'stand-for' relation, and of the sign as representation, to the foreground. We can, however, complete this preliminary survey of the semiotic sign with some writers closer to the exchange between Derrida and Saussure. In his translator's introduction to *Speech and Phenomena,* David Allison writes that: 'the sign or signifier in general is always a sign *for* something' (xxxiv). And in that same book, Derrida cites Husserl as stating that: 'every sign is a sign for something' (Husserl, qtd in *S&P*: 23). Using language closer to Derrida's own, Bennington suggests that: 'For simplicity's sake, let us provisionally accept Saussure's terminology' (1993: 25). But what is that terminology? For Bennington, 'the sign must stand in for the thing in its absence . . . The function of the sign is to represent the thing during its absence' (1993: 25). He goes as far as to suggest that Saussure's terminology would describe a 'tripartite division . . . which Saussure receives, like the law, from the tradition' (1993: 26). While none of these writers can be said to speak for Derrida, it does alert us to the possibility that Derrida's use of the Saussurean terms 'signifier' and 'signified' might pertain to a 'stand-for' relation. Such a relation may not sit easily with the relationship between these terms indicated by the *Course*.

A comparison of Peirce and Saussure

While Peirce is clearly the main source of the conceptual foundations for the science of semiotics, Saussure is nevertheless present in a subordinate role in most semiotic texts. In many cases, the role of Saussurean linguistics within semiotics is the same as Saussure himself envisaged: that of a part to the whole. Eco, for example, restricts Saussurean insight to that part of semiotics in which communication is *intentional*, whereas semiotics as a whole also admits *unintentional* and *natural* sources of signs. He defines the Saussurean sign as 'a twofold entity (signifier and signified or *sign-vehicle* and *meaning*)', and states that, for Saussure:

> the sign is implicitly regarded as a communication device taking place between two human beings intentionally aiming to communicate or to express something. It is not by chance that all the examples of semiological systems given by Saussure are without any shade of doubt strictly conventionalized systems of artificial signs, such as military signals, rules of etiquette and visual alphabets. Those who share Saussure's notion of *sémiologie* distinguish sharply between intentional, artificial devices (which they call 'signs') and other natural or unintentional manifestations which do not, strictly speaking, deserve such a name. (Eco 1976: 14–15)

If that is so, then Guiraud's definition of the sign would more accurately delimit Saussure's role within semiotics: 'A sign is a stimulus – that is, a perceptible substance – the mental image of which is associated in our minds with that of another stimulus. The function of the former stimulus is to evoke the latter with a view to communication' (22). And those who share Saussure's notion of semiology would limit the scope of their research to those signs which not only stand for something else, but also are messages with senders and receivers: *aliquid stat pro aliquo*, plus the intention of communication. For Eco, however, the proper basis of semiotics includes natural phenomena, and as such, he draws sharp distinctions between Peircean and Saussurean semiotics:

Peirce's definition offers something more. It does not demand, as part
of a sign's definition, the qualities of being intentionally emitted and
artificially produced. (Eco 1976: 15)

Those who reduce semiotics to a theory of communication acts cannot
consider symptoms as signs. (16)

In this sense events coming from a *natural source* must also be listed as
signs: for there is a convention positing a coded correlation between an
expression (the perceived event) and a content (its cause or its possible
effect). An event can be a sign-vehicle of its cause or its effect provided
that both the cause and the effect are not actually detectable. Smoke is
a sign of fire to the extent that fire is not actually perceived along with
the smoke: but smoke can be a sign-vehicle standing for non-visible fire,
provided that a social rule has necessarily and usually associated smoke
with fire. (17)

As with Sless's and Deely's definitions, the sign and the referent-signified
cannot be self-same; something must be *revealed* in signification. In Eco's
example of smoke and fire, the fire must be absent for smoke to function as
a sign of it; if the fire is present, then we learn nothing from the smoke and
hence it is not a sign. Following Peirce, Eco's definition of the sign includes
both unintentional and natural *sources* of signs, but at all times requires
a human *receiver*, or interpreter. For this reason, Eco is forced to exclude
'stimuli' such as the ring of the bell by a Pavlovian experimenter to a dog:

The sound of the bell is a stimulus for the dog, which salivates independently of any social code, while the psychologist regards the dog's
salivation as a sign (or symptom) that the stimulus has been received
and has elicited the correct response. (Eco 1976: 20)

The sound of the bell – to the dog – is a 'stimulus' and not a 'sign' because
it is not established by a 'social code'. This is despite the fact that we know
that the bell will not stimulate the dog until it is established (to the dog's
satisfaction) that it *stands for* something not present. One wonders exactly
what kind of 'social code' would exclude such a scenario as 'stimulus', and
yet at the same time specify that smoke is a 'sign' of fire – as long as the fire is
absent – because of the 'convention' established between cause and effect. If I
am not saying too much too soon, Eco's efforts here seem to demonstrate the
morbid difficulties of upholding a social and conventional definition of the
sign with naturally occurring phenomena. It is little wonder that Eco begins
Semiotics and the Philosophy of Language with the section: '1.1. Crisis of a
Concept' (14).

Harris argues that since the *Course* defines semiology simply as the science which studies the role of signs as part of social life, there is no reason for it to exclude meteorological or medical signs, such as spots 'meaning' measles (Harris 1987: 27). What the *Course* says on the topic is this:

> It is therefore possible to conceive of a science *which studies the role of signs as part of social life* . . . We shall call it *semiology* (from the Greek, *sēmeîon*, 'sign'). It would investigate the nature of signs and the laws governing them. Since it does not yet exist, one cannot say for certain that it will exist. But it has a right to exist, a place ready for it in advance. Linguistics is only one branch of this general science. The laws which semiology will discover will be laws applicable in linguistics, and linguistics will thus be assigned to a clearly defined place in the field of human knowledge. (15–16/33)

It is certainly true, as Harris suggests, that the *Course* never specifies 'intentional communication' or any other characteristics that a sign ought to have, other than being part of social life. However, Eco is correct in claiming that all the examples of general semiology offered by Saussure at this point are of conventional, intentional communication: 'writing, the deaf-and-dumb alphabet, symbolic rites, forms of politeness, military signals, and so on' (15/33). Further on in the *Course*, however, Saussure considers whether signs that are not wholly arbitrary, such as mime, genuflection or the scales of justice, fall within the province of semiology. Saussure concludes that such signs 'although often endowed with a certain natural expressiveness . . . are none the less fixed by rule' (*Course*: 68/101), and in this respect *do* form part of his science of signs. Knowing that Peirce's highest categorisation of signs takes in *symbols* (arbitrary signs), *icons* (those signs with a resemblance to what they represent, such as the scales of justice), and *indices* (those signs with a causal relationship, such as smoke and fire), then the Saussurean definition of the sign would seem to admit both symbols and icons, with the most arbitrary signs such as language demonstrating the semiological process best. But what is essential here is that Saussure never mentions causality, symptoms, or signs that have a physical or objective relationship between signifier and signified. Sebeok's comments on indexical signs are useful here:

> An index is that kind of a sign that becomes by virtue of being really (i.e., factually) connected with its object. 'Such is a symptom of disease' (Peirce 1965: 8.119). All 'symptoms of disease', furthermore, 'have no utterer', as is also the case with signs of the weather' (8.185). We have an index, Peirce prescribed in 1885, when there is 'a direct dual relation of the sign to its object independent of the mind using the sign . . . of this nature are all natural signs and physical symptoms' (3.361). (Sebeok 2001: 70–1)

To form an indexical sign, such as between smoke and fire, or between symptoms and their disease, a causal or 'factual' connection between signifiers and signifieds must be established. Culler comments on the unlikelihood of such a connection falling within Saussurean explanation:

> Indices are, from the semiologist's point of view, more worrying. If he places them within his domain he risks taking all human knowledge for his province, for all the sciences which attempt to establish causal relations among phenomena could be seen as studies of indices. (Culler 1975: 17)

To be fair to all parties here, it is not *at all* clear from the *Course* whether unintentional communication or natural relationships of cause and effect would have been considered by Saussure as part of 'the role of signs in social life'. All we know is that the laws of such a general semiology would have to apply equally well to linguistics. And as we shall see, if applying such a test means that Saussurean semiology excludes causal, objective, or logical relationships, then the basic operational example of semiotics, that 'smoke is a sign of fire', may thereby also be the least applicable to Saussurean semiology.

This comparison of the Peircean and Saussurean sign suggests that the most contentious issue in any analysis of the 'stand-for' relation is the status of the 'referent', or the 'object', or simply, 'the thing itself'. In her introduction to *Of Grammatology*, Gayatri Chakravorty Spivak claims that Derrida's work on the sign demonstrates that: 'the sign cannot be taken as an homogenous unit bridging an origin (referent) and an end (meaning), as "semiology", the science of signs, would have it' (xxxix). This perhaps indicates the influence that Derrida has had in the contemporary reading of Saussure. Because the first ever critical readers of Saussure, Ogden and Richards in *The Meaning of Meaning*, found that exactly what was missing was a theorisation of the referent: 'this theory of signs, by neglecting entirely the things for which signs stand, was from the beginning cut off from any contact with scientific methods of verification' (6). To correct Saussure's lacuna, they suggest a triangular system consisting of the symbol, the thought, and the referent. In such a system, the symbol 'stands for' the referent, by way of the thought. The Ogden and Richards schema would seem, then, to replicate the Scholastic elaboration of the classical definition of the sign as *vox significat mediantibus conceptibus* (cf. Harris 1987: 63). What is important for our understanding of Saussure is that the problem of neglecting the referent, at least for Ogden and Richards, is the problem of verification of the truth of the representation with the object represented.

Saussure's place within the field of semiotics is, then, perhaps less easily summarised than is usually thought. This field is dominated by the 'stand-for' relation, and the medieval maxim *aliquid stat pro aliquo*, broadened by

Peirce to include the process of interpretation between the sign-object and the referent-signified. In this sense, the semiotic sign is indivisibly tripartite and referential, whereas Saussure's model is bipartite and formed only by mental entities. We also see how the field of semiotics is characterised by its abundance of forms and means of signification. Such abundance puts into question the unity of the science of which Saussure is supposed to be part. Harman has gone as far as suggesting that Peircean semiotics attempts to encompass incompatible elements under a single general theory:

> Smoke means fire and the word *combustion* means fire, but not in the same sense of *means*. The word *means* is ambiguous. To say that smoke means fire is to say that smoke is a symptom, sign, indication, or evidence for fire. To say that the word *combustion* means fire is to say that people use the word to mean fire. Furthermore, there is no ordinary sense of the word *mean* in which a picture of a man means a man or means that man. This suggests that Peirce's theory of signs would comprise at least three rather different subjects: a theory of the intended meaning, a theory of evidence, and a theory of pictorial depiction. There is no reason to think that these theories must contain common principles. (93)

This possibility of non-unification is suggested somewhat by Peirce:

> In consequence of every representamen being thus connected with three things, the ground, the object, and the interpretant, the science of semiotic has three branches. The first is called by Duns Scotus *grammatica speculativa*. We may term it *pure grammar*. It has for its task to ascertain what must be true of the representamen used by every scientific intelligence in order that they must embody any *meaning*. The second is logic proper. It is the science of what is quasi-necessarily true of the representamina of any scientific intelligence in order that they may hold good of any *object*, that is, may be true. Or say, logic proper is the formal science of the conditions of the truth of representations. The third . . . I call *pure rhetoric*. Its task is to ascertain laws by which in every scientific intelligence one sign gives birth to another, and especially one thought brings forth another. (2.229)

Such a collection of subordinate studies may indeed form a unified whole, or may not. But perhaps the main difference between Saussurean and Peircean semiotics highlighted here lies in Peirce's interest in logic, that is, in a scientific or verifiable relationship with objects. For as Guiraud states: 'Saussure emphasises the social function of the sign, Peirce its logical function' (2). And Normand argues that Saussure's aim was:

to separate the linguistic point of view from any direct relationship with the 'real' world. For logicians it is this relationship to the 'real' world which is the very matter of semantics. Saussure's steadfastly repeated position sets him apart among scholars who are fascinated by language – if not in a realm entirely on his own. (104)

The difference between logic and convention is no small matter, and Derrida's opinion on the matter will be critical.[1]

Saussurean linguistics can therefore be distinguished from Peircean semiotics in a number of ways. First, that the basic unit of Peircean semiotics is the stand-for relation, or in classical terms, *aliquid stat pro aliquo*. The development of semiotics is the development of how this standing-for functions. Saussure's adherence to such a scheme has already been examined, in part, under the name of classical semiology; clearly there is more work to do here within the contemporary science of signs. Second, Peircean semiotics takes into its schema natural signs, or those in which there is a causal or object-to-object relationship between a stimulus and meaning. In other words, we have learned to distinguish between indexical signs and conventional signs, and understand why Saussurean semiology might be limited to the latter. Third, Peircean semiotics specifically and necessarily negotiates, through the process of *interpretation*, a stimulus object and a referential object; while Saussurean semiology seems to forgo a relationship with objects entirely. Implied in this distinction also is the horizon of logic as it is phrased within the science of signs: as a verifiable relationship between a representation and its object. Considering all of the differences, it becomes possible to believe that Peirce and Saussure were not working in the same field at all.

Derrida on Peirce and Saussure

Derrida has a way of speaking about the Saussurean sign which, rightly or wrongly, can confound and aggrieve the Saussurean reader. But I feel that Derrida's engagement with Saussure is more easily understood in the context of the above discussion of Peircean semiotics. To begin with an example, the first section of the essay 'Différance' is dedicated to Saussure's construction of the sign – and yet the terminology and presuppositions of this section seem to defy the text of the *Course*. Derrida writes that:

> The sign is usually said to be put in place of the thing itself, the present thing, 'thing' here standing equally for meaning or referent. The sign represents the present in its absence. It takes the place of the present. When we cannot grasp or show the thing, state the present, the being-present, when the present cannot be presented, we signify, we go through the detour of the sign. We take or give signs. We signal. The sign, in this sense, is deferred presence. (Diff: 9)

The model of the sign that Derrida's interrogation of Saussure *begins* from resembles the classical definition of the sign as *aliquid stat pro aliquo*, in that the sign is put in place of the thing itself. Already we can recognise a semiotic structure which seems closer to that of the Peircean tradition. At the same time, however, Derrida's classical sign describes a relationship between two elements only – the sign and the thing itself – which is quite unlike Peirce's tripartite system. For Derrida, 'the thing itself' holds equally for the sense-signified and the object-referent. We have already seen, in Chapter 1, how such a justification can be made: that the concept and the thing itself are undifferentiated within universal experience, hence Aristotle can speak as easily of signs for things as he does of signs for concepts. My objections to such a view have already been made. However, in addition to the way the difference between meaning and referent is effaced in the classical structure of the sign, Derrida provides further evidence of the effacement of the signifier within 'modern linguistics':

> The *signatum* always referred, as to its referent, to a *res*, to an entity created or at any rate first thought and spoken, thinkable and speakable, in the eternal present of the divine logos and specifically in its breath. If it came to relate to the speech of a finite being . . . through the *intermediary* of a *signans*, the *signatum* had an immediate relationship with the divine logos which thought it within presence and for which it was not a trace. And for modern linguistics, if the signifier is a trace, the signified is a meaning thinkable in principle within the full presence of an intuitive consciousness. The signified face, to the extent that it is still originarily distinguished from the signifying face, is not considered a trace; by rights, it has no need of the signifier to be what it is. (*OG*: 73)

Modern linguistics, in other words, might do away with the tripartite Aristotelian structure of word, meaning, and thing, but only by making the meaning interchangeable with the thing itself, a signified independent of a signifier, thinkable in the presence of the divine *logos*. In other words again, all that modern linguistics achieves – in making the sign a bipartite relationship between sound-pattern and sense – is the transference of the units of the sign from external realities to psychological entities within a full intuitive consciousness. What this gesture allows Derrida to do, under the rubric of 'Saussurean psychologism' (S&G: 22–3), or the reduction of physical entities to mental entities, is to conflate tripartite and bipartite models of the sign, and to allow the 'thing itself' to hold equally for the concept or the object. And if the originality of Saussure is merely psychologism, then the classical structure of the sign as a *signans* divided from its *signatum*, which is put in place of the thing itself, which represents the present in its absence, is maintained.

What I specifically want to take issue with, *here*, is that Saussure's sole originality is to internalise the classical sign. To make such a point is to argue against the general misunderstanding of what Saussure has done in making the sign bipartite. As we have seen, the criticism of Ogden and Richards is that Saussure ought to have developed a triangular relationship between the word, the concept, and the thing. Harris, for one, believes that Saussurean semiology offers something more than the transfer of linguistic units from the physical world to the mind. First, he acknowledges the criticism of Ogden and Richards, that 'Saussure's great mistake' was to retain a bipartite model of the sign:

> According to critics of this school, Saussure correctly perceived the inadequacy of the old 'name-and-thing' model of the linguistic sign, but wrongly supposed that the simple solution was to transpose both terms of this duality into the mental sphere ... Thus, far from solving the problem of the linguistic sign, Saussure simply perpetuated an old error in a new disguise. (Harris 1987: 62)

Harris clearly agrees with Derrida's suggestion that the nomenclaturist view of language is not renounced by simply making the sign psychological. Whether the sign stands for a thing or stands for a concept, it would adhere to the nomenclaturist view as long as the name follows, and does not affect, the prior unity of the referent. But Harris also believes that, far from perpetuating an old error in a new disguise, the *Course*'s admonition of nomenclaturism is precisely an attempt to correct the misconception that 'speakers' linguistic concepts are just private pictorial images of corresponding things in the external world' (Harris 1987: 61). Exactly how this rejection of nomenclaturism is achieved, for Saussure, 'will not be fully explained until the chapter on *La valeur linguistique*' (Harris 1987: 61). In other words, it is Saussure's theory of linguistic value which ought to prevent one from interpreting his sign as a simple binarism between name and referent, whether that referent is a physical object or a mental concept. As Harris says of the difference between Locke and Saussure:

> Where Saussure's speech circuit marks an advance over Locke is that Locke's account is still basically a form of nomenclaturism. For Locke, words 'stand for' ideas in the mind: but the mind forms its ideas independently of language. Saussure rejects this psychocentric surrogationalism in favour of giving theoretical priority to the linguistic sign itself (envisaged as an indissoluble combination of *signifiant* and *signifié*). (Harris 1987: 213)

Quite clearly, what Derrida calls 'psychologism', Harris calls 'psychocentric surrogationalism'. And for Harris, it is the theory of linguistic value, or the indissoluble (and reciprocal) combination of a signifier and a signified, which enables the Saussurean sign to escape such a charge. To this end, the warning quotes which Harris places around the phrase 'stand for' are significant. Harris problematises the phrase here because it is specifically the theory of value which prevents one from speaking of a signifier which 'stands for' an object or idea which is stable and real prior to the introduction of linguistic structure. Clearly, in rejecting psychocentric surrogationalism, and in turn nomenclaturism, we must reject the view that the Saussurean sign unites a name and thing – whether the thing holds for the sense or the object – and so, to the same extent, reject the sign as an order of representation.

Perhaps the most comprehensive argument against the sign as an order of representation is one I have already cited, being Samuel Weber's. It is useful to recall Weber's observation of the pre-Saussurean, nomenclaturist tradition:

> the fundamental category of that tradition has always been that of *representation*, with its logical and ontological implication of the priority of the thing named, as extralinguistic referent, over the process of naming itself. (Weber 1976: 919–20)

And that:

> In the chapters which follow Saussure's initial rejection of the conception of language as nomenclature, the traditional model of language as representation remains unshaken . . . Indeed, it is only when Saussure proceeds from his description of what the sign is – a concrete linguistic *entity* – to how it *works*, that this representational-denominational conception of language is put into question. And this step coincides with his introduction of the notion of 'linguistic value'. (920)

Weber revisits this point in *Return to Freud* (1991). He writes that for 'Aristotle – and by much of the metaphysical tradition that will follow', language only functions 'as symbol – that is, as a substitute for things . . . as representation, and more precisely, representation in the sense of a substitute, proxy, deputy, or stand-in' (24). However, 'It is precisely this question which defines the point of departure of Saussure's reflections upon language' (25). This is because for Saussure:

> the primary distinction is neither that of representation and referent, nor that of signifier and signified. Rather, it is that of *difference* as the principle upon which the function of the signifier as well as that of the signified is 'founded' . . . Thought in this way, signification is no longer conceived of as a process of representation, but as one of articulation. (Weber 1991: 27)

To summarise: the Saussurean sign does not simply replace an extralinguistic referent with a mental concept; the Saussurean sign rejects the logical and ontological priority of the thing named; the Saussurean signified is not self-identical and constituted anterior to and independently of its designation by a signifier; and as such, the Saussurean sign breaks from the representational-denominational conception of language. Or as Simon Critchley puts it: 'In breaking the bond that ties meaning to representation, Saussure breaks with the classical theory of the sign' (36).

But how are we then to understand language? If the Saussurean sign is not an order of representation, then what is it? Do signs *consist* of something, *express* something, *convey*, *communicate* something? If these are supposedly synonyms, they are uneasy ones, glossing over perhaps the central question of semiology. If the sign does not represent a concept or a thing, then what does it do? Weber argues that, after Saussure, signification is no longer an act of representation – with its implication of substitution or standing for – but an act of articulation. It is worth noting, then, that the section of the *Course* in which Saussure defines semiology as the 'science which studies the role of signs as part of social life' immediately follows Saussure's definition of the language faculty as *articulation*:

> This idea [that the language faculty is not by nature phonic] gains support from the notion of *language articulation*. In Latin, the word *articulus* means 'member, part, subdivision in a sequence of things'. As regards language, articulation may refer to the division of the chain of speech into syllables, or to the division of the chain of meanings into meaningful units. (10/26)

The next time that articulation appears in the *Course* is in the chapter 'Linguistic Value', where Saussure states that:

> Linguistic structure might be described as the domain of articulations, taking this term in the sense defined earlier (10/26). Every linguistic sign is a part or member, an *articulus*, where an idea is fixed in a sound, and a sound becomes the sign of an idea. (111/156)

In other words, as Weber suggests, the theory of linguistic value determines that the relationship between the signifier (which is no longer equivalent to a 'name') and the signified (which is no longer equivalent to a 'referent') is not one of representation, or of standing-for, but of articulation. Hence, it would be appropriate to rephrase general semiology as the science of articulation. If so, then there is already support for such a view. Malmberg, for example, distinguishes between the 'symbol' and the 'sign', where the former is used for representation, and the stand-for relation, while the latter is kept for 'those units which, like the signs of language, have a double articulation and owe their existence to an act of signification' (Malmberg, qtd in Eco 1976: 21). And Barthes states that:

We know that linguists refuse the status of language to all communication by analogy – from the 'language' of bees to the 'language' of
gesture – the moment such communications are not doubly articulated,
are not founded upon a combinatory system of digital units as phonemes are. (Barthes 1977: 149)

Together, between Harris, Weber, Barthes, and Malmberg, this argument *for*
the sign-as-articulation is, at the same time, an argument *against* the sign-as-
representation *and* Derrida's evaluation of the Saussurean sign as psycholo-
gistic binarism.

I have argued that Derrida's writings on the sign, even when specifically
associated with Saussure's name, imply a semiotic structure which seems
closer to that of the Peircean tradition. Derrida never draws attention to the
sharp divide between Saussure and Peirce, nor between bipartite and tripartite models of the sign, nor between arbitrary and natural signification, nor
even between the legitimation of logic and of convention. Instead, he will
insist on an essentially a priori referential and representative notion of the
sign. The degree to which Derrida's reading of Saussure has contributed to
the jumble of classical, Peircean, and Saussurean terminology in contemporary semiotics is only to be guessed at. But what is necessary now is to restore
specificity and power to Saussure's model of the sign, from within the imprecision of the Derridean reading.

What did Derrida want of Peirce?

As I have suggested, Derrida's engagement with Saussure is more easily
understood in the context of Peircean semiotics. But what exactly does
Derrida obtain from Peirce's writings, or want from Peircean semiotics? The
only time that Derrida cites Peirce directly is in his chapter on Saussure in *Of
Grammatology*, in which he attests that: 'Peirce goes very far in the direction
that I have called the de-construction of the transcendental signified, which,
at one time or another, would place a reassuring end to the reference from
sign to sign' (*OG*: 49). Derrida cites Peirce's definition of the sign:

   Anything which determines something else (its interpretant) to refer to
   an object to which itself refers (its object) in the same way, this interpretant becoming in turn a sign, and so on ad infinitum. (Peirce, *Element
   of Logic*, qtd in *OG*: 50)

The sign determines a relationship between the interpretant and an object.
This object, however, becomes an interpretant of another object, and the
original interpretant becomes a sign. Smoke is a sign of fire, a relationship
which then becomes a sign for, say, 'combustion', which might then become

a sign for 'scientific method', and so on. Derrida calls this infinite flow from objects to interpretants to signs the 'indefiniteness of reference,' and applies it to the deconstruction of the transcendental signified:

> Peirce considers the indefiniteness of reference as the criterion that allows us to recognize that we are indeed dealing with a system of signs. *What broaches the movement of signification is what makes its interruption impossible. The thing itself is a sign* . . . There is thus no phenomenality reducing the sign or the representer so that the thing signified may be allowed to glow finally in the luminosity of its presence. The so-called 'thing itself' is always already a *representamen* shielded from the simplicity of intuitive evidence. The *representamen* functions only by giving rise to an *interpretant* that itself becomes a sign and so on to infinity. (*OG*: 49)

Let us try to examine how the 'indefiniteness of reference' deconstructs the transcendental signified. If we start from the (necessarily imprecise) position that the sign-signifier *stands for* the signified-thing-referent, then that signified is transcendental because it refers to no signifier, and so reference-signification comes to rest in a fully intuitive consciousness in proximity to the divine *logos*. What Derrida gains from Peirce is that reference is indefinite, that reference does not come to rest, but continues 'from sign to sign', and hence the 'thing itself' is never simply present in itself because it is always already in the position of also being an interpretant, and, in turn, a sign.

In Saussurean terminology, we would therefore say that the transcendental signified is deconstructed when one realises that the signified is also in the position of a signifier. The importance of this manoeuvre is indicated by Derrida's inclusion of this formula in at least two of his major interactions with Saussure: in *Of Grammatology* and in 'Semiology and Grammatology'. Derrida writes that the concept of the sign is deconstructed:

> from the moment that the trace affects the totality of the sign in both its faces. That the signified is originarily and essentially . . . trace, that it is *always already in a position of the signifier*, is the apparently innocent proposition within which the metaphysics of the logos, of presence and consciousness, must reflect upon writing as its death and its resource. (*OG*: 73)

If the 'essence' of the transcendental signified is to refer to no signifier, and no longer function as a signifier, then:

> On the contrary, though, from the moment that one questions the possibility of such a transcendental signified, and that one recognizes

that every signified is also in the position of a signifier, the distinction between signified and signifier becomes problematical at its root. (S&G: 20)

In addition, there are references to putting into question the opposition between the signifier and signified by this means in 'Structure, Sign, and Play' (280) and in 'The Original Discussion of "Différance"' (88), all of which strengthens the position that it is Peirce's semiotic logic which provides, for Derrida, the means to disrupt the sign's complacent relationship with presence, and hence to deconstruct the transcendental signified. Culler, for one, marks the importance of Peirce's observation for Derrida's redoubling of the signified as a signifier, and confirms, too, that this redoubling is dependent on an act of *interpretation*. He cites the same passage of Peirce on infinite semiosis (*Elements of Logic*: 1, 2, 302), and then cautions that 'infinite semiosis':

> does not propose indeterminacy of meaning in the usual sense: the impossibility or unjustifiability of choosing one meaning over another. On the contrary, it is only because there may be excellent reasons for choosing one meaning rather than another that there is any point in insisting that the meaning chosen is itself also a signifier that can be interpreted in turn. The fact that any signified is also in the position of a signifier does not mean that there are no reasons to link a signifier with one signified rather than another; ... The structural redoubling of any signified as an interpretable signifier does suggest that the realm of signifiers acquires a certain autonomy, but this does not mean signifiers without signifieds, only the failure of signifieds to produce closure. (Culler 1982: 189)

In short, the signified chosen (Peirce's *interpretant*) is always a sign of something, and hence it is always in the position of a signifier (Peirce's *representamen*). The role of interpretation in Peircean semiotics is, then, every bit as essential as the logical relationship with a referent. And here we recall Sebeok's assessment that: 'To the classic notion of *substitution* featured in this famous phrase – Roman Jakobson called it *renvoi*, translatable as 'referral' – Peirce here added the criterion of *interpretation*' (33).

On the contrary, however, Saussure's semiology is no more a matter of interpretation than it is of reference. Ogden and Richards, again, display incredulity at Saussure's second lacuna – that of interpretation:

> A sign for de Saussure is twofold, made up of a concept (*signifié*) and an acoustic image (*signifiant*), both psychical entities. Without the concept, he says, the acoustic image would not be a sign (*Cours*: 100). The disadvantage of this account is ... that the process of interpretation is included by definition in the sign! (5)

And for Deely, similarly, it is the failure to identify the process in which referents become signs, and in turn other signs, which precludes Saussurean linguistics acting as the model for semiotics:

> [Saussure] compromised his proposal for the enterprise by making of linguistics 'le patron générale [sic] de toute sémiologie', raising the 'arbitrariness of signs' into a principle of analysis for all expressive systems ... The duality of *significant* [sic] and *signifié*, in a word, lacked the thirdness whereby the sign in its foundation ... undergoes transformation into first an object and then into other signs. (115)

Saussurean semiology lacks what Peirce calls *thirdness*, that is, the interpretative function, by which objects become signs for ideas. Such a system is absolutely necessary when 'smoke' is said to *stand for* 'fire'. Smoke is an object – external, extralinguistic – which becomes a sign when it stimulates the idea 'fire' in the mind of the observer; in this case, responding to the 'social code' that fire is necessary to produce smoke.

I am not challenging Derrida's appropriation of Peircean semiotics *for its own sake*, for I believe that insofar as Peircean semiotics describes a coherent science, then the infinite semiosis from sign to sign is a necessary and worthwhile step to take. In other words, if what Derrida wants from Peirce is the problematisation of the relationship between the sign and the referent, then to that end I have no disagreement. However, I would counter that no such problematisation needs to take place within the *confines*, and *limitations*, of Saussurean semiology. Culler usefully quotes Saussure from a passage 'which he actually wrote':

> The ultimate law of language is, dare we say, that nothing can ever reside in a single term. This is a direct consequence of the fact that linguistic signs are unrelated to what they designate, and that therefore *a* cannot designate anything without the aid of *b* and vice versa, or in other words that both have value only by the difference between them, or that neither has value, in any of its constituents, except through this same network of forever negative differences. (*Cahiers* 12: 63, qtd in Culler 1986: 52)

If Saussure's rejection of the referent is not explicit enough in chapter one of the *Course*, then surely this statement makes up for that deficit. The absence of the referent is no lacuna in the *Course*; it is deliberate, theoretical, and anything but 'naïve', as Ogden and Richards suggest (5). Sturrock's example is that if an animal is called *horse* and *cheval* on different sides of the English Channel, 'we cannot and must not conclude from that that they are two signifiers with a common signified' (15), because a signified is something which is found in the collective consciousness of a language community, and 'neither signified is to be found standing in a field' (16). And neither is Saussurean semiology an act of interpretation because it does not involve a relationship from sign to sign, on the same level. It is a particular kind of transaction, called articulation, which forms units simultaneously and reciprocally as an intermediary between abstract sound and abstract thought. The relationship between the already-articulated objects 'smoke' and 'fire', or between 'flowers' and 'love', or between 'flag' and 'nation' no doubt requires an explanation, but that explanation has nothing at all to do with Saussurean semiology.

The interpretation of dreams

I have argued, in this chapter, that Saussurean semiology is not an order of representation, nor of interpretation, but of articulation. There exists a single example of Derrida's intervention in semiology which helps to sharpen the division between Peircean representation-interpretation and Saussurean articulation. This occurs in the essay 'Freud and the Scene of Writing' in the moment when Derrida discusses Freud's advancement of the language, or the code, or the semiology of dreams. Rejected by Freud for its permanence and its simplicity, the 'popular method' for interpreting dreams is described by him as this:

> It might be described as the 'decoding' method, since it treats dreams as a kind of cryptology in which each sign can be translated into another sign having a known meaning, in accordance with a fixed key. (Freud, qtd in F&SW: 207)

In contrast, for Freud:

> My procedure is not so convenient as the popular decoding method which translates any given piece of a dream's content by a fixed key. I, on the contrary, am prepared to find that the same piece of content may conceal a different meaning when it occurs in various people or in various contexts. (Freud, qtd in F&SW: 209)

According to Freud, the popular decoding method assigns fixed codes of meaning to certain dream-symbols, for example, that a 'serpent', when it appears in a dream, signifies 'disease'. In contrast, Freud's method allows for the fact that a single dream-symbol can 'conceal a different meaning when it occurs in various people or in various contexts', and hence 'the correct interpretation can only be arrived at on each occasion from the context' (Freud, qtd in F&SW: 209). Derrida's interpretation of this passage goes much further, however, and it is necessary to quote it at length:

The absence of an exhaustive and absolutely infallible code means that in psychic writing, which thus prefigures the meaning of writing in general, the difference between signifier and signified is never radical. Unconscious experience, prior to the dream which 'follows old facilitations', does not borrow but produces its own signifiers; does not create them in their materiality, of course, but produces their status-as-meaningful. Henceforth, they are no longer, properly speaking, signifiers. And the possibility of translation, if it is far from being eliminated . . . is nevertheless in principle and by definition limited . . . Translation, a system of translation, is possible only if a permanent code allows a substitution or transformation of signifiers while retaining the same signified, always present, despite the absence of any specific signifier. This fundamental possibility of substitution would thus be implied by the coupled concepts signified/signifier, and would consequently be implied by the concept of the sign itself. Even if, along with Saussure, we envisage the distinction between signified and signifier only as the two sides of a sheet of paper, nothing is changed. Originary writing, if there is one, must produce the space and the materiality of the sheet itself. (209–10)

What Freud objects to is a fixed cryptology of dreams, for all people and at all times, which is perhaps a rather weak object for criticism to begin with. For both Freud and Derrida, on the contrary, a relationship between a 'dream-content' and a 'dream-thought' is spontaneously produced within the dream. For Derrida, the fact that this relationship is not permanent (from dream to dream) or universal (from dreamer to dreamer) means that dream-contents are no longer, properly speaking, signifiers of dream-thoughts. The obvious objection to make here is that languages are not like the popular decoding method of interpreting dreams. For that would be to say that languages do not change over time, nor could there be multiple languages in existence at any one time. More seriously, the reason why Freud's dream-symbols are not, properly speaking, signifiers, at least in the Saussurean sense, is because the relationship between dream-content and dream-meaning is not a semiological one, again in the Saussurean sense. The question that burns throughout this discussion of dream codes is whether, in this temporary idiomatic grammar, any of the elements are differential. Are what Freud calls 'dream-content' and 'dream-thought' differential and mutually articulated units, or are they – like 'serpent' and 'disease', or 'flowers' and 'love' – already determined as stable entities prior to the moment of their association? And are the dream-content and dream-thought connected to one another as the contact between two different planes, as in Saussure's analogy of air and water, or are they related to one another on the same level, both being pictorial perhaps? Even Freud speaks of the relationship between dream-thought and dream-content not as *signification* but as *translation*:

The dream-thoughts and the dream-content (the latent and manifest) are presented to us like two versions of the same subject-matter in two different languages. Or, more properly, the dream-content seems like a transcript of the dream-thoughts into another mode of expression, whose characters and syntactic laws it is our business to discover by comparing the original and the translation. The dream-thoughts are immediately comprehensible, once we have learned them. The dream-content, on the other hand, is expressed as it were in a pictographic script, the characters of which have to be transposed *individually* into the language of the dream-thoughts. (Freud 1953–75: 4.277, my emphasis)

I emphasise the word 'individually' in order to highlight the un-Saussurean nature of this operation. As Weber notes: 'A closer reading of *The Interpretation of Dreams*, however, shows that the so-called original constituted by the latent dream thoughts always takes the form of grammatically correct sentences' and that Freud 'never called into question the existence of an original text' (Weber 1991: 2). In other words, Freud's interest is in how 'serpent' comes to *stand for* 'disease', not in their original constitution as meaningful entities.

In order to demonstrate the Freudian destabilisation of Saussurean logocentrism, Derrida will – without explanation – map the words 'signifier' and 'signified' onto the Freudian 'dream-content' and 'dream-thought'. Hence, the manifest becomes a signifier of the latent, the relationship is one of signification, and the pair forms a sign. Derrida does not pose any questions into the nature of the units of dream-language, in being differential or not, arbitrary or not, bipartite or tripartite; he does not inquire into the difference between translation and signification, between logic and convention, or between reference and articulation. Derrida, in a process which becomes tiresomely familiar, fails to engage with any semiological questions at all on the way to announcing his semiological conclusions.

Conclusion

Derrida's appropriation of Peirce occurs at a key moment in his deconstruction of the Saussurean sign. According to Derrida, Saussure merely 'psychologises' the referent in making the sign a binary and mental entity. In doing so, Saussure maintains a transcendental signified, and a relationship with presence, with truth and the *logos*. Peirce, on the other hand, 'goes very far in the direction that I have called the de-construction of the transcendental signified' by showing that 'The thing itself is a sign' (*OG*: 49). Derrida appropriates the 'indefiniteness of reference' to show that the signified is always already in the position of a signifier, and hence the difference between signifier and signified is never radical. Derrida is only able to make this declaration, however, by adopting a classical and Peircean semiotic in which 'signification' is the process by which one symbol is substituted for another, as a stimulus-object for a referential-object, and so on to infinity, *on the same level*. On the contrary, within Saussurean semiology, the signified is never in the position of a signifier, because the sign is formed by the exchange of abstract sound and abstract thought, as two *different* materials, like the contact of air and water. If the signified chosen to match the signifier *means* something, it is not in the same sense of *means* as signification itself. As a result, both the semiotic object of Derrida's deconstruction, and the means by which is it deconstructed, remain within the representative view of language, which is dominated by a 'stand-for' relation between already-constituted entities on the same level.

In conclusion, it is impossible for Peircean semiotics to do without the 'stand-for' relation, and impossible for Saussurean linguistics to accept it. Put another way, the semiotic acts of *representation* and *interpretation* are incompatible with Saussure's theory of value and its manifestation in language as *articulation*. The *Course* takes enormous trouble to define its entities, and yet this trouble is disregarded by Derrida, who continues to deal with 'signs' of 'things' as if these were perfect synonyms for signifiers and signifieds. Derrida appropriates Peirce in order to problematise the one-to-one relationship between concept and object proposed by Aristotle, and the logocentric drive to unite the word of man with the word of God. Such appropriation, however, sharpens the contrast between the explanatory power of Peirce and Saussure. It is, then, not simply a matter of showing how Peirce is wrong, or that his project is impossible or incongruent, although I have my doubts. Rather, it is a matter of making a choice: between the sign-as-articulation and the sign-as-representation; or between an explanation that sets language as its horizon and one that attempts to mediate between what is within and what is without language. The role of the object-referent, and all that follows from that relationship, which is the relationship with verifiability, with logic, or with truth, is divisive here. Elucidating the nature of this choice, and its philosophical and political consequences, is a task that will be renewed and extended in the conclusion to this book.

Note

1. See for example, Derrida's comment in *Speech and Phenomena* that: 'Husserl would not deny the signifying force of such formations [such as 'abracadabra' or 'green is where']: he would simply refuse them the formal quality of being expressions endowed with *sense*, that of being logical, in the sense that they have a relation with an *object*' (*S&P*: 99).

6 Linguistic Identity

The work of the preceding five chapters has, I believe, gone some of the way towards demonstrating my claim that Derrida's engagement with Saussure is fragmented, tangential, and implicit. To make Derrida's writings engage more fully and directly with the *Course*, to gather together the threads of engagement from disparate sources and turn them towards the arguments of the *Course*, has required something of the 'interminable hesitations' that Derrida found in Saussure (*OG*: 329). If this hesitating work has allowed us to argue that Derrida's commentary on Saussure is not always attentive to the detail of the *Course*, then in return, it encourages us to restore something of the originality and specificity of Saussure within the epoch of the sign. Restoring this originality makes possible the two related ambitions of this book. The first was, and is, to demonstrate how Derrida, in attempting to apprehend the general project of Western metaphysics, *goes too far* in assimilating Saussure within a 'classical' tradition of the sign; a tradition which itself is of doubtful unity. The second ambition goes further: it is to suggest that Saussure's contribution to the epoch of the sign is *not just* more specific, but also not containable in its entirety by Derrida's discourse. In other words, elements of the *Course*'s originality *exceed* Derrida's capacity to apprehend and contain them within his discourse of classical metaphysics. This second project becomes the priority from this chapter onwards.

There is one ongoing concern of the *Course in General Linguistics* which explains more about the limits of engagement between Derrida and Saussure than any other, which is with the determination of linguistic identity. The linguistic discourse urges us to specifically consider how we determine sameness and difference, how two things are said to be the same and two things are said to be different; how we might say that these two things are both 'rivers' but that third thing is a 'stream', to borrow Culler's example (1986: 24). The determination of linguistic identity is the essence of any theory of language, and Saussure, as a linguist, is explicit about his method. Derrida, as a philosopher of language, is not quite so explicit, and yet there is enough writing on meaning, identity, and ideality for us to make some judgements about Derrida's position. The point that I am going to make is that there is an essential incommensurability between Derrida's approach and Saussure's in the handling of what Saussure calls 'the language user' in the determination of linguistic identity. We can begin by opening out Derrida's engagement with linguistic identity, or the determination of meaning, as it appears in 'Signature Event Context', 'Freud and the Scene of Writing', and *Speech and Phenomena*.

Context, repetition, ideality

Derrida's essay 'Signature Event Context' begins with an interrogation of the meaning of the word 'communication', and he wonders whether any meaning of this word could be 'unique, univocal, rigorously controllable, and transmittable: in a word, communicable' (1). In doing so, he notes that even proposing such a question anticipates a definition of the word communication as 'a vehicle, a means of transport or transitional medium of a *meaning*, and moreover of a *unified* meaning' (1). Derrida acknowledges the polysemic aspects of the word – such as to 'communicate a movement' or a 'tremor', or that we also speak of different places 'communicating with each other by means of a passage or opening' (1) – but asks whether the 'semantic field' (1) of this word might not be reduced by its *context*: 'It seems self-evident that the ambiguous field of the word "communication" can be massively reduced by the limits of what is called a context' (2). In other words, the context of usage determines the specific meaning of the word. Already we are starting to see some of the parameters of, let us say in advance, the 'classical' method of determining linguistic identity. There exists a 'semantic field' associated with a word – that is, there is a finite range of meanings available – and Derrida wonders if the variability, or the indeterminacy, of a word's meaning could be reduced by the *context* of its use. However, Derrida immediately moves to undermine this classical model: 'But are the conditions of a context ever absolutely determinable? That is, fundamentally, the most general question that I shall endeavour to elaborate. Is there a rigorous and scientific concept of *context*?' (2–3). What Derrida questions here is the model of communication-as-transport, in which a sender encodes a message (by assigning signifiers to thought) and sends it to the receiver, who faithfully decodes the message and recovers the intentions of the sender. In doing so, it is necessary for the receiver to reconstruct the conditions of the original utterance, in order to reduce polysemy to a unique, unified meaning. And so 'communication', by this definition, is achieved to the degree that such restoration of context is accurate and complete.

The process by which Derrida deconstructs this classical structure of communication is both unexpected and ingenious. He observes that writing, 'in its currently accepted sense . . . can only be seen as a *means of communication*. Indeed, one is compelled to regard it as an especially potent means of communication, *extending* enormously, if not infinitely, the domain of oral or gestural communication' (3). The written form of communication develops, as a stage in the evolution of representational forms, specifically in response to the need to communicate with receivers who are *absent*. In contrast to spoken communication, which exhausts itself in the moment of its utterance, writing retains its meaning far beyond the limits of its original context and communicative intentions. Derrida deconstructs this classical formulation by arguing that this quality of writing – its ability to radically break from any particular context and to be received within entirely new contexts – equally applies to all forms of communication, whether written, spoken, or gestural. In doing so, Derrida reverses and displaces the traditional subordination of writing to communication, as a specificity within a category, so that all those concepts under the 'classical discourse' of communication are better understood as forms of writing-in-general (7).

This argument, which is built around the notion of 'absence', will be examined in closer detail shortly. What is important in understanding Derrida's theory of linguistic identity is that by placing the restoration of context in question, he also places communication-as-transport in question, and hence also the possibility of an absolutely determinable meaning. Derrida writes:

> Every sign, linguistic or non-linguistic, spoken or written . . ., in a small or large unit, can be *cited*, put between quotation marks; in so doing it can break with every given context, engendering an infinity of new contexts in a manner which is absolutely illimitable. This does not imply that the mark is valid outside of a context, but on the contrary that there are only contexts without any centre or absolute anchoring. (SEC: 12)

The sign might be valid only within a context, but there is no single context, or even a finite range of contexts, to unify and control meaning. To take Derrida's example: which would be the correct context in which to place the word 'communication'? In the philosophical colloquium, in geological science, or in medicine? Which is the true centre of meaning, against which all other connotations must take a position? In other words, how can fully determinate meanings be transmittable or recoverable when utterances can be endlessly placed in new contexts, without centre or anchoring? Already it is clear that the first step to take will be to engage Saussure on the determination of meaning within *contexts*.

What Derrida is working towards in 'Signature Event Context' is a notion of linguistic identity in which an essential 'citationality' divides the sign from itself. We only recognise the identity, or unity, of a signifying form:

> by virtue of its iterability, by the possibility of its being repeated in the absence not only of its 'referent', which is self-evident, but in the absence

of a determinate signified or of the intention of actual signification, as well as of all intention of present communication. This structural possibility of being weaned from the referent or from the signified (hence from communication and from its context) seems to me to make every mark, including those which are oral, a grapheme in general. (SEC: 10)

What defines the grapheme – the unit of writing-in-general – is its ability to be weaned from all empirical communicative contexts and grafted onto others. And it is this structural possibility of citation which gives the mark its communicative power. But this citationality also divides the 'event' of signification from itself, in that the 'original' signification is *already* a citation of a general form, and hence the value of 'originality' becomes questionable. For Derrida, the now-ness of the event is already divided from itself in its general citationality or iterability:

In order to function, that is, to be readable, a signature must have a repeatable, iterable, imitable form; it must be able to be detached from the present and singular intention of its production. It is its sameness which, by corrupting its identity and its singularity, divides its seal. (SEC: 20)

Rephrasing this into the language of communication theory, it would no longer be a matter of comparing the message received with the message sent, but of understanding that both events are citations of a general form.

In 'Signature Event Context' the concept of 'iteration' is presented as a development of citationality, although the two often seem synonymous. Derrida helps to locate the specificity of iteration by noting that: '*iter*, again, probably comes from *itara*, *other* in Sanskrit, and everything that follows can be read as the working out of the logic that ties repetition to alterity' (SEC: 7). And so iteration is a general citationality in which an essential 'drift' acts upon the unity of the sign, so that the utterance/grapheme can be grafted into an infinity of new contexts to produce illimitable new meanings. The apparently contained moment of (written, oral, gestural) communication is only *made possible* by the power of repetition, by an essential citationality which divides the event of language from itself, which relies on past and future iterations of the language. Derrida's notion of iteration is developed further in 'Freud and the Scene of Writing' in his analysis of Freud's construction of the mystic writing-pad. In a thought experiment that spans thirty years, from the *Project* (1885) to the 'Note on the Mystic Writing-Pad' (1925),[1] Freud attempts to furnish a neurological explanation of perception and memory. He begins the *Project* with the question of how neurones can hold memory while staying open to new experience: 'It would seem, therefore, that neurones must be both influenced and also unaltered, unprejudiced' (Freud 1953–75: 1.299). For Derrida, 'The crux of such an explanation, what makes such an apparatus almost imaginable, is the necessity of accounting simultaneously, as the "Note" will do thirty years later, for the permanence of the trace and for the virginity of the receiving substance' (F&SW: 200). The 'original' impression, that is, its identity as an utterance, or a grapheme, only functions on the basis that it is already a memory: 'For repetition does not *happen* to an initial impression; its possibility is already there' (F&SW: 202). For linguistic identity, the implication is that it only appears, only apparently functions, due to the primordial possibility of repetition, a repetition without a pure origin. Such a schema reverses the classical model, in which the possibility of repetition is based upon an originary identity, or presence. Or as Derrida phrases it here: 'Life must be thought of as trace before Being may be determined as presence' (F&SW: 203).

We can bring this talk of iteration (and of drift, trace, citation, etc.) closer to a semiological model by observing Derrida's deconstruction of the ideality of signs in *Speech and Phenomena*. There is a passage in the chapter 'Meaning and Representation' which will guide all of the discussion of linguistic identity that will follow, in which Derrida reveals the logocentric basis of linguistic identity in the classical model:

A sign is never an event, if by event we mean an irreplaceable and irreversible empirical particular. A sign which would take place but 'once' would not be a sign; a purely idiomatic sign would not be a sign. A signifier (in general) must be formally recognizable in spite of, and through, the diversity of empirical characteristics which may modify it. It must remain the same, and be able to be repeated as such, despite and across the deformations which the empirical event necessarily makes it undergo. A phoneme or grapheme is necessarily always to some extent different each time that it is presented in an operation or a perception. But, it can function as a sign, and in general as language, only if a formal identity enables it to be issued again and to be recognized. This identity is necessarily ideal. (*S&P*: 50)

Once again, Derrida defines representation as the possibility of repetition, of substitution and iteration; he speaks of 'the primordially repetitive structure of signs in general' (*S&P*: 51). A sign that can occur only once is not a sign, and does not function as language. For Husserl, repetition is not the source of ideality, as it is for Derrida, but is *made possible* by ideality. Linguistic identity, or repetition as the same, is made possible by the entirety of phenomenological processes which reduce the physical indeterminacy of sounds and things to an ideality within consciousness. As Derrida remarks:

The concept of ideality naturally has to be at the center of such a question. According to Husserl, the structure of speech can only be described in terms of ideality. There is the ideality of the sensible form (for example, the word), which must remain *the same* and can do so only as an ideality. There is, moreover, the ideality of the signified (of the *Bedeutung*) or intended sense . . . But this ideality, which is but another name for the permanence of the same and the possibility of its repetition, *does not exist* in the world, and it does not come from another world; it depends entirely upon acts of repetition. It is constituted by this possibility. Its 'being' is proportionate to the power of repetition; absolute ideality is the correlate of a possibility of indefinite repetition. (*S&P*: 52)

A sign's power, which is carried by its ideality, is proportional to its power of repetition. A sign that can be infinitely repeated must also be infinitely, or absolutely, ideal. In deconstructing Husserl's phenomenological project, Derrida argues that repetition is not made possible by an originary presence, but rather, that presence is an effect of the primordial possibility of repetition. Or again, that identity can never be fully present when it is determined by something not present, determined by the possibilities of the system in which identity appears.

Let us now summarise, as we return to Saussure, Derrida's intervention in the classical determination of meaning. First, Derrida's argument against a fully determinable context means that the presumed possibility, and metaphysical necessity, of 'full' communication – in which the sender's context and intentions are properly restored – becomes suspect. In proposing infinite and decentred contexts in which to place utterances, Derrida replaces polysemy with dissemination, or a meaning which is radically cast adrift from the conditions of its utterance. Second, Derrida reveals that it is iteration, or all that ties repetition to alterity, that gives utterances their communicative power at all. The identity of any utterance cannot be located in any specific event, but only in the ability to break from any specific context and be grafted onto others, and hence in a general iteration of past and future events. Third, that it is such a primordial possibility of repetition which makes possible ideality and hence identity, and all linguistic distinctions which follow. Linguistic identity is therefore to be thought on the basis of this repetition, and not the other way around. It will be necessary, then, as a minimum, to pay particular attention to the concepts of *context, repetition*, and *ideality*, as they appear or fail to appear in the *Course in General Linguistics*.

Sameness and difference

Saussure is, in a sense, concerned with the determination of linguistic identity at all points in the *Course*, whether discussing the location of linguistic units, synchronic and diachronic identity, syntagmatic and associative relations, the role of the community and the role of time, or the difference between *la langue* and *la parole*. But there is one chapter of the *Course*, titled 'Identities, Realities, Values', where we specifically discover what, for Saussure, marks an utterance as the same. He speaks of the case of '*Messieurs!*', where one might imagine a lecture theatre or parliament, and all the different uses and inflexions of that word, as in '*Gentlemen!*'. Saussure states that with each slight variation in intonation or in context, the word will have a slightly different meaning:

> We feel that in each case that it is the same expression, and yet there are variations of delivery and intonation which give rise, in the several instances, to very noticeable phonic differences. Differences which are as marked as those which in other cases serve to differentiate one word from another (e.g. *pomme* from *paume*, *goutte* from *goûte*, *fuir* from *fouir*, etc.). Furthermore, this feeling of identity persists in spite of the fact that, from a semantic point of view too, there is no absolute reduplication from one *Messieurs!* to the next. A word can express quite different ideas without seriously compromising its own identity (cf. *adopter une mode, adopter un enfant; la fleur du pommier, la fleur de la noblesse*). The mechanism of a language turns entirely on identities and differences, the latter are merely counterparts of the former. (*Course*: 106–7/150–1)

The question being addressed here seems quite similar to Derrida's in 'Signature Event Context', of how, 'through empirical variations of tone, voice, etc., possibly of a certain accent, for example, we must be able to recognize the identity, roughly speaking, of a signifying form' (SEC: 10). Saussure's notion of 'sameness' also seems to be dependent, like Derrida's classical model of communication, upon *repetition*, where two instances of an expression can be recognised as being the *same*. Dependent also, it would appear, upon a formal identity, or upon a reduction of physical abundance to idealities, and so again falling within the framework identified by Derrida. On the contrary, there is much in this simple example, and how it is developed in the succeeding pages, to indicate that Saussure's theory of linguistic identity offers considerable resistance to Derrida's critique of classical or phenomenological ideality.

The first issue to be addressed is how Saussure deals with the issue of *context*. Interestingly, Saussure never uses the word context, and his example of the situations into which an utterance can be placed is not typical. For the 'contexts' of the word '*Messieurs!*' follow each other almost immediately: they are not divided by time or place like a parchment, and take place seemingly with the same conditions of sending and receiving. If two utterances of '*Messieurs!*' so close together can be considered different 'contexts', then there must be very many contexts indeed. Derrida suggests that contexts ought to be infinite and illimitable, and it seems possible that Saussure would

say the same thing. He says this about what happens each time one says
'*Messieurs!*':

> I renew its material being, it is a new act of phonation and a new psy-
> chological act. The link between two uses of the same word is not based
> upon material identity nor upon exact similarity of meaning, but upon
> factors the linguist must discover, if he is to come anywhere near to
> revealing the true nature of linguistic units. (*Course*: 107/152)

Saussure's position is that each time we say '*Messieurs!*', not only is the material form different, but so is the meaning. If the situations of '*Messieurs!*'
can be called contexts at all, then Saussure's view of meaning would depend
upon not just multiple but *infinite* contexts; not merely polysemy, but
closer to what Derrida calls 'dissemination'. But more important still is
that Saussure's model of linguistic identity doesn't seem to depend upon
the *recovery* of contexts. Each utterance of '*Messieurs!*' produces a new,
original, '*Messieurs!*' in both sound and meaning. The meaning of an utterance might be valid only within a context, but that meaning seems subject
to the kind of drift proposed by Derrida. But if linguistic identity doesn't
depend on contexts, and certainly not on a centre-and-periphery model
that Derrida suggests we should expect, then it *does* depend upon 'factors
the linguist must discover', and these will come to play a decisive role
shortly.

The second point is to take up the issue of 'repetition', which seems to be
the guarantee of linguistic identity in the example of '*Messieurs!*'. For even
if Saussure's theory points to infinite contexts, there would appear to be a
formal identity recognisable in spite of any variation in the material or the
meaning. However, the last sentence in the citation, that: 'the mechanism of
a language turns entirely on identities and differences, the latter are merely
counterparts of the former', begins to indicate the degree to which any previous notions of identity, sameness, and difference will be problematised in the
Course. Indeed, in a chapter titled 'Identities, Realities, Values', one might
expect an explication of the distinction between the three terms. Saussure, in
fact, attempts the opposite. He attempts to show how, when dealing with linguistic units, all existing notions of 'identity', 'entity', and 'difference' merge
with his proposal for 'value':

> the notions discussed above [identity and reality] do not differ in essen-
> tials from what we have elsewhere referred to as *values* . . . Thus it can
> be seen that in semiological systems, such as languages, where the ele-
> ments keep one another in a state of equilibrium in accordance with
> fixed rules, the notions of identity and value merge.
>
> That is why in the final analysis the notion of value covers units, con-
> crete entities and realities. There is no fundamental difference between

these notions, but they allow the same problem to be formulated in a variety of different ways. (*Course*: 108–9/153–4)

Saussure previously suggested that 'the mechanism of a language turns entirely on identities and differences, the latter are merely counterparts of the former' (*Course*: 107/151). Here, according to the *Course*'s general method of successive reformulations, he furthermore states that the notions of 'identity', 'entity', and 'reality' merge with Saussure's wholly original designation of 'value'. In order to appreciate this operation, it is necessary to also consider Saussure's deliberate and subtle distinction between 'value' and 'meaning':

> Are *value* and *meaning* synonymous terms? Not in our view, although it is easy to confuse them. For the subtlety of the distinction, rather than any analogy between the two terms, invites confusion.
>
> Value, in its conceptual aspect, is doubtless part of meaning. It is by no means easy, indeed, to draw the distinction in view of this interconnexion. Yet it must be drawn, if a language is not to be reduced to a mere nomenclature.[2] (*Course*: 112/158)

A 'value' is different from a 'meaning', in that a 'value' is a product of the interplay of all the elements in a semiological system, that is, of semiological difference. Saussure says that 'A language is a system in which all the elements fit together, and in which the value of any one element depends on the simultaneous coexistence of all the others' (*Course*: 113/159). In such a scheme, 'The content of a word is determined in the final analysis not by what it contains but by what exists outside it. As an element in a system, the word has not only a meaning but also – above all – a value. And that is something quite different' (*Course*: 114/160). 'Meaning' is like the exchange of a token; it is the bipartite correspondence between the signifier and the signified. 'Value', however, recognises that these are not positive terms, but differential and mutually determining units of language. And for Saussure, at least, that is something quite different. Weber is attentive to this gesture of Saussure's, and here compares 'value' with 'meaning' (which Weber translates as 'signification'):

> If 'signification', despite a certain vagueness, appears to designate the representational, denominational, referential and semantic aspect of language, it is in elaborating his notion of 'value' that Saussure will call that aspect into question. Not by rejecting it outright, but by reinscribing it in a process of articulation which it no longer dominates. For it is not signification, according to Saussure, which produces value, but value which enables language to signify. In order for signs to function as representations, they must delineate themselves with regard to other signs: 'Its content is only truly determined in concurrence with

what exists outside of it' (*Course (B)*: 115) ... It is only when this has been established that the full import and uniqueness of Saussure's notion of the '*arbitraire du signe*' begins to emerge. (Weber 1976: 926–7)

Weber concludes that: 'Identity thereby appears as a function of the position of the sign with regard to other signs, and Saussure names it 'value'. The notion of *value* thus comes to replace that of *identity*, or *entity*, for Saussure' (Weber 1976: 921). And if value comes to replace identity, or entity, or reality, then Derrida's critique of the classical determination of identity may not be entirely applicable to Saussure.

In *Speech and Phenomena*, Derrida writes that the identity of the sign – that which allows it to be recognised as the same despite empirical differences – is necessarily ideal. In his *Introduction* to *The Origin of Geometry*, Derrida cites Husserl on (what we could call) the singularity of ideality:

The word *Löwe* (lion) occurs only once in the German language; it is identical throughout its innumerable utterances by any given persons. (Husserl, qtd in *Intro*: 67)

And Derrida responds:

Thus, the word has an ideal Objectivity and identity, since it is not identical with any of its empirical, phonetic, or graphic materializations. It is always the *same* word which is meant and recognized through all possible linguistic gestures. (*Intro*: 67)

From the empirical fact of language to the ideality of language, Husserl's ideal is that which:

is founded with regard to spatiotemporal appearance in a specifically real thing but which can appear in different realities as identical – not merely as similar. (Husserl, qtd in *Intro*: 91n)

After the phenomenological reduction, the formal idealities of language exist singularly; they occur only once in the language. The ideal word – in its form and its meaning – is not merely similar but *identical* throughout all of its empirical utterances.

Can we say, then, that for Saussure there is a single, pure, ideal form of the word 'lion'? We can take as an example Saussure's description of the signifying force of the letter 't'. In this example, the priority of Saussurean inquiry is on *difference* rather than sameness, identity, or entity. Saussure makes no reference to the reduction of empirical abundance to formal singularities. On the contrary, he writes: 'The values of the letters are purely negative and differential . . . The one essential thing is that his *t* should be distinct from his *l*, his *d*, etc' (*Course*: 118/165). In each utterance of '*Messieurs!*', and in each iteration of the letter *t*, linguistic identity is determined differentially and negatively:

> instead of *ideas* given in advance, [there] are *values* emanating from a linguistic system. If we say that these values correspond to certain concepts, it must be understood that the concepts in question are purely differential. That is to say they are concepts not defined positively, in terms of their content, but negatively by contrast with other items in the same system. What characterises each most exactly is being whatever the others are not. (*Course*: 115/162)

What is most radical about 'value', conceived as above, is that linguistic identity is no longer a matter of 'sameness'. That is, the emphasis on identity, entity, and repetition-as-the-same is replaced by an emphasis on difference, or, the sum total of what it is not. Derrida's assumption throughout his engagement with Saussure is that something like the phenomenological reduction is occurring in the transformation from abstract sound to linguistic ideality. On the contrary, Saussure's notion of linguistic identity is subject to values, and to semiological difference, and the 'entities' of language are formed in a system of differences without positive values. When we hear a sound, all we have to do is differentiate it from others, not identify it as a kind of *singularity*. What results from this is a *variety*, apparently infinite, of forms which can be distinguished from other forms. There is no ideal or singular form which would be reduced to ideality from empirical experience – only the play of differences in a system:

> The processes of linguistic change amply demonstrate this correlation. It is precisely because two signs *a* and *b* are never grasped as such by our linguistic consciousness, but only the differences between *a* and *b*, that each sign remains free to change in accordance with laws quite unconnected with their signifying function . . . The reason is that all that matters is the difference between the signs . . . These signs thus function not according to their intrinsic value but in virtue of their relative position. (*Course*: 116/163–4)

In this way, it is the play of differences, not identities, which are the units of language; units which can only be derived from knowledge of the system as a whole.

The degree to which Derrida fails to engage with the subtleties of the notion of value is evident in the following passage from 'Différance', which can be contrasted with Saussure's, above. Here, Derrida writes of the *silence* of difference, the *inaudibility* of difference:

Saussure had only to remind us that the play of difference was the functional condition, the condition of possibility, for every sign; and it is itself silent. The difference between two phonemes, which enables them to exist and to operate, is inaudible. The inaudible opens the two present phonemes to hearing, as they present themselves. If, then, there is no purely phonetic writing, it is because there is no purely phonetic phone. The difference that brings out phonemes and lets them be heard and understood itself remains inaudible. (Diff (A): 133)

But difference *is* audible, and is what is being transcribed by, for example, the letter 'a'. The letter 'a' in a purely phonetic writing would transcribe the sum total of all phonic differences in an alphabet. Or as Culler puts it: 'the phoneme /b/ is the intersection of the contrasts that differentiate *bat* from *pat*, *cat*, *fat*, etc' (1988: 223). It is useful, I think, to consider the case of Morse code. Derrida states that the differences between phonemes remain inaudible, and as such, cannot be transcribed in a phonetic writing. On the contrary, in Morse code, the silence of the spacing between words *is* a phoneme: its silence is audible, the silence is discerned through hearing. The extended silence between words is different to the shorter silence between letters, and as such, the audible difference between two silences is heard, and that difference can be transcribed. But *only* – and this is the key to Saussurean value – as part of a system of differences. Heard on its own, a Morse silence, or the letter 'a', has no force and no meaning, and no identity. As Saussure says: 'two signs *a* and *b* are never grasped as such by our linguistic consciousness, but only the differences between *a* and *b*' (*Course*: 116/163). Or again, as Culler has discovered in Saussure's manuscripts:

> The ultimate law of language is, dare we say, that nothing can ever reside in a single term. This is a direct consequence of the fact that linguistic signs are unrelated to what they designate, and that therefore *a* cannot designate anything without the aid of *b* and vice versa, or in other words that both have value only by the difference between them, or that neither has value, in any of its constituents, except through this same network of forever negative differences'. (*Cahiers* 12: 63, qtd in Culler 1986: 52)

What we hear or read, precisely, is not the sameness between two utterances, but the sum total of differences within a system.

To summarise, if it has previously been argued that the most important and radical originality of the *Course* lies in the construction of linguistic value, then this radicality is most pronounced when compared with any previous notions of the determination of linguistic identity. For Saussure, linguistic units are not determinable as ideal singularities occurring only once in the language, nor as positive correlations between a signifier and a signified, nor as the positive correlation between two instances of the same phoneme, but only in any single instance as the sum of what they are not within a system of differences. Harris makes this point about the Saussurean method:

> the reader is never told exactly what *la langue* is at any point in the *Cours*: there is no definitive or final formulation. All we find are successive reformulations which bring out different contrasts between *la langue* and everything which *la langue* is not. The procedure is an object-lesson in Saussurean methodology, and in this sense the *Cours* itself is the great masterpiece of Saussurean linguistics. (Harris 1987: 15)

The degree to which Derrida applies a critique of phenomenological ideality to the Saussurean sign marks the degree to which he fails to engage with Saussurean insight. What I have attempted here is to restore our attention to the Saussurean originality in the determination of linguistic identity which Derrida overlooks. However, any attempt to resist Derrida's application of such a metaphysico-phenomenological scheme to Saussurean linguistics is necessarily only preliminary. This is because the most important and decisive originality of Saussure's is still to come. It is never *directly* critiqued in any text of Derrida's, and yet it is this originality which will best define the tensions between the Derridean and Saussurean approaches to language. And that is the consideration of the role of the language user.

Identity and identification

The place to start considering the role of the language user in Saussurean theory comes in his intriguing statement, in the chapter 'Identities, Realities, Values', that linguistic identity 'is not based upon material identity nor upon exact similarity of meaning, but upon factors the linguist must discover if he is to come anywhere near to revealing the true nature of linguistic units' (107/152). Saussure says that: 'We feel that in each case it is the same expression' (106/150), and it is precisely this recourse to what *we* feel that is the heart of the matter. Let us consider Saussure's example of the 8.45 train from Geneva to Paris, which follows his '*Messieurs!*' example, from the same chapter:

> Let us examine the problem of identity in linguistics in the light of some non-linguistic examples. We assign identity, for instance, to two trains ('the 8.45 Geneva to Paris'), one of which leaves twenty-four hours after the other. We treat it as the 'same' train, even though probably the locomotive, the carriages, the staff etc. are not the same. . . .

A quite different kind of case would be, say, a suit of mine which is stolen, but which I find subsequently on a second-hand stall. That suit is indeed a material object, made up simply of various inert substances – cloth, lining, facings, etc. Any other suit, however similar, would not be my suit. Now linguistic identity is not the kind of identity the suit has, but the kind of identity the train [has]. (*Course*: 107/151–2)

Culler makes a point about the Geneva-to-Paris analogy. He says that the identity of the train, like language, is determined *differentially*, in this case by its position in the timetable:

What gives the train its identity is its place in the system of trains, as indicated by the timetable. And note that this relational identity is indeed the determining factor: the train remains the same train even if it leaves half an hour late . . . What is important is that it can be distinguished from, say, the 10:25 Geneva-to-Paris Express, the 8:40 Geneva-to-Dijon local, etc. (Culler 1986: 27)

For Culler, this shows that identity is not physical or positive, but 'wholly a function of differences within a system' (28). What Culler's analysis confirms is the originality of the Saussurean sign, with respect to all antecedent notions of context, repetition, and ideality, just discussed. And while I believe this to be true, the Geneva-to-Paris analogy reveals, I believe, a more profound originality in Saussure's formulation of linguistic identity.

Saussure says that linguistic identity functions like the analogy of the train, rather than of the suit. This is because according to the theory of value, the former examples are identified by their relative position, and the latter by its physical continuation. But what is not yet accounted for is the role of the language user in making such an *identification*. Harris remarks that:

linguistic units do not, like garments or people or buildings, have an identity which can be defined in terms of spatio-temporal continuity. On the contrary, whether we are dealing with the same linguistic unit or two different linguistic units seems to be far more dependent on identification. (Harris 1987: 166)

Here Harris introduces a distinction between 'identity' and 'identification', in which linguistic units are far more a matter of identification. Or even, he somewhat reluctantly acknowledges, for a radical Saussurean, *entirely* a matter of identification:

Provided that identifiability is guaranteed, it seems superfluous – and even nonsensical – to look for any *further* criteria of linguistic identity.

So any contrast between the objectivity of identity and the subjectivity of identification, which holds good generally for our dealings with the physical world, immediately becomes blurred in the case of language. (Harris 1987: 166)

Of course, it is possible to go further than this, and argue that both in language and in 'our dealings with the physical world', the subjectivity of identification is all that is possible.

Let us examine the strength of Saussure's position on the point of view of the language user:

the arbitrary nature of the sign enables us to understand more easily why it needs social activity to create a linguistic system. A community is necessary in order to establish values. Values have no other rationale than usage and general agreement. (*Course*: 111–12/157)

And similarly, that:

in order to have a language, there must be a *community of speakers*. Contrary to what might appear to be the case, a language never exists even for a moment except as a social fact, for it is a semiological phenomenon. (*Course*: 77/112)

And that it is illogical to say that:

'the language does this or that', to speak of the 'life of the language', and so on, because a language is not an entity, and exists only in its users. (*Course*: 5n/19n)

Finally, and most importantly:

Synchrony has only one perspective, that of the language users; and its whole method consists of collecting evidence from them. In order to determine to what extent something is a reality, it is necessary and also sufficient to find out to what extent it exists as far as the language users are concerned. (*Course*: 89/128)

Collected together, this is a remarkable and resolute commitment to a concept of linguistic identity which is no more or less than the point of view of language users. We begin to understand that, for Saussure, linguistic identity is better understood as linguistic *identification*.

Harris provides an example of this operation when he cites Bloomfield's rejection of a hypothetical informant's supposition that 'cran-' in 'cranberry' means red. Bloomfield wants to stress the limits of interrogating language users in developing a theory of language. Harris says that:

Bloomfield held that it was no use asking speakers for the meaning of a linguistic form . . . Bloomfield's example is a hypothetical informant's supposition that *cran-* in *cranberry* means 'red'. Bloomfield is evidently not willing to accept either (1) that if a speaker thinks that *cran-* means 'red' then *ipso facto* it *does* mean 'red' for that speaker, or (2) that *cran-* might have different meanings for different speakers. (Harris 2001: 114–15)

A second example, on Lacan's dictum that 'the unconscious is structured like a language', helps to imagine the size of this problem. Harris cites Lacan, that language is 'imperative in its forms, unconscious in its structure', meaning that we obey linguistic rules but don't understand why, and couldn't explain why. Harris is highly sceptical of these claims and states, among other things, that this dictum 'reduces, in fact, to the rather trite claim that speakers who have not had the benefit of a course in modern linguistics will not be able to state the phonemic rules of their own language' (Harris 2001: 118). He counters that it is simply the ability to distinguish *pin* from *bin* that counts as showing consciousness of phonological structure (Harris 2001: 119). If being aware of what the scientific grammarian knows indicates consciousness, then consciousness equates to whatever theory is current in academic circles: 'That would be rather like claiming that villagers are unconscious of the topography of the locality where they live until a municipal surveyor has been sent along to map it' (Harris 2001: 120). In short, the imperative of the Saussurean investigator is to affirm the point of view of the language user as the only reality which has any linguistic legitimacy. To put it another way, the only possible test of the proposition 'a dog is an animal' is to collect evidence from language users.

The language user

As I have suggested, it is this role assigned to the language user that best captures the incommensurability between Derrida's and Saussure's approaches to language. For it emerges that for Derrida, the determination of linguistic identity is *independent* of language users. This gesture of independence from language users appears throughout the linguistic texts of Derrida, and we can begin with 'Signature Event Context', in which Derrida argues that:

In order for my 'written communication' to retain its function as writing, i.e., its readability, it must remain readable despite the absolute disappearance of any receiver, determined in general. My communication must be repeatable – iterable – in the absolute absence of the receiver or of any empirically determinable collectivity of receivers. (SEC: 7)

How this argument proceeds is worth noting. Derrida begins by citing Condillac on the origins of the specificity of writing: 'Men in a state of communicating their thoughts by means of sounds, felt the necessity of imagining new signs capable of perpetuating those thoughts and of making them *known* to persons who are *absent*' (qtd in SEC: 4, Derrida's italics), and responds that: 'I underscore this value of *absence*, which, if submitted to renewed questioning, will risk introducing a certain break in the homogeneity of the system' (SEC: 4). Following from Condillac's definition, Derrida remarks that the 'absence' in such a communication is first of all the absence of a *receiver*. But Derrida notes that the absence of the *sender* is not a condition examined by Condillac, nor are the absences of the initial conditions of writing (the context), or of the writer's intentions. In Condillac's linguistic history, where gestures become sounds, which in turn become graphic symbols, the 'absence' in writing is presented as what Derrida calls 'the continuous modification and progressive extenuation of presence' (SEC: 5). That is, writing is simply an extension of the foundational and defining form of communication, that of two people facing each other, communicating by gestures or sounds. Derrida's intervention in this classical scheme is to pursue Condillac's notion of 'absence' to its limit, to the point where absence is radical and absolute. He writes:

> What holds for the receiver holds also, for the same reasons, for the sender or the producer. To write is to produce a mark that will constitute a sort of machine which is productive in turn, and which my future disappearance will not, in principle, hinder in its functioning, offering things and itself to be read and to be rewritten. When I say 'my future disappearance', it is in order to render this proposition more immediately acceptable. I ought to be able to say my disappearance, pure and simple, my nonpresence in general, for instance the nonpresence of my intention of saying something meaningful, of my wish to communicate, from the emission or production of the mark. For a writing to be a writing it must continue to 'act' and to be readable even when what is called the author of the writing no longer answers for what he has written, for what he seems to have signed, be it because of a temporary absence, because he is dead or, more generally, because he has not employed his absolutely actual and present intention or attention, the plenitude of his desire to say what he means, in order to sustain what seems to be written 'in his name'. (SEC: 8)

Writing continues to function as writing, as marks which produce meaning, in the case of the absence of the receiver, by definition, but also in the absence of the sender, the sender's intention to communicate, and the conditions of the sender's communication. In other words, writing continues to function as writing in the radical absence of the possibility of recovering any aspect of the context of its inscription.

It is interesting to note the similarity of this schema to the one held by Umberto Eco. As we have seen (above), Derrida considers that the 'first condition' of a sign's functioning is:

> its delineation with regard to a certain code; but I prefer not to become too involved here with this concept of code which does not seem very reliable to me; let us say that a certain self-identity of this element (mark, sign, etc.) is required to permit its recognition and repetition ... [T]his unity of the signifying form only constitutes itself by virtue of its iterability, by the possibility of its being repeated in the absence not only of its 'referent', which is self-evident, but in the absence of a determinate signified or of the intention of actual signification, as well as of all intention of present communication. (SEC: 10)

This view seems either to have been adopted by Eco, or to be fundamental to a certain view of signs. For Eco writes: 'A sign is everything which can be taken as significantly substituting for something else. This something else does not necessarily have to exist or to actually be somewhere at the moment in which a sign stands for it' (Eco 1976: 7). And furthermore:

> When – on the basis of an underlying rule – something actually presented to the perception of the addressee *stands for* something else, there is *signification*. In this sense the addressee's actual perception and interpretive behaviour are not necessary for the definition of a signified relationship as such: it is enough that the code should foresee an established correspondence between that which '*stands for*' and its correlate, valid for every possible addressee even if no addressee exists or will ever exist. (Eco 1976: 8)

Eco's semiotic schema allows for the permanence of the code in the radical absence of referents and receivers, and even the *possibility* of a receiver. And for Derrida, the essential predicate of writing-in-general 'is a mark that subsists, one which does not exhaust itself in the moment of its inscription and which can give rise to an iteration in the absence and beyond the presence of the empirically determined subject who, in a given context, has emitted or produced it' (SEC: 9).

Of course, for Derrida, the 'code' is not permanent but adrift; yet whatever meaning will be possible subsists or resides within the mark itself, as 'a sort of machine' (SEC: 8), sustained by the inherent possibilities of the system which gave it life. For Saussure, on the other hand, meaning, and the potential for meaning, resides solely within the brain of the language user; marks which are cut adrift of consciousness, and hence from *la langue*, are meaningless. What is *la langue*?

It is a fund accumulated by the members of the community through the practice of speech, a grammatical system existing potentially in every brain or more exactly in the brains of a group of individuals, for the language is never complete in any single individual, but exists perfectly only in the collectivity. (*Course*: 13/30)

The language system is a social and collective production, and yet it is stored within the brain of each individual of that community: 'The associations ratified by collective agreement which go to make up the language are realities localised in the brain' (*Course*: 15/32). Such an arrangement invites a critique of the relationship between the individual and the community, the degree to which they might be different, how this difference is resolved, and so on.[3] But the critical point of difference with Derrida is that 'marks' are meaningless unless subject to the discrimination of consciousness. Whether or not a mark has been inscribed with a particular intention, or with the intention to communicate at all, does not play a part in the determination of linguistic identity. Sounds and writing are determined as meaningful in the moment of their production, and again in the moment of their perception. As Saussure's example illustrates, the status of the sound sequence 'sižlaprã' as meaningful is not given in advance of its perception (*Course*: 103/146). Its division into meaningful units – in this case, as *si je l'apprends* (if I learn it) – is not linguistically a priori, but is determined by what the hearer finds significant, in 'the rapid and subtle interplay of units' (*Course*: 104/148). What is transported from one user to another in speech is *not* a signifier, but only a sequence of abstract sounds. For as we have just noted, it is illogical to say that ' "the language does this or that", to speak of the "life of the language", and so on, because a language is not an entity, and exists only in its users' (*Course*: 5n/19n). If the receiver should determine some meaning in the sounds it is because abstract sound and abstract thought are able to be mutually articulated within a language structure, *la langue*, which is stored in their brain. This accords with the Saussurean dictum that 'any linguistic entity exists only in virtue of the association between signifier and signified. It disappears the moment we concentrate exclusively on just one or the other' (*Course*: 101/144), and hence that 'it is impossible in a language to isolate sound from thought, or thought from sound' (*Course*: 111/157).

Derrida offers an interesting philosophical puzzle, which you might want to consider for a moment before I give you his answer. He writes:

A writing that is not structurally readable – iterable – beyond the death of the addressee would not be writing. Although this would seem to be obvious, I do not want it accepted as such, and I shall examine the final objection that could be made to this proposition. Imagine a writing whose code would be so idiomatic as to be established and known, as secret cipher, by only two 'subjects'. Could we maintain that, following the death of the receiver, or even of both partners, the mark left by one of them is still writing? (SEC: 7)

It is an interesting enough philosophical puzzle, and one which does not have a clear answer, precisely because of the liminality of the use of the word 'writing' here. Derrida's answer is this:

> Yes, to the extent that, organised by a code, even an unknown and non-linguistic one, it is constituted in its identity as mark by its iterability, in the absence of such and such a person, and hence ultimately of every empirically determined 'subject'. (SEC: 7–8)

The mark is constituted by its iterability, its ability to be weaned from its original context and grafted onto entirely new contexts. Its status as writing, in other words, is determined by the conditions of the possibility of meaning. What is essential about writing is external to and independent from any particular language user, or from any possible language user. But what I feel that Derrida avoids responsibility for here – and this is crucial for understanding the incommensurability of the two positions – is the 'we' of the previous quotation. He asks: 'Could *we* maintain that, following the death of . . . both partners, the mark left by one of them is still writing', but doesn't identify who the *we* is. He posits a writing that must be structurally 'readable' beyond the death and in the absence of every empirically determined subject, and yet who is determining this readability? Who, in short, reads? Does Derrida call upon an empirical, historical subject or consciousness, or can readability be determined prior to subjectivity, prior to consciousness?

For me, the argument against Derrida here takes two forms. The first objection takes the point of view of the language user, as I have just recently invited you – the reader – to do. On what basis does one decide that a phenomenon is writing or not? Derrida wants to exclude any kind of subjective point of view, which might include empirical evidence, or more information, or context: does it look like writing, could it eventually be deciphered, are there clues to its origins, and so on. In short, Derrida will not allow writing's status to be in the hands of an empirically determined subject. There is no doubt, of course, that what Derrida is working towards in 'Signature Event Context', and elsewhere, is a system in which the reader, and not the sender, is *privileged* in the determination of a specific meaning. However, the very status of the utterance as meaningful is placed outside of the domain of the language user, to the system of possibility which gives rise to language users and to consciousness itself. The second is the theoretical and linguistic objection that readability requires subjectivity as a *co-dependent* value. Without readers, there is no reading; without reading there are no readers. As such, it may not be possible to separate the question of reading from the question of readers. These arguments, when fully tested, will occupy the final two chapters of this book.

Conclusion

Derrida deconstructs classical conceptions of meaning and communication through intensive challenges to the notions of 'context', 'repetition', and 'ideality'. In place of communication and presence, Derrida's philosophy considers iteration and absence; in the place of polysemy, Derrida proposes dissemination, and a meaning which is radically cast adrift from the conditions of its utterance. Such challenges serve to deconstruct the classical conception of identity thought on the basis of presence. In doing so, however, Derrida removes authority of meaning from any specific language user, or from language users in general. Derrida speaks of the *self*-identity that is inherent in iteration, and of how a mark contains its own repeatability; how it *subsists*, in the absence of any empirically determined subject. In Derrida's schema, communication is only made possible because of *primordial* difference and the de jure possibility of repetition. In the *Course*, on the other hand, Saussure's view of meaning as 'value' is radicalised in his privileging of language users. For Saussure, linguistic identity resides *entirely* within consciousness – both in the individual and the collective. In this way, Saussurean linguistics offers an equally radical reappraisal of the assumptions of classical communication. In place of classical notions of identity, entity, meaning, and sameness, Saussure offers value, difference, identification, and the privileging of the language user.

Of course, when we say that meaning is determined by language users, we might also say that meaning resides in the mind of the language user, or in consciousness. This is, no doubt, precisely the criticism that Derrida would make: that for Saussure and for structuralism, meaning may not reside in the thing itself, but rather, in a full intuitive consciousness; that Saussurean language theory fails to put into question the prior unity of consciousness; that Western metaphysics, from the *Phaedrus* onward, is founded upon 'consciousness as the ultimate authority' (SEC: 8). Perhaps it is sufficient to reflect that when Saussure states that 'In order to determine to what extent something is a reality, it is necessary and also sufficient to find out to what extent it exists as far as the language users are concerned', we recognise a proposition that would be rejected by post-structuralism: for failing to question the origins and sediments of the point of view of the language user, and of the production of a self-present consciousness. This is no doubt true, from a certain *point of view*. And yet, there may be something in the Saussurean determination of linguistic identity as the point of view of the language user that is able to both resist and exceed the Derridean critique of context, ideality and identity. This confrontation – between iteration and value, or between

Derridean and Saussurean systematicity – takes place around the question of 'structure'.

Notes

1. The *Project* and the 'Note on the Mystic Writing-Pad' are included in *The Standard Edition of the Complete Psychological Works of Sigmund Freud*, trans. James Strachey, London: Hogarth Press, 1953–75, vols 1 and 19, respectively.
2. The editors refer the reader to the *Course* (65/97): 'For some people a language, reduced to its essentials, is a nomenclature: a list of terms corresponding to a list of things . . . This conception is open to a number of objections. It assumes that ideas already exist independently of words'. And indeed, this passage contains a reference to the *Course* (110/155), chapter four: 'Linguistic Value'.
3. And it is clear that Saussure does not completely resolve these questions. To move forward with Saussurean theory, some discussion of this would be essential. See Harris (1987: 219–37) for a comprehensive opening out of this problem.

7 The Sign and Time

The lecture titled 'Différance' was first presented to the Société française de philosophie on 27 January 1968, and published in the Société's *Bulletin* in July 1968. In June 1968, in between the presentation of 'Différance' as a lecture and its first publication, Julia Kristeva interviewed Jacques Derrida for the journal *Information sur les sciences sociales*, which was later reprinted in *Positions* as 'Semiology and Grammatology'. In this interview, Kristeva suggests to Derrida that: 'Semiology today is constructed on the model of the sign and its correlates: *communication* and *structure*' (Kristeva, qtd in S&G: 17). 'Semiology and Grammatology' itself is oriented towards questions of communication as the transport of pure signifieds, and hence towards the classical concept of the sign, the transcendental signified, and phono-logocentrism. In response to the question of structure, Derrida refers the reader to the essay 'Différance', and to the work of *différance* upon the theory of synchronic structure proposed by Saussure. This work is summarised in 'Semiology and Grammatology' as follows:

> The activity or productivity connoted by the *a* of *différance* refers to the generative movement in the play of differences. The latter are neither fallen from the sky nor inscribed once and for all in a closed system, a static structure that a synchronic and taxonomic operation could exhaust. Differences are the effects of transformations, and from this vantage the theme of *différance* is incompatible with the static, synchronic, taxonomic, ahistoric motifs in the concept of structure. (S&G: 27)

And so it is to the essay 'Différance', and to Derrida's intervention in the static, synchronic, taxonomic, and ahistoric motifs in the concept of *structure*, that we will now turn.

In his introductory remarks to 'Différance', Derrida describes the essay as a 'sheaf' of utilisations of *différance*, which is neither a word nor a concept. The term 'sheaf' marks that 'the assemblage to be proposed has the complex structure of a weaving, an interlacing which permits the different threads and different lines of meaning – or of force – to go off again in different directions, just as it is always ready to tie itself up with others' (Diff: 3). The contents of this sheaf, which refuse to be bound and closed, are sketched here as:

> the juncture – rather than the summation – of what has been most decisively inscribed in the thought of what is conveniently called our 'epoch': the differences of forces in Nietzsche, Saussure's principle of semiological difference, differing as the possibility of (neurone) facilitation, impression and delayed effect in Freud, difference as the irreducibility of the trace of the other in Levinas, and the ontic-ontological difference in Heidegger. (Diff (A): 130)

Différance, therefore, is an assemblage of forces, of plural utilisations of a graphic intervention, and is directed towards the philosophy of five named theorists. It is certainly not trivial to note that within this sheaf, the first and longest section of 'Différance' is addressed to Saussurean difference. It is even worth considering that Saussure's premier position in the discourse of *différance* might be something that Derrida cannot do without. However, the ambition of these final two chapters is absolutely *not* to overturn Derrida's motif of *différance* in its entirety. It is, rather, to gather together, from a vantage point somewhere in between Derrida and Saussure, all of Derrida's commentary, critique and work upon the notions of *structure* and *synchrony* found in the *Course*. After this it might be possible, as with the other chapters of this book, to question the authority of the Derridean reading, and to offer alternative pathways of investigation.

Différance

Derrida prefigures his engagement with the five named theorists with a 'simple and approximate semantic analysis' of *différance* (Diff: 7). Derrida notes that, according to the *Littré* dictionary, and following its Latin roots, the verb *différer* offers two distinct meanings: to differ and to defer. The sense of deferring relates to an interval of time; of, as Derrida suggests, 'a detour, a delay, a relay, a reserve, a representation – concepts that I would summarize here in a word I have never used but that could be inscribed in this chain: *temporization*' (Diff: 8). The sense of differing, on the other hand, implies the non-identical, that which is other, in which 'an interval, a distance, spacing, must be produced between the elements' (Diff: 8). The economy of *différance*, then, would be to bring together these intervals of time and space within an irreducible polysemia. *Différance*, up to this point, would therefore be positioned in between and among the 'spatial' and the 'temporal'. But additionally, the '*-ance*' of *différance* indicates the sense of deferring the activity associated with the present participle, *différant*: 'because it brings us close to the infinitive and active kernel of différer, *différance* (with an a) neutral-izes what the infinitive denotes as simply active' and that the ending '*-ance*' 'remains undecided *between* the active and the passive . . ., announcing or rather recalling something like the middle voice' (Diff: 9). And so *différance* is more correctly that which economises not just the spatial and the temporal, but also the more active orientations of the becoming-spatial and the becom-ing-temporal. But as Derrida asks, and it is the reason for his engagement with Saussure, '*Différance* as temporization, *différance* as spacing. How are they to be joined? Let us start, since we are already there, from the problem-atic of the sign and of writing' (Diff: 9). What Derrida wants from, and does with, the Saussurean sign can be well understood and even schematised, at least initially. In 'Différance', Derrida deals first with the *différance* of tem-porisation and later with the *différance* of spacing, but here my re-writing and schematisation will begin with spacing.

Saussure is, according to Derrida, the thinker who instituted the field of semiology which is based on the arbitrary and differential character of the sign. The system of signs is arbitrary, in that meaning is not constituted in any essential and naturalistic relationship, or as Derrida says, not in their 'pleni-tude', but rather in 'the network of oppositions that distinguishes them, and then relates them one to another' (Diff: 10). Derrida then assembles a citation from the *Course*, within the limitation, 'let us cite Saussure only at the point which interests us':

> The conceptual side of value is made up solely of relations and differ-ences with respect to the other terms of language, and the same can be said of its material side . . . Everything that has been said up to this point boils down to this: in language there are only differences. Even more important: a difference generally implies positive terms between which the difference is set up; but in language there are only differences *without positive terms*. Whether we take the signified or the signifier, language has neither ideas nor sounds that existed before the linguistic system, but only conceptual and phonic differences that have issued from the system. The idea or phonic substance that a sign contains is of less importance than the other signs that surround it. (*Course (B)*: 117–18, 120, qtd in Diff: 10–11)

And Derrida responds that:

> The first consequence to be drawn from this is that the signified concept is never present in and of itself, in a sufficient presence that would refer only to itself. Essentially and lawfully, every concept is inscribed in a chain or in a system within which it refers to the other, to other concepts, by means of the systematic play of differences. Such a play, *différance*, is thus no longer simply a concept, but rather the possibility

of conceptuality, of a conceptual process and system in general . . . The
difference of which Saussure speaks is itself, therefore, neither a concept
nor a word among others. The same can be said, a fortiori, of *différance*.
(Diff: 11)

In 'Semiology and Grammatology', Derrida states that the Saussurean
concept of the sign marks 'a simultaneous impediment and progress' (S&G:
17). In this passage, Saussure appears in the light of progress, as the inau-
gurator of the *différance* of spacing. Here, *différance* acts as an elaboration of the potential of Saussurean difference – as the *play* of difference
– if it can be released from its logocentric grounding in a transcendental
signified.

The relationship between *différance* and difference is, therefore, beginning
to form. As Derrida continues at this point: 'we are thereby led to explicate
the relation of one to the other' (Diff: 11). If Saussurean semiology suggests
the play of difference in the *différance* of spacing, then what of the *différance*
of temporisation? For Derrida, it is precisely this problem that remains
untheorised in Saussure:

> The sign represents the present in its absence. It takes the place of the
> present. When we cannot grasp or show the thing, state the present, the
> being-present, when the present cannot be presented, we signify, we go
> through the detour of the sign. We take or give signs. We signal. The
> sign, in this sense, is deferred presence. Whether we are concerned with
> the verbal or the written sign, with the monetary sign, or with electoral
> delegation and political representation, the circulation of signs defers
> the moment in which we can encounter the thing itself, make it ours,
> consume or expend it, touch it, see it, intuit its presence. What I am
> describing here in order to define it is the classically determined struc-
> ture of the sign in all the banality of its characteristics – signification as
> the *différance* of temporization. (Diff: 9)

This last phrase is the most important: 'signification as the *différance* of
temporization'. As I have already argued, in the Derridean model of the
Saussurean sign, the principle of difference *between* signs is economised as
the *différance* of spacing. Here, Derrida defines signification – the movement
within the sign, between the signifier and signified, where the signified stands
for either the concept or the thing itself – as the *différance* of temporisation.
And this completes the schema to which I earlier referred. The progress in
Saussure is the formulation of the differential and arbitrary characteristics of
the sign, which are constituted by the *différance* of spacing. The impediment
in Saussure results from the formulation of signification, or the division and
movement between the signifier and signified, which is constituted by the *différance* of temporisation. In Saussure's semiological system, differences can

be considered synchronically – as momentarily structured in their entirety. But Derrida, importantly, does not see this as a structure but as a process, a structuring; not as a system of differences, but as the 'systematic play of differences', and calls this *différance* (Diff: 11).

The deferral in *différance* also contains the sense of unfulfilled desire that is carried by *vouloir-dire* in French, that is, by 'wanting to say':

> *Différer* in this sense is to temporize, to take recourse, consciously or unconsciously, in the temporal and temporizing mediation of a detour that suspends the accomplishment or fulfilment of 'desire' or 'will', and equally effects this suspension in a mode that annuls or tempers its own effect. (Diff: 8)

Signification – as the movement from signifier to signified – would then imply the suspension of desire, or the deferral of moment when we can encounter the thing itself. As Robert Young puts it, 'Derrida's interest is precisely in the movement of passage that always defers the arrival of the signified. A perpetual play and instability occurs in the unending drift across the traverse' (16). The sign would then imply a deferral of presence, that is, a deferral of the moment when the sign can be (re-)joined to a truth, or reality. Signs are utilised when we cannot show or grasp the thing, and they hold this place until such time as this originary presence is restored. Because of this classical implication of an originary presence, Derrida writes that: 'One could no longer include *différance* in the concept of the sign, which always has meant the representation of a presence, and has been constituted in a system (thought or language) governed by and moving toward presence' (Diff: 10). On the contrary, the intervention of *différance* undermines this presence, this transcendental signified as the origin of differences, and even this presumption of a simple origin. *Différance* cannot be thought of in any terms of classical metaphysics, as it is *différance*, or the simultaneous origin and play, and cause and effect, of differences which allows metaphysics to appear.

To summarise the relationship between *différance* and difference:

> With its *a*, differance more properly refers to what in classical language would be called the origin or production of differences and the differences between differences, the *play* of differences. (Diff (A): 130)

And that:

> In a conceptuality adhering to classical strictures '*différance*' would be said to designate a constitutive, productive, and originary causality, the process of scission and division which would produce or constitute different things or differences. (Diff: 8–9)

In this way, *différance* makes possible the differences between presence and absence, activity and passivity, synchrony and diachrony, subject and object, and so on, that Saussure seems to presume and require for his theory of language. Semiological differences are constituted in and produced by *différance*, in a history without origins. Already it is possible, therefore, to suspect the straightforwardness of Derrida's intervention of 'history' and the 'temporal' within the synchronic, or 'spatial', distribution of meaning. There is already the thought that the temporality that precedes semiological 'presence' is not simply historical but is causal, not simply de facto, but de jure. Both possibilities, and not simply both, but also what gives rise to their difference, will have to be examined. But first we will exhaust Derrida's intervention of time within no-time, within synchrony.

Derrida's temporal intervention

The starting point for any discussion of Derrida's temporal intervention within synchronic structure must be his principle, or axiom, that 'differences have not fallen from the sky'. Derrida uses this phrase twice in 'Différance', and again when summarising the work of *différance* in 'Semiology and Grammatology'. First:

> In a language, in the *system* of language, there are only differences. Therefore a taxonomical operation can undertake the systematic, statistical, and classificatory inventory of a language. But, on the one hand, these differences *play*: in language, and in speech too, and in the exchange between language and speech. On the other hand, these differences are themselves *effects*. They have not fallen from the sky fully formed, and are no more inscribed in a *topos noētos*, than they are prescribed in the gray matter of the brain . . . What is written as *différance*, then, will be the playing movement that 'produces' – by means of something that is not simply an activity – these differences, these effects of difference. (Diff: 11)

And shortly following this:

> Since language, which Saussure says is a classification, has not fallen from the sky, its differences have been produced, they are produced effects, but they are effects which do not find their cause in a subject or substance, in a thing in general, a being that is somewhere present, thereby eluding the play of *différance*. If such a presence were implied in the concept of cause in general, in the most classical fashion, we then would have to speak of an effect without a cause, which very quickly would lead to speaking of no effect at all. (Diff: 11–12)

And finally, as we have already seen:

> The activity or productivity connoted by the *a* of *différance* refers to the generative movement in the play of differences. The latter are neither fallen from the sky nor inscribed once and for all in a closed system, a static structure that a synchronic and taxonomic operation could exhaust. Differences are the effects of transformations, and from this vantage the theme of *différance* is incompatible with the static, synchronic, taxonomic, ahistoric motifs in the concept of *structure*. (S&G: 27)

A number of elaborations must be made if we are to make Derrida's intervention engage as fully as possible with Saussurean theory. Derrida says that, in a certain restricted sense, a taxonomical operation could be performed upon a language system. Such an inventory might resemble a dictionary, albeit one which also classifies and cross-references phonemes and grammatical rules. Saussure suggests that: 'If we could collect the totality of word patterns stored in all those individuals, we should have the social bond which constitutes their language' (*Course*: 13/30); and that such a language 'takes the form of a totality of imprints in everyone's brain, rather like a dictionary of which each individual has an identical copy' (*Course*: 19/38); and that it is 'a grammatical system existing potentially in every brain' (*Course*: 13/30). There would seem to be little about Derrida's description of a 'systematic, statistical, and classificatory inventory of a language' for Saussurean readers to disagree with.

But, 'on the other hand', writes Derrida, these differences are *effects*. That is, they have not fallen from the sky, they have been produced in a history, something has *caused* them. A great deal of caution must, and will, be taken on this point. But we can assert *first*, as a brute fact, that anyone who writes that Saussure thought that linguistic differences had fallen from the sky ought not to be writing on the subject at all. For the author of the *Mémoire sur le système primitif des voyelles dans les langues indo-européennes* is unquestionably more qualified to write about linguistic evolution than Derrida, or Peirce, or Condillac, or Jakobson, or any of the other major theorists of language in play in this investigation. The historical evolution of various languages is analysed so richly and fruitfully in the *Course*[1] that this criticism – in its crudest form – must be rejected without hesitation. If it is beyond question that languages evolve over time, then what *exactly* is Derrida suggesting? The question that Derrida's intervention begs at this point is how the knowledge that languages evolve, and that the state of a language today is the modification of a previous state, proscribes making a taxonomy at one moment in time. That is, how the knowledge that differences are 'the effects of transformations' makes them 'incompatible with the static, synchronic, taxonomic, ahistoric motifs in the concept of *structure*' (S&G: 27).

To begin, the assumption that we would hope to make – that Derrida's reminder of the evolution of language is *not* crude – does not start at all well. Derrida writes that differences are not 'inscribed once and for all in closed system, a static structure' (S&G: 27). This remark seems to accord with Derrida's observation of the 'permanent code' of classical semiology, which Freud's dream language would disturb (F&SW: 210). But in what possible sense, we must ask, does Derrida mean 'once and for all' or 'permanent', when the constant evolution of language is such a prominent feature of the *Course*? The complete citation from 'Freud and the Scene of Writing', which Derrida addresses specifically to Saussure and the *Course*, reveals that this permanence derives from a wholly classical schema of signification:

> Translation, a system of translation, is possible only if a permanent code allows a substitution or transformation of signifiers while retaining the same signified, always present, despite the absence of any specific signifier. This fundamental possibility of substitution would thus be implied by the coupled concepts signified/signifier, and would consequently be implied by the concept of the sign itself. (F&SW: 210)

The 'permanence' of signification becomes clearer, then, when we understand it to be a relationship between signs and things, or between signs and absolute ideality. Signifiers can be substituted for other signifiers – it is this which explains linguistic evolution – but the signified must be permanent, infallible, and hence transcendental. Or to recall Aristotle's terms, the correspondence between 'things' and 'mental experiences' (which are the *images* of things) is 'the same for all men'. Derrida maintains the view that, despite the constant evolution and arbitrary connection between the signifier and signified, semiology would wish to maintain a permanent and infallible relationship between the signified and its referent. Derrida's engagement with the temporality of signification therefore presumes a classical model of the sign in which 'permanence' and 'infallibility' ensure the metaphysical relationship with presence and truth.

Second, as we have already seen, Derrida defines linguistic identity as essentially diachronic, as a manifestation of *the same*. This definition of signification as repetition is necessarily also an argument for an irreducible temporality within the sign. An utterance is not contained within the moment of its event, but is an iteration of general form, made possible by a structural and primordial citationality. The event of signification is already divided from itself in a general citationality or iterability. Derrida argues, therefore, for an essential relationship between the sign in the present with the sign in the past and the future:

> It is because of *différance* that the movement of signification is possible only if each so-called 'present' element, each element appearing on the scene of presence, is related to something other than itself, thereby

keeping within itself the mark of the past element, and already letting
itself be vitiated by the mark of its relation to the future element, this
trace being related no less to what is called the future than to what is
called the past, and constituting what is called the present by means of
this very relation to what it is not: what it absolutely is not, not even a
past or a future as a modified present. (Diff: 13)

It might be possible, shortly, to propose a semiological engagement with
the problem of (what Derrida might call) the non-simple *derivation* of 'the
present'. But for the moment, Derrida's temporal intervention, and his
reminder that 'differences have not fallen from the sky', can be more richly
understood. A sign is never an event, but rather, is an iteration of a general
form, which cannot be contained within any synchronic moment. If each
element in a semiological system did not enact a repetition, or iteration,
of *the same*, it would cease to function as signification. Each element in a
semiological system is inscribed in a chain, a trace, of substitutions, always
nostalgic for and moving towards presence, or the reunification of language
with a present intuition or reality. Until such time, the sign takes the place,
and holds the place, and defers the accomplishment, of its own desire to say.
Above all, such a schema would reveal that present significations cannot
reside or rest in a simple presence, and hence are unable to be contained by a
synchronic and taxonomical operation.

It is not necessary to undertake a reversal of each of these supposed characteristics of the Saussurean sign. It is enough to observe that Derrida's relationship with semiological temporality is determined by, and contained by,
the presumption of a classical relationship with presence. To put it another
way, Derrida's understanding of semiological *structure* is determined by his
view of semiological *communication*. To whatever degree Derrida's reading
of semiological communication is valid or not, then the same would apply to
his reading of semiological structure. However, if the Saussurean sign does
not reproduce these characteristics of logocentrism, if *la langue* is neither
transcendental nor inscribed in a *topos noētos*, if Saussurean value does not
equate to phenomenological ideality, then Derrida's efforts are not appro-
priately engaged with the theory that actually appears in the *Course*. What
Derrida proposes, in summary, is that: 'the play of differences' is not enclosed
in a system which 'a synchronic and taxonomic operation could exhaust'
(S&G: 27). Some closer scrutiny of the *Course*, and of these synchronic and
taxonomic operations, is now necessary.

Temporality in the *Course*

To begin, we can confirm that Saussure acknowledges the constant evolution
of languages. Aside from his frequent recourse to examples of linguistic evo-

lution, Saussure also explicitly states that: 'languages are always changing, however minimally' (*Course*: 100/142); and more thoroughly, that:

> Language at any given time involves an established system and an evolution. At any given time, it is an institution in the present and a product of the past. At first sight, it looks very easy to distinguish between the system and its history, between what it is and what it was. In reality, the connexion between the two is so close that it is hard to separate them. (*Course*: 9/24)

In this way, language might be analogous to the movement of an object in space. The object is simultaneously in motion *and* at a position; always at a single point and always part of a movement which is connected to the past and to the future. Indeed, the *Course* provides several analogies in the attempt to explain how a single language could be considered from two contrasting points of view, with the best known of these being the game of chess. Saussure argues that:

> In a game of chess, any given state of the board is totally independent of any previous state of the board. It does not matter at all whether the state in question has been reached by one sequence of moves or another sequence. Anyone who has followed the whole game has not the least advantage over a passer-by who happens to look at the game at that particular moment. In order to describe the position on the board, it is quite useless to refer to what happened ten seconds ago. All this applies equally well to a language, and confirms the radical distinction between diachronic and synchronic. (*Course*: 88/126–7)

In this analogy, Saussure is quite aware that the position on the board was *caused* by certain actions; actions which took place as recently as ten seconds ago. But such information about the past is *useless* in attempting to describe the present. Language hasn't fallen from the sky, but it wouldn't make any difference if it had.

Saussure says that an evolving system, like language or a chess game, can be viewed from two points of view which are irreducible: the historical or diachronic point of view, and the structural or synchronic point of view. Saussure says that despite the difficulty of doing so, we *must* separate the structural from the historical in language, and he provides substantial and complex reasoning for this necessity. Derrida's intervention in the static, structural point of view is carried by the work of *différance* upon the Saussurean sign, as the play of what is both productive and produced. But what is missing from the Derridean intervention is any discussion or critique of the *reasons* that Saussure gives for the radical distinction between the synchronic and diachronic points of view. These are worth considering, however, as they not only defend the structural view of language, but also carry with them a critique of history, causality, and origins that serves to destabilise the presuppositions of Derrida's reading.

The first of these continues from the chess analogy, where Saussure remarks that: 'There is only one respect in which the comparison is defective. In chess, the player *intends* to make his moves and to have some effect upon the system. In a language, on the contrary, there is no premeditation. Its pieces are moved, or rather modified, spontaneously and fortuitously' (*Course*: 88–9/127). This qualification is far from trivial for Saussure. On the contrary, the 'fortuitous' nature of language change is an important principle which reflects its arbitrary character.[2] Saussure makes the point that linguistics, in this regard, is like few other disciplines. Physical sciences like geology do not need to strictly divide static analysis from the analysis of change. But language is more like economics, which is forced to recognise this duality. We are obliged to: 'divide linguistics into two parts, each based upon a principle of its own. The reason is that, as in the study of political economy, one is dealing with the notion of value' (*Course*: 79–80/115). The mechanism of *value* – which derives from the *arbitrary* and *differential* character of the sign – means that it is simply not possible to consider any single unit of language without considering at the same time the entire system of which it is part. Saussure says that: 'All this confirms the principles already formulated above, which may be summed up as follows' (*Course*: 86/124):

> A language is a system of which all the parts can and must be considered as synchronically interdependent.
>
> Since changes are never made to the system as a whole, but only to its individual elements, they must be studied independently of the system [but] it is true that every change has a repercussion on the system. (*Course*: 86/124)

And to once again draw an analogy with chess:

> in order to pass from one stable position to another or, in our terminology, from one synchronic state to another, moving one piece is all that is needed. There is no general upheaval . . . In spite of that, the move has a repercussion upon the whole system. (*Course*: 88/126)

In this way, Saussure problematises the whole notion of *staying the same*. Even when it would appear that the form or the meaning of a word has remained unchanged, it *will* have actually changed due to other changes in the form or meaning of neighbouring words. In structural analysis it becomes impossible to say that the word for 'the same thing' has changed, or that the word has stayed the same while the idea has changed, because in each case *same* and *different* refer to structural position, not individual existence. In the case of the chess game, the value of *every* piece changes after *each* move, even though only one piece has been moved. With language the problem of diachronic identity is even more obscure, without the aid of physical pieces to assure some continuity in time.

The argument here – which is conducted in the *Course* against nineteenth-century linguistics – is between atomism and systematicity. Harris sums up the atomist view with a citation from Whitney, who writes that signs are 'isolated and independent entities', and with Gilliéron's famous aphorism, that: 'every word has its own history' (qtd in Harris 1987: 85). For nineteenth-century linguists, there was 'nothing problematic at all in the notion of a word "surviving" over the centuries, irrespective of its incorporation at different times into different linguistic systems' (Harris 1987: 85–6). On the contrary, Saussure describes diachronic identity as a 'delicate question':

> For in order to be able to say that a given unit has remained the same over time, or that, while remaining a distinct unit, it has changed in form or meaning – any of which is possible – I must know on what I base the claim that an element taken from one period – e.g. the French word *chaud* ('hot') – is the same as an element taken from another period – e.g. the Latin *calidum* . . . It is doubtless correct to say that Latin *mare* ('sea') ought to appear in French in the form *mer* on the grounds that Latin *a* became *e* in French under certain conditions, that final unstressed *e* fell, etc. But to state that these connexions *a → e, e →* zero, etc. constitute the identity in question is to put the cart before the horse. On the contrary, one judges that *a* became *e*, that final *e* fell, etc. in the light of the correspondence *mare* : *mer*. (*Course*: 180/249)

Saussure's objection to the general method of historical linguistics, a method he had previously used himself, is profound and devastating. Harris's conclusion is that: 'Far from being uncontroversial, it raises the dire question of the extent to which diachronic linguistics is possible at all' (Harris 1987: 163). An essential part of the historical method is to prove that, for example, the French *mer* is a descendant of the Latin *mare*, on the basis of them both being names of 'the same thing'. On the contrary:

> The point Saussure is making is that even if trees had not changed in any significant respect between Caesar's day and Napoleon's, and even if the thing designated by the word *arbor* is the same as the thing designated by the word *arbre*, this does not mean that there has been no change of meaning *unless we also assume that identity of things designated guarantees identity of ideas* (as Aristotle, for one, appears to have maintained, to judge by *De Interpretatione* . . .). (Harris 1987: 57–8)

The Saussurean theory of diachronic identity states that *both* the form (signifier) *and* the meaning (signified) will inevitably have undergone evolution between one state of the language and another. Hence, neither element can be held constant while we investigate the other, as diachronic linguistics would like to. To make matters more complicated, we must also face the knowledge that both faces of the sign *will* have changed, even in cases where they *appear* unchanged, due to changes in the system around it. Attempting to follow the history, or the diachronic identity, of 'a' word, the 'same' word, would be like trying to solve an equation with exactly two variables and two unknowns.

The second implication of the Saussurean approach to time follows from the first. For Saussure's radical problematisation of diachronic identity is also, to some degree, a problematisation of historical explanation in general. Culler makes the important point that history is ordinarily concerned with cause and effect, whereas the language system is founded in arbitrariness:

> Historical or causal explanation is not what is required; it bears on the elements of a language, not the language, and bears on them only as elements. Explanation in linguistics is structural: one explains forms and rules of combination by setting out the underlying system of relations, in a particular synchronic state, which create and define the elements of that synchronic system. (Culler 1986: 45)

Explanation in linguistics is structural and not historical because causality is not relevant in a system of arbitrary and differential values. A language system did not fall from the sky, but there is nothing outside of the present structure which is meaningful. We would also want to recall at this point the relationship with causality which was critical in distinguishing Saussurean semiology from Peircean semiotics. To exclude causality is to exclude Peircean indexical signs – as in the relationship between smoke and fire – from the domain of Saussurean explanation. That is, Saussurean semiology does not include phenomena such as symptoms, where a logical or interpretive relationship is postulated between two referents.

The contrast with the view of nineteenth-century linguistics is stark. In 1891, the neogrammarian linguist Hermann Paul wrote:

> It has been objected that there is another view of language possible besides the historical. I must contradict this. What is explained as an unhistorical and still scientific observation of language is at bottom nothing but one incompletely historical, through defects partly of the observer, partly of the material to be observed. (Paul, qtd in Harris 2001: 35)

And to this, Harris remarks:

> Saussure must have seemed to many of his contemporaries (including his editors) to be denying what nearly all nineteenth-century scholar-

ship, from Darwin onwards, had recognised; namely, that evolution was the indispensable factor in understanding current states of affairs.

Although the intellectual spanner that Saussure had deliberately thrown into the evolutionary works was crude, it was also impossible to ignore. (Harris 2001: 35–6)

Which brings us back to Derrida. For whether or not it is reasonable to say that Derrida has *ignored* this 'spanner' of systematicity, there are several issues that the *Course* raises that Derrida chooses to not comment on *directly*. Derrida's intervention in static, ahistoric, taxonomic structure is carried by *différance*, and by the demonstration that in the (classical) semiological model, linguistic identity is built upon a relationship between past and future elements, between iterations of a singular ideality, implying also a relationship of causality, and of the suspension of the fulfilment of the will. But Derrida makes no defence of diachronic identity, or of historical explanation in general, against Saussure's reasoning for synchrony and systematicity. Indeed, in the essay 'Différance', Derrida cites only two passages from the *Course*: the first is reproduced above, concerning the definition of 'value' as differences without positive terms; and the second is a two-line excerpt on the relationship between language and speech (Diff: 15). At no point in 'Différance' – the essay charged with demonstrating the mistake of static, synchronic structure – does Derrida make an attempt to engage with any part of the theory of synchrony which occupies such a substantial proportion of the *Course*. Instead, Derrida relies upon the work of *différance* to exceed and to neutralise the detailed arguments of the semiological discourse.

Conclusion

The final and most important reason for Saussure's insistence upon the strict division between synchrony and diachrony will take us into questions that will be addressed in the final chapter of this book. This reason is, of course, that synchrony is privileged because it is the viewpoint of the language user. Saussure says that the synchronic and diachronic 'are not of equal importance. It is clear that the synchronic point of view takes precedence over the diachronic, since for the community of language users that is the one and only reality' (*Course*: 89/128). This passage from the *Course* is cross-referenced to another:

The first thing which strikes one on studying linguistic facts is that the language user is unaware of their succession in time: he is dealing with a state. Hence the linguist who wishes to understand this state must rule out of consideration everything which brought that state about, and pay no attention to diachrony. Only by suppressing the past can he

enter into the state of mind of the language user. The intervention of
history can only distort his judgement. (*Course*: 81/117)

The theory of synchrony does not so much fix the language at one point in
time as *follow* the point of view of language users, who determine linguistic value by acts of differentiation within the system of language stored in
their brains *at any moment in time*. And so when Derrida refers to static
and taxonomic operations, these are in fact the operations of the ordinary
language user, which are then mimicked by the linguist. Elaborating on
this permanently synchronic state of language users, Harris observes that:
'the Saussurean identification of synchrony with the viewpoint of current
language users', is wholly based upon the principle, or assumption, that:
'the only reality of a system is the reality it has for its present users: to this
reality the past contributes nothing' (Harris 1987: 202). Or, as Culler phrases
it, whatever the language system has inherited from the past is currently
incorporated into and functions only within the state of the language at the
moment of signification:

> a knowledge of previous meanings and of the particular causes of
> change would not be relevant to an account of the semantic relations
> of a synchronic state (except insofar as previous meanings were still
> present in the system, in which case they would be considered syn-
> chronically, not diachronically). (Culler 1986: 45)

The Saussurean theory of language has, then, two mutually determining
principles: the point of view of the language user, and synchrony. The only
meaningful 'identity' in a language is the differential value determined by
language users. And the only point of view available to language users – or
as Harris says, 'the only relevant psychological reality for current speakers of
the language' (Harris 2001: 197) – is the synchronic.

However, in concluding this chapter and opening out the next, we need to
note that it is precisely these mutually determining principles and assumptions that Derrida would wish to question, and more specifically, question the
origin of. From where have these principles arrived? Have they fallen from
the sky, or are they divine, inscribed in a *topos noëtos*? What becomes critical at this point is Derrida's subtle play with the notions of precedence and
determination. For to say that some event *preceded* some other event is not
the same as to say that some fact *determines* another fact. For example, it is
one thing to say that event A took place prior to event B; it is another thing
to say that *if* A equals X *then* B equals Y. The first is a concept of (de facto)
history and succession, the second is a concept of (de jure) determination and
causation.[3] Derrida's engagement with Saussurean structure, then, opens out
these two questions, and also the question of the difference between them.
The first, addressed in this chapter, concerns the intervention of the temporal

within the synchronic: the involvement of a temporal interval within semiological, or spatial, difference. The second is the question of metaphysical
determination: of where the principles of Saussurean theory, or any other
deterministic theory of meaning, have come from; of what enables or produces the axioms of semiology. *Différance*, as we shall see, poses a question of
the *origins* of linguistic identity, and reveals a chain within the *determination*
of linguistic identity that is not simply historical or causal. Derrida situates
différance as prior (either de facto or de jure) to difference, as the non-simple
origin and production of differences. This question of priority, the ultimate
question that Derrida's philosophy poses to metaphysics, will occupy the
ultimate chapter of this book.

For the moment, however, at least two points have emerged from this
analysis of temporality which will encounter no reason to be revoked. The
first is that Derrida's intervention of *différance* is directed wholly towards
classical, rather than Saussurean, semiology. Against Saussure's highly original and subtly detailed critiques of diachronic identity, of staying the same,
of historical explanation, and of origins, Derrida will continue to interrogate
an Aristotelian schema of signification, in which 'a permanent code allows a
substitution or transformation of signifiers while retaining the same signified,
always present, despite the absence of any specific signifier' (F&SW: 210).
For Derrida, the sign is put in the place of the thing itself, and it is this relationship between 'signs' and things, or absolute idealities, which reveals the
temporality of signification in the deferral of presence. In resisting Derrida's
reading, one would say that Saussurean signification does not pertain to a
relation between signs and things, nor does Saussurean linguistic identity
depend upon repetition-as-the-same, nor upon a phenomenological relationship with idealities. In short, there is no deferral and no delay, simply because
Saussurean semiology is not a referential semiotic.

The second point is that Derrida's intervention of temporality misses its
mark in describing Saussurean theory as 'ahistoric'. Derrida's engagement
with Saussure specifically overlooks his radical engagement with time by
insisting upon a classical and Aristotelian model. But as Harris states, on
the contrary, Saussurean synchronic linguistics 'rejects a conflation of data
pertaining to different historical states. But it is at the same time "radically
historical" in that it proposes an analysis based solely on data which are historically coherent in the sense of belonging to a single system' (Harris 1987:
10). Similarly, Culler argues that:

> It has been suggested that in distinguishing rigorously between these
> two perspectives and in granting priority to the synchronic study of
> language, Saussure was ignoring, or at least setting aside, the fact that
> a language is fundamentally historical and contingent, an entity in
> constant evolution. But on the contrary, it was precisely because he
> recognized, more profoundly than his critics, the radical historicity of

language that he asserted the importance of distinguishing between facts about the linguistic system and facts about linguistic evolution, even in cases where the two kinds of facts seem extraordinarily intertwined. (Culler 1986: 35)

Harris goes as far as to suggest that the *Course* 'gives rise to the impression that this is a text written by someone with a nagging obsession about time, and specifically about the relationship between temporality and systematicity' (Harris 1987: 199–200). Derrida's critique of Saussurean structuralism *begins* from the point that Saussure either fails to recognise, or represses, the origin and constitution of differences. Such is the result of Derrida's decision to not address, or even acknowledge, the *Course*'s comprehensive argumentation in relation to temporality and systematicity.

Notes

1. See the *Cours*: 15, 23, 45–6, 49–54, 59–61, 64, 77–9, 102, 109–10, 119–23, 127, 129–33, 135–8, 163, 167, 184, 193–262, 270–5, 282–9, 291–303, 308–10, 316–17.
2. Such a qualification would also, surely, answer Weber's criticism of the chess analogy as not taking into account *whose move it is next* (Weber 1976: 931ff).
3. Such a distinction could also be made along the lines that Derrida observes of Husserl: 'First (Erste) nearly always designates in Husserl either an undetermined primacy, or most often, a *de facto* chronological priority in constituted cosmic time, i.e., an original factuality. Proto-, Arch-, and Ur- refer to phenomenological primordiality, i.e., to that sense of ground, of the *de jure* after the reduction of all factuality' (*Intro*: 37).

8 The Horizon of Language

Let us start again, one final time, from the conclusions and questions of the previous chapters. First, in examining how Derrida and Saussure each approach the question of linguistic identity, it was discovered that the role allocated to the language user is critical. We understand that, for Saussure, linguistic identity is more a matter of linguistic *identification*, and is solely in the hands (or brains) of the language user. And when we say that meaning is determined by language users, we might also say that meaning resides within consciousness. However, it is precisely this privilege given to language users, and to consciousness, that Derrida's discourse would wish to question. The critique that has been deferred – to this point – is that Saussurean language theory fails to question the origin and constitution of 'consciousness'. Hence, the apparent unity of consciousness is only a metaphysical presupposition which depends upon a more originary potentiality.

Second, in responding to Derrida's critique of the temporality of the sign, it was discovered that – while certainly acknowledging the constant evolution of languages, and the derivation of the current state of the language from a previous state – Saussure continues to assert the radical synchrony of the language system. To do so is also, as we have seen, to radically problematise the determination of diachronic identity and the value of historical explanation in language. What is important for this final chapter is understanding that to privilege the point of view of language users is, at the same time, to privilege synchrony as: 'the only relevant psychological reality for current speakers of the language' (Harris 2001: 197). The Saussurean theory of language would have, then, two corresponding, mutually determining, and logically coherent principles: the point of view of language users, and synchronic structure. But again, from where have these principles arrived? Have they fallen from the sky, or are they divine, inscribed in a *topos noētos*? What, in short, has produced or created them, or what has allowed them to appear as present entities?

To address this final critique is to begin again from the moment that Derrida summarises the relationship between *différance* and difference:

> With its *a*, differance more properly refers to what in classical language
> would be called the origin or production of differences and the differ-
> ences between differences, the *play* of differences. (Diff (A): 130)

And that:

> In a conceptuality adhering to classical strictures '*différance*' would be
> said to designate a constitutive, productive, and originary causality, the
> process of scission and division which would produce or constitute dif-
> ferent things or differences. (Diff: 8–9)

The question of this final chapter can then be asked: if subject and object,
synchrony and diachrony, writing and speech, are utilised by Saussure as
already present entities, then what is it that created or produced or enabled
them? If Saussurean semiology as a theory relies on the prior existence of
these entities, then, Derrida would claim, this prior existence requires an
explanation.

The work of *différance* upon Western metaphysics is, of course, irreducibly
complex and variegated. As such, the ambition of this chapter is, again, absolutely *not* to overturn Derrida's motif and work of *différance* in its entirety.
The work of this chapter is to bring the Derridean intervention of strategic
primordiality to bear against the Saussurean assertion of radical systematicity. As we shall see, to make such distinct philosophies engage, or even to
understand what makes them different, it will be necessary to place Derrida's
reading of Saussure within the problematics of systematicity, axiomatics, and
the horizon of language.

Consciousness and the present

Derrida situates *différance* as being the non-simple origin of taxonomic and
ahistoric semiological difference: the cause and effect, the differing and deferring, of differences. It is *différance*, which is neither a word nor a concept,
which allows the metaphysical and linguistic conditions of Saussurean theory
to appear and to function. In relation to the question of *structure*, the two
mutually determining principles of Saussurean theory come sharply into
view: the point of view of the language user, and synchrony. And so, in relation to the structural discourse and its assumptions, what Derrida would
specifically want to question is the origin and constitution of *consciousness*
and the *present*.

To begin with the question of the consciousness, Derrida asks: 'Differences,
thus, are "produced" – deferred – by *différance*. But *what* defers or *who*
defers?' (Diff: 14):

If we answered these questions before examining them as questions, before turning them back on themselves, and before suspecting their very form, including what seems most natural and necessary about them, we would immediately fall back into what we have just disengaged ourselves from. In effect, if we accepted the form of the question, in its meaning and its syntax ('what is?' 'who is?' 'who is it that?'), we would have to conclude that *différance* has been derived, has happened, is to be mastered and governed on the basis of the point of a present being, which itself could be some thing, a form, a state, a power in the world to which all kinds of names might be given, a *what*, or a present being as a *subject*, a *who*. And in this last case, notably, one would conclude implicitly that this present being, for example a being present to itself, as consciousness, eventually would come to defer or to differ . . . (Diff: 14–15)

If questions about the possibly transcendental status of *différance* are held for the moment, then Derrida's logic is irrefutable: if *différance* is the very question of the origins of consciousness, then *différance* cannot be thought of on the basis of a linguistically prior and stable consciousness. What seems most natural about the question 'who differs?' is only the naturalisation of the metaphysical presupposition of a conscious entity, prior to linguistic differences, prior to the play of differences. In such a classical scheme, differences are thought on the basis of presence, and in particular, on the basis of the self-presence of consciousness.

   Such a scheme would, then, conform to Derrida's engagement with classical metaphysics *in general*. But it is once again in his textual engagement with the *Course* that Derrida's argument appears least careful and precise. He writes:

Now if we refer, once again, to semiological difference, of what does Saussure, in particular, remind us? That 'language (which only consists of differences) is not a function of the speaking subject'. This implies that the subject (in its identity with itself, or eventually in its consciousness of its identity with itself, its self-consciousness) is inscribed in language, is a 'function' of language, becomes a *speaking* subject only by making its speech conform . . . to the system of the rules of language as a system of differences. (Diff: 15)

This citation and argument also appear in 'Semiology and Grammatology':

It confirms that the subject, and first of all the conscious and speaking subject, depends upon the system of differences and the movement of *différance*, that the subject is not present, nor above all present to itself before *différance*, that the subject is constituted only in being divided

from itself, in becoming space, in temporizing, in deferral; and it confirms that, as Saussure said, 'language (which consists only of differences) is not a function of the speaking subject'. (S&G: 29)

Derrida does not provide a reference for this citation from the *Course*,
either in 'Différance' or in 'Semiology and Grammatology'. However, the
original phrase '*la langue n'est pas une fonction du sujet parlant*' is taken
from Saussure's discussion of the roles of the individual and the community
in determining the difference between *la langue* and *la parole*. This passage
appears in the Harris translation as:

> The language itself is not a function of the speaker. It is the product
> passively registered by the individual . . . Speech, on the contrary, is an
> individual act of the will and the intelligence . . . (*Course*: 14/30–1)

This opposition of language to speech is then rephrased as:

> The study of language thus comprises two parts. The essential part
> takes for its object the language itself, which is social in its essence and
> independent of the individual. This is a purely psychological study.
> The subsidiary part takes as its object of study the individual part of
> language, which means speech, including phonation. This is a psycho-
> physical study. (*Course*: 19/37)

That is, *la langue* is not a function of the speaking subject because it is a function of the *masse parlante*, which the speaking subject passively adopts. There
is never any doubt, however, that for Saussure, *la langue* is an entity which
resides solely in the brains of speaking subjects: 'A language, as a collective
phenomenon, takes the form of a totality of imprints in everyone's brain . . .
Thus it is something which is in each individual, but is none the less common
to all' (*Course*: 19/38).
    The implication that Derrida draws from this sentence is, however, some-
what different. What Derrida wants to do with this citation is, in effect,
to stage the debate over which has *priority*: consciousness, or the play of
differences. The question that Derrida poses is whether or not Saussurean
consciousness exists as a stable entity prior to the play of differences in language. The conclusion that Derrida draws from this citation – truncated,
interjected, and piteously out of context – is that Saussure would want to
claim that linguistic differences *precede* subjective consciousness, and hence
that consciousness is not self-present, because 'language is not a function of
the speaking subject'. Derrida makes the point on behalf of Saussure, here:

> the subject becomes a *speaking* subject only in its commerce with the
> system of linguistic differences; or yet, the subject becomes a *signifying*

... subject only by inscribing itself in the system of differences. Certainly in this sense the speaking or signifying subject could not be present to itself, as speaking or signifying, without the play of linguistic or semiological *différance*. (Diff: 16)

According to this argument, consciousness is not a present and stable entity prior to language because the subject only becomes a signifying subject by inscribing itself within, or *subjecting* itself to, the play of differences. However, Derrida immediately moves to undermine this argument:

> But can one not conceive of a presence, and of a presence to itself of the subject before speech and signs, a presence to itself of the subject in a silent and intuitive consciousness?
>   Such a question therefore supposes that, prior to the sign and outside it, excluding any trace and any *différance*, something like consciousness is possible. And that consciousness, before distributing its signs in space and in the world, can gather itself into its presence. But what is consciousness? What does 'consciousness' mean? Most often, in the very form of meaning, in all its modifications, consciousness offers itself to thought only as self-presence, as the perception of self in presence. (Diff: 16)

Opposing the argument that consciousness is subject to the play of differences, Derrida 'conceives' of a specific meaning of consciousness as the already-formed receptacle of signs and meanings, as self-presence itself. Consciousness, then, would be that very thing which must precede differences, as the space into which differences are distributed.

This characterisation of 'consciousness' is not, of course, to be found in the *Course*, and Derrida offers no examples of this usage, except to note that: 'the category of the subject cannot be, and never has been, thought without the reference to presence as *hupokeimenon* or as *ousia*, etc., so the subject as consciousness has never manifested itself except as self-presence' (Diff: 16). Such a definition and characterisation of 'consciousness' would be implicit in Derrida's entire engagement with the metaphysics of presence, and is not something I would wish to disagree with, *in general*. But two points must be made before continuing:

1. That the argument that Derrida constructs on behalf of Saussure – that the play of differences precedes subjectivity – is not Saussure's. And nor is it even possibly Saussurean: a conclusion which I hope to draw out in the latter part of this chapter.
2. That the form and construction of the debate that Derrida stages is *revealing*. What it reveals is that, for Derrida, the relationship between the play of differences and consciousness must be phrased as a choice: that

one, and *only* one, must have priority, or must come *first*. In regard to Saussure, the *only* way to escape the implications of a transcendental and logocentric consciousness is to rethink consciousness as an entity derived from the primordial play of difference. Already we are starting to see how systematicity and axiomatics will be decisive here.

Derrida's objection to the primordiality of consciousness is now clear, and is best summarised in his critique of Husserl, in which: 'the certitude of inner existence, Husserl thinks, has no need to be signified. It is immediately present to itself. It is living consciousness' (*S&P*: 43). And against which, Derrida argues:

> this determination of 'absolute subjectivity' would also have to be crossed out as soon as we conceive the present on the basis of difference, and not the reverse. The concept of *subjectivity* belongs *a priori and in general* to the order of the *constituted*. (*S&P*: 84n)

In short, consciousness is not a present entity, simply available for theorisation, as metaphysics would like to think.

Second, and following the logic of classical metaphysics, the self-presence of consciousness is communicated to self-presence in time, to the present:

> The privilege granted to consciousness therefore signifies the privilege granted to the present ... Thus one comes to posit presence – and specifically consciousness, the being beside itself of consciousness – no longer as the absolutely central form of Being but as a 'determination' and as an 'effect'. (Diff: 16)

According to the logic of classical metaphysics, the self-presence of the present is determined by the self-presence of consciousness, by 'the category of the subject'. Derrida therefore posits consciousness and the present as not only inextricably related entities, but inextricably related throughout their entire histories.[1] As such, the present is as vulnerable as consciousness to Derrida's critique of self-presence.

Derrida describes the work of *différance* upon temporality as that: 'which can no longer be conceived within the horizon of the present' (Diff: 10), and which liberates 'the transcendental horizon of the question of Being ... from its traditional, metaphysical domination by the present and the now' (Diff: 10). Derrida writes of the moment of timelessness, the moment of structure, in relation to Husserl:

> If the punctuality of the instant is a myth, a spatial or mechanical metaphor, an inherited metaphysical concept, or all that at once, and if the present of self-presence is not *simple*, if it is constituted in a primordial

and irreducible synthesis, then the whole of Husserl's argumentation is threatened in its very principle. (*S&P*: 61)

And you would say: so would Saussure's argumentation be threatened, as even more do his distinctions – between *la langue* and *la parole*, synchrony and diachrony, and so on – rely on the difference between continuity and systematicity, or between the 'axis of succession' and the 'axis of simultaneity' (*Course*: 80/115). In opposition to Saussure, and to 'the history of the Occident', Derrida reveals that it is *différance* which constitutes the instant, which constitutes and distinguishes between the intervals of time and space:

> An interval must separate the present from what it is not in order for the present to be itself, but this interval that constitutes it as present must, by the same token, divide the present in and of itself, thereby also dividing, along with the present, everything that is thought on the basis of the present, that is, in our metaphysical language, every being, and singularly substance or the subject. In constituting itself, in dividing itself dynamically, this interval might be called *spacing*, the becoming-space of time or the becoming-time of space (*temporization*). And it is this constitution of the present, as an 'originary' and irreducibly nonsimple (and therefore, *stricto sensu* nonoriginary) synthesis of marks, or traces of retentions and protensions . . . that I propose to call archi-writing, archi-trace, or *différance*. (Diff: 13)

In other words, there is a difference between the present and what it is not, and so the production of differences must precede the category of the present. It will be necessary, shortly, to propose a semiological solution to the problem of (what Derrida might call) the non-simple *derivation* of 'the present'. But for the moment, it is enough to note that the metaphysical presupposition, or myth, or metaphor, of the timelessness of the present, is derived from the category of the subject; it is 'the being beside itself of consciousness'. As such, the horizon of the present, as much as the horizon of consciousness, must be understood as derived, or produced, and which belongs '*a priori and in general* to the order of the *constituted*'.

The transcendental status of *différance*

The question that we have reached concerns the derivation of consciousness and the present, and the implications for a theory of language which seems to rely upon the prior constitution of such entities. Derrida's intervention is to bring the work of *différance* to bear against the simple presence of Saussure's presuppositions. But what kind of entity is this *différance* which allows differences to appear; which is not simply active, or productive of differences, in the sense of causing differences, nor passive, in the sense of being the effects of differentiation? It is useful, before calling upon the *Course* to answer Derrida's critique, to reflect upon the special status of *différance*, which makes itself felt between presence and absence, between subject and object, and between the synchronic and diachronic. To offer just a sample, we would note that *différance* is prior to, or constitutive of, the opposition of subject to object:

> Nothing – no present and in-different being – thus precedes *différance* and spacing. There is no subject who is agent, author, and master of *différance*, who eventually and empirically would be overtaken by *différance*. Subjectivity – like objectivity – is an effect of *différance*, an effect inscribed in a system of *différance*. (S&G: 28)

Prior to passivity and activity:

> Differance is not simply active (any more than it is a subjective accomplishment); it rather indicates the middle voice, it precedes and sets up the opposition between passivity and activity. (Diff (A): 130)

Prior to truth:

> it inaugurates the destruction, not the demolition but the de-sedimentation, the de-construction, of all the significations that have their source in that of the logos. Particularly the signification of *truth*. (*OG*: 10)

And essence:

> for if the sign in some way preceded what we call truth or essence, there would be no sense in speaking about the truth or essence of the sign. (*S&P*: 24)

Prior to the opposition between presence and absence:

> The gram as *différance*, then, is a structure and a movement no longer conceivable on the basis of the opposition presence/absence. (S&G: 27)

Prior to opposition in general:

> the movement of *différance*, as that which produces different things, that which differentiates, is the common root of all the oppositional concepts that mark our language, such as, to take only a few examples, sensible/intelligible, intuition/signification, nature/culture, etc. (Imp: 9)

And again, prior to presence, prior to science, and hence to every *thing* in general:

> This arche-writing, although its concept is *invoked* by the themes of 'the arbitrariness of the sign' and of difference, cannot and can never be recognized as the *object of a science*. It is that very thing which cannot let itself be reduced to the form of presence. (*OG*: 57)

And so, how to engage Saussurean thought with a potentiality that exceeds every opposition of Saussure's discourse? This is not a simple task. But there is, at least, one point in the characterisation of *différance* where Saussurean semiology is qualified to make a response. This is at the point where Derrida states that: 'as we shall see, *différance* is literally neither a word nor a concept' (Diff: 3). Indeed, as we shall see, *différance* 'is' not at all. However, examining the procedure of this most linguistic of claims – that *différance* is neither a word nor a concept – will bring us closest to understanding the relationship between *différance* and difference, and between Derrida's presuppositions and Saussure's.

Derrida's justification for the particularity of *différance* resumes the argument in which the difference between the *e* and the *a* of *différance* is inaudible. That is to say:

> the play of difference, which, as Saussure reminded us, is the condition for the possibility and functioning of every sign, is in itself a silent play. Inaudible is the difference between two phonemes which alone permits them to be and to operate as such. The inaudible opens up the apprehension of two present phonemes such as they present themselves . . . The difference which establishes phonemes and lets them be heard remains in and of itself inaudible, in every sense of the word. (Diff: 5)

And so, according to this logic, the differences between phonemes are inaudible. But furthermore:

> It will be objected, for the same reasons, that graphic difference itself vanishes into the night, can never be sensed as a full term, but rather extends an invisible relationship, the mark of an inapparent relationship between two spectacles. Doubtless. But, from this point of view, that the difference marked in the 'differ()nce' between the *e* and the *a* eludes both vision and hearing perhaps happily suggests that here we must be permitted to refer to an order which no longer belongs to sensibility. (Diff: 5)

My objection to the inaudibility of differences between phonemes has already been made.[2] The same objection would apply to Derrida's notion of the invisibility of differences between graphemes. I believe that Saussurean theory suggests – or rather, explicitly states on a number of occasions – that it is *precisely* differences which are heard and seen. Derrida's rhetoric here is important, for it allows him to place *différance* beyond the order of the sensible and intelligible with some legitimacy. My objection to this manoeuvre stands, but even if we were to accept Derrida's argument, then we could only conclude that the difference between *any* phonemes or graphemes – not just between the *e* and *a* of *différ( )nce* – must be inaudible or invisible. And *différance* would then lose the particularity that Derrida requires of it in the following pages, in claiming that *différance* is 'neither a concept nor a word *among others*' (Diff: 11, my italics).

But we will continue to attempt to understand the special status of *différance*. Derrida continues:

> What am I to do in order to speak of the *a* of *différance*? It goes without saying that it cannot be *exposed*. One can expose only that which at a certain moment can become *present*, manifest, that which can be shown, presented as something present, a being-present in its truth, in the truth of a present or the presence of the present. Now if *différance* ~~is~~ (and I also cross out the '~~is~~') what makes possible the presentation of the being-present, it is never presented as such. It is never offered to the present. Or to anyone. Reserving itself, not exposing itself, in regular fashion it exceeds the order of truth at a certain precise point, but without dissimulating itself as something, as a mysterious being. (Diff: 5–6)

Once again, Derrida moves perhaps too swiftly through a logical or rhetorical progression. In the previous passage, it was 'the difference between the *e* and *a*' of '*différ( )nce*' that escaped the order of the sensible and the intelligible. Here, it is simply 'the *a* of *différance*' which cannot be exposed, shown, presented as something present, which 'goes without saying'. For the same reason, no doubt, *différance* is never offered to the present, and in turn, exceeds the order of truth. Without pausing too long on any particular statement, we can continue again to explore the special status of *différance*. For as Derrida will say next, *différance* 'is' not:

> Already we have had to delineate *that différance is not*, does not exist, is not a present-being in any form; and we will be led to delineate also everything *that* it *is not*, that is, *everything*; and consequently that it has neither existence nor essence. It derives from no category of being, whether present or absent. (Diff: 6)

Différance is neither word nor concept. It cannot be revealed at all. It exceeds the order of truth, but is not a mysterious being. As if anticipating the objection that might be forming, Derrida states that *différance* is not theological:

> And yet those aspects of *différance* which are thereby delineated are not theological, not even in the order of the most negative of negative theologies . . . *Différance* is not only irreducible to any ontological or theological – ontotheological – reappropriation, but as the very opening of the space into which ontotheology – philosophy – produces its system and its history, it includes ontotheology, inscribing it and exceeding it without return. (Diff: 6)

In a process that has become familiar, *différance* cannot be theological, for the reason that it is *prior* to theology; it gives rise to the difference between theology and what theology is not. Similarly, in *Of Grammatology*, Derrida writes that: 'the trace must be thought before the entity', but that: 'This formulation is not theological, as one might believe somewhat hastily. The "theological" is a determined moment in the total movement of the trace' (*OG*: 47). The trace, or *différance*, is formulated by Derrida to stand in the place of the transcendental origin, so that subject, sign, time, and theology, are all derived from *différance*, and only *différance* escapes derivation.

A difficult question needs to be asked at this point; the last within the horizon of semiological sense. Does Derrida mean that '*différance*' in its entirety – as letters on a page, which are joined to some conceptualisation in the mind of the reader, that is, what Saussure would call the *sign* of *différance* – is neither a word nor a concept, or only that what is evoked by the *word différance* is the *concept* of being neither a word nor a concept? Derrida makes some challenging comments:

> For us, *différance* remains a metaphysical name, and all the names that it receives in our language are still, as names, metaphysical . . . 'Older' than Being itself, such a *différance* has no name in our language. But we 'already know' that if it is unnameable, it is not provisionally so, not because our language has not yet found or received this *name*, or because we would have to seek it in another language, outside the finite system of our own. It is rather because there is no *name* for it at all, not even the name of essence or of Being, not even that of '*différance*', which is not a name, which is not a pure nominal unity, and unceasingly dislocates itself in a chain of differing and deferring substitutions. (Diff: 26)

Différance is 'unnameable', hence it is an object or concept, not a name. But, 'remains a metaphysical name', hence it is a name.[3] And it is 'unnameable', but at the same time, *not* 'ineffable', and not theological, because it precedes God: 'This unnameable is not an ineffable Being which no name could approach: God, for example' (Diff: 26). Is *différance* ineffable, or that which gives rise to the difference between the nameable and unnameable, or the horizon of language?

Put simply, semiology is ill-equipped to critique this formulation. Any citation from the *Course* at this point would immediately be made ineffective by the terms of Derrida's engagement. And it is extremely difficult to refute Derrida's formulation of *différance*, even when limited to its relationship with semiological difference, when Derrida's discourse nullifies semiology's capacity to respond. There are two almost irreconcilable tasks at hand here: to allow *différance* its full force, including that which exceeds semiology; and to allow the semiological discourse at least the possibility of resistance, to give the text of the *Course pertinence*. In order to continue, then, we are faced with the necessity of understanding and characterising Derrida's general method, the general form and presuppositions of his intervention in semiology, and to understand its logic and procedures.

The logic of antecedence in Derrida's engagement with Saussure

Let us start with this summary of the work of *différance*, from 'Semiology and Grammatology':

> At the point at which the concept of *différance*, and the chain attached to it, intervenes, all the conceptual oppositions of metaphysics (signifier/ signified; sensible/intelligible; writing/speech; passivity/activity; etc.) . . . become nonpertinent. They all amount, at one moment or another, to a subordination of the movement of *différance* in favor of the presence of a value or a meaning supposedly antecedent to *différance*, more original than it, exceeding and governing it in the last analysis. This is still the presence of what we called above the 'transcendental signified'. (S&G: 29)

Just as with the debate that he stages between the priority of consciousness and the play of differences, Derrida phrases the work of *différance* as the question of *antecedence*. The only way to escape the transcendental signified is to rethink all the conceptual oppositions of metaphysics on the basis of an antecedent *différance*, and not the other way around. Or, as Derrida phrases it here:

> Play is always play of absence and presence, but if it is to be thought radically, play must be conceived of before the alternative of presence and absence. Being must be conceived as presence or absence on the basis of the possibility of play and not the other way around. (SS&P: 292)

Such a formulation of antecedence is the logical consequence of the form of the question that Derrida poses to metaphysics: from where have your pre-suppositions fallen? But perhaps what seems most natural about this question is also what might make Saussurean structuralism so original and transform-ing. For what Saussure's radical systematicity *reveals* is the dependence of Derridean thought upon a certain model of causality, and furthermore, the possibility of freedom from that model.

The final task of this book is, then, to argue that Derrida takes a *deter-mined position* on the nature of causality and systematicity throughout his engagement with Saussurean semiology. Derrida's *position* – which he does not present as a position in general – is that the constitution of a system must precede the system. Or, that the terminology and methods and pre-sumptions of the semiological system have not fallen from the sky, and therefore demand an explanation of their prior appearance. As we have seen, Derrida's construction of *différance* – as the non-simple and non-present origin of differences, as that very potentiality which is not derived – exceeds and invalidates semiology's capacity to respond. However, the questions of systematicity and axiomatics are very much within the purview of Saussure's work, and are questions for which the *Course* provides novel answers.

Derrida's *position* on systematicity – as the question of the constitution of linguistic differences, or the question of what is antecedent to the axioms of linguistic discourse – is made most explicit in his earliest work, in *Edmund Husserl's Origin of Geometry: An Introduction*. In *Speech and Phenomena*, Derrida's work begins from a critique of Husserl's 'essential distinctions', and asks, essentially, from where have they fallen? In the *Introduction*, however, Derrida examines Husserl's relationship with systematicity *in general*. The *Origin of Geometry* is concerned with the question of the unity of *the* geometrical science, or as Derrida phrases it: 'how, *historically*, have all geometries been, or will they be, geometries?' (*Intro*: 52). In response, Derrida suggests that Husserl's attempt to define geometry as the science of exhaus-tive deductivity was compromised 'when Gödel discovered the rich possibil-ity of *"undecidable"* propositions in 1931' (*Intro*: 53). Let us allow Derrida to phrase the problematic:

> if the primordial act of grounding that Husserl wishes to elicit here was the institution of an axiomatic and deductive field or even the institu-tion of axiomatics and the ideal of deductivity in general . . . then the Husserlian project would be seriously threatened by the evolution of axiomatization toward a total formalization within which one necessar-ily comes up against the limits stated by Gödel's theorem (and related theorems). (*Intro*: 54)

In other words, if Husserl were attempting only to establish the appropriate axioms for geometrical investigation, or of phenomenological investigation in general, then Gödel's critique of axioms would work to diminish such an achievement as merely local and finite, rather than universal and infinite. 'But that is not so!' as Derrida remarks here (*Intro*: 54). Husserl's project goes beyond or prior to the grounding of axioms, where axioms are only a '*secondary* grounding':

> There is no doubt, in any case, that the kinds of primordial evidence he investigates here are for him prior to those of axioms and serve as their ground . . . Axiomatics in general (from which alone every ideal of exhaustive and exact deductibility can take its sense, from which alone every problem of decidability can then spring) already supposes, therefore, a sedimentation of sense: i.e., axiomatics supposes a primordial evidence, a radical ground which is already past. (*Intro*: 54–5)

In other words, the very nature of deductability or decidability presupposes a ground of primordial evidence. It is towards such primordial evidence that Husserl attempts to return.

Gödel's incompleteness theorem appears again in ' "Genesis and Structure" and Phenomenology', where Derrida notes again that Husserl's project precedes the axiomatic ground of geometry or mathematics:

> From the start, Husserl refuses, and will always refuse, to accept the intelligibility and normativity of this universal structure as manna fallen from a 'heavenly place' (*topos ouranios*), or as an eternal truth created by an infinite reason. To seek out the subjective origin of arithmetical objects and values, here, is to turn back toward perception, toward perceptual ensembles, and toward the pluralities and totalities found in perception in a premathematical organization. (GS&P: 157)

That is, mathematical axioms have not fallen from the sky, and so demand an explanation of their constitution. Against this, however, Derrida warns:

> Here, we cannot enter into the intramathematical difficulties always raised by this Husserlian conception of mathematical 'definitude', especially when confronted by certain later developments of axiomatics and by Gödel's discoveries. (GS&P: 162)

Derrida's appropriation of Gödel is interesting, not least because of its recourse to evidence from mathematical axiomatics. The editor of Kurt Gödel's *Collected Papers* recently wrote that:

> Like Heisenberg's uncertainty principle, Gödel's incompleteness theorem has captured the public's imagination, supposedly demonstrating that there are absolute limits to what can be known. More spe-

cifically, it is thought to tell us that there are mathematical truths which can never be proved. These are among the misconceptions that proliferate around Gödel's theorem and its consequences. (Feferman 2006: 30)

Gödel's theorem, in broadly logical terms, posits that there can exist statements of finite truth which are unprovable within certain systems of axioms. Or, more technically: 'if S is any consistent formal system which contains number theory, and A is a statement that asserts its own unprovability in S, then A is indeed not provable in S' (Feferman 2006: 31), therefore the formal system is incomplete. The implications for philosophy arising from Gödel's incompleteness theorem are many and varied. Derrida's interest in Gödel's theorem, and in axiomatics in general, arises from the suggestion that the *explanation* of a system must *precede* the system. That is, wherever axioms are involved, then something prior to those axioms must have produced them, constituted them, allowed them to appear. At its limit, Derrida's entire engagement with Saussure, and perhaps even with Western metaphysics, could be phrased in terms of Gödel's theorem:

> If, for example, mathematics is to be founded on systems of axioms, on what basis are those systems to be chosen? The incompleteness theorems tell us that whatever system is accepted, one will need further axioms to arrive at previously unprovable truths. But which axioms, and why? (Feferman 2006: 31)

In relation to linguistics, Derrida phrases the consequences of this question as:

> It is because arche-writing, movement of differance, irreducible arche-synthesis, opening in one and the same possibility, temporalization as well as relationship with the other and language, cannot, as the condition of all linguistic systems, form a part of the linguistic system itself and be situated as an object in its field. (*OG*: 60)

Derrida's *position* is that the conditions of a linguistic system cannot be situated as objects within that linguistic field; the conditions of a linguistic system must precede (de facto and de jure) its appearance and functioning. And this, finally, is the proposition that we can take to Saussurean linguistics.

The radical systematicity of Saussurean linguistics

We already understand the role of priority in the work of *différance*. We know that the presuppositions of Saussurean semiology only appear on the scene of presence as effects of a more primordial potentiality. We know, for example, that *différance*: 'does not depend on any sensible plenitude, audible or visible, phonic or graphic. It is, on the contrary, the condition of such a plenitude' (*OG*: 62). *Différance* is, therefore, prior to the signifier; but also prior to the signified, in that *différance*: 'is thus no longer simply a concept, but rather the possibility of conceptuality, of a conceptual process and system in general' (Diff: 11). *Différance* is, then, neither a word nor concept among others, but rather, the *condition* and *possibility* of their appearance. What is important here is that Derrida would also grant this priority and particularity to semiological difference. After citing this passage from the *Course* –

> Everything we have said so far comes down to this. *In the language itself, there are only differences.* Even more important than that is the fact that, although in general a difference presupposes positive terms between which the difference holds, in a language there are only differences, *and no positive terms.* (*Course*: 118/166)

– Derrida responds that: 'The difference of which Saussure speaks is itself, therefore, neither a concept nor a word among others (Diff: 11). For Derrida, the organising principle of the semiological system is difference. As such, it is thus neither a word nor a concept among others, but the central and reassuring, transcendental signified of any semiological system. Semiological difference must therefore *precede* the system of meaning to which it gives birth. And it is this de jure sense of semiological difference which Derrida brings to bear against Husserl's essential distinctions, and which he names 'primordial' difference (*S&P*: 46). It is this, and *only* this, that Derrida wants to take from Saussure and the *Course*, as the loosening of metaphysics: the 'restoration' of the primordiality of the sign, and of the non-derivative character of difference. In Derrida's hands, primordial difference must be used against metaphysics – against Husserl's essential distinctions, for example – before 'one inevitably encounters "the logocentric and ethnocentric limits" of such a model. At this point, perhaps, the concept is to be abandoned' (S&G: 17). What Derrida does with semiological difference, and with the concept of the sign, is to delay, as long as possible, its inevitable fall back into the language and logic of metaphysics. As Derrida phrases it here:

> The formal essence of the signified is *presence*, and the privilege of its proximity to the logos as *phonè* is the privilege of presence. This is the inevitable response as soon as one asks: 'what is the sign?' . . . One cannot get around that response, except by challenging the very form of the question and beginning to think that the sign ix that ill named thing, the only one, that escapes the instituting question of philosophy: 'what is . . .?' (*OG*: 17–18)

The only way of escaping metaphysics is to think of the sign as prior to the institution of philosophy, prior to the question of Being, prior to all the oppositions of metaphysics. In pursuing this, difference becomes *différance*. And in upholding the principle and possibilities of primordial difference, in restoring the non-derivative character of signs, Derrida believes that: 'The concept of *différance* even develops the most legitimate principled exigencies of "structuralism"' (S&G: 28).

But what if it didn't? What if *différance* and primordiality did not develop, but worked against, the most legitimate principled exigencies of structuralism? What if the difference of which Saussure speaks was not primordial, or originary, but *was* just a word or concept like any other? What if 'difference', 'consciousness', the 'present', 'value', and all the other elements of Saussurean theory were *caught up* in the system of language, as much as 'tree' or 'horse'? What if – to phrase the question most precisely – the conditions of a linguistic system *did not* precede, *were not* logically antecedent, but *were* situated as objects within that linguistic field?

The *Course*, unfortunately, does not provide an unequivocal answer to this question. Indeed, Saussure's point of view here, on a question he was never faced with, must ultimately remain unclear. The best evidence for this proposal is that nothing appears in the *Course* to contradict it. That is, there is nothing in the *Course* to suggest that the particular words that Saussure uses to construct his theory of language should be exempt from the social-synchronic play of differences in a language system. And if they are not exempt, then the terms of Saussurean language theory are just as subject to the innovation of individuals and the ratification of the language community as any others. Harris makes this point about the Saussurean method in the definition of *la langue*:

> the reader is never told exactly what *la langue* is at any point in the *Cours*: there is no definitive or final formulation. All we find are successive reformulations which bring out different contrasts between *la langue* and everything which *la langue* is not. The procedure is an object-lesson in Saussurean methodology, and in this sense the *Cours* itself is the great masterpiece of Saussurean linguistics. (Harris 1987: 15)

There is no suggestion here of an ideal, infinite, or transcendental sense of *la langue*. There is never any indication in the *Course* that the elements, units, or words of his theory of language should be immune to the social-synchronic play of language. In which case, language must be described using language, and no *mastery* is ever possible, in the sense of exceeding or preceding language, or of containing the social and political forces of linguistic evolution. No individual owns or controls or *finalises* the language, including Saussure, and the language is not, and has never been, fixed for all people for all time. When Derrida writes: 'Play is always play of absence and presence, but if it is to be thought radically, play must be conceived of before the alternative of presence and absence' (SS&P: 292), we ought to ask when and where the alternative of presence and absence takes place. In French, in 1966? Or everywhere and always? Does Derrida allow that there will be a time *after* the alternative of 'presence' and 'absence'?

The proposition at stake is whether or not the conditions of a linguistic system – the possibility and production of 'consciousness', the 'present', and of 'difference' – can be situated as objects within that linguistic field. To imagine the 'what if' of this proposal is at the same time to allow all the previous possibilities of the resistance to Derrida's reading of Saussure to have force. It is necessary to also imagine that there is no such entity as 'the concept of the sign'. Not only does empirical evidence point to substantial changes in both 'the' word and 'the' concept of 'sign', but Saussure's observations on diachronic identity demonstrate why neither element can be held constant while we investigate the other. We could then believe that the Saussurean sign does not maintain the medieval formula of *aliquid stat pro aliquo*. And if the sign does not *stand for* something else, something not present, then the sign would not be a detour, a secondary and provisional placeholder, until such time as language is reunited with presence. It would mean that Saussurean semiology could be distinguished from Peircean semiotics, and from a logical dependence upon a referent, and a relationship with verifiability, and hence with the truth. It would then be possible to believe that the Saussurean sign is not riven by temporality, in the movement from signs to things. Above all, we would believe that linguistic identity is more a matter of identification, and that, as the *Course* states: 'Values have no other rationale than usage and general agreement' (112/157).

The question of whether or not the conditions of a linguistic system can be situated as objects within that linguistic field is necessarily also a question of horizons. This question, like the question of axiomatics, arises most distinctly in the *Introduction*. Derrida says this about the horizon of phenomenology:

> It is not by chance that there is no phenomenology of the Idea. The latter cannot be given in person, nor determined in an evidence, for it is only the possibility of evidence and the openness of 'seeing' itself; it is only *determinability* as the horizon for every intuition in general . . . If there is nothing to say about the Idea *itself*, it is because the Idea is that starting from which something in general can be said. Its own particular presence, then, cannot depend on a phenomenological type of evidence. (*Intro*: 138–9)

And so:

> Accordingly, *phenomenology* cannot be grounded as such in itself, nor can it *itself* indicate its own proper limits . . . That a phenomenological determination of the Idea itself may be radically impossible from then

on signifies perhaps that phenomenology cannot be reflected in a phenomenology of phenomenology . . . The *Endstiftung* of phenomenology
(phenomenology's ultimate critical legitimation: i.e., what its sense,
value, and right tell us about it), then, never directly measures up to a
phenomenology. (*Intro*: 140–1)

Phenomenology is unable to investigate the primordial ground of its own
axioms, and therefore does not measure up to a phenomenology. As such, the
constitution of phenomenology precedes or exceeds the horizon of phenomenology. Phenomenology cannot be grounded in itself, and therefore fails to
provide an explanation of its present appearance.

But can such a critical construction be applied to the *Course*: that semiology cannot be grounded in a system of signs, or that semiology fails to put
into question the constitution of its own axioms? Sturrock puts this very
question to structuralism:

A certain kind structuralism is here hoist with its own petard since the
'centre' which it claims to have located for structures no longer forms
part of them. From being an element among others caught within the
play of relations, it is elevated above the structure to a point of privilege
from where it is held to determine the play as a whole. (150)

In other words, whatever elements we organise our semiological model
around – be they 'difference', or 'consciousness', or 'presence' – must exist
outside of the system itself, outside of the play of relations, thus ruining
the notion of the sign at the moment it is established. Derrida anticipates
this question, or at least, the problems of such an intralinguistic closure. In
'Semiology and Grammatology', and again in 'Différance', Derrida cites this
passage from the *Course*:

Language is necessary for speech to be intelligible and to produce all
of its effects; but speech is necessary for language to be established; historically, the fact of speech always comes first. (*Course (B)*: 37)

In 'Semiology and Grammatology', Derrida responds that:

There is a circle here, for if one rigorously distinguishes language and
speech, code and message, schema and usage, etc., and if one wishes
to do justice to the two postulates thus enunciated, one does not know
where to begin, nor how something can begin in general, be it language
or speech. Therefore, one has to admit, before any dissociation of
language and speech, code and message, etc. (and everything that goes
along with such a dissociation), a systematic production of differences,
the *production* of a system of differences – a *différance* – within whose

effects one eventually, by abstraction and according to determined motivations, will be able to demarcate a linguistics of language and a linguistics of speech, etc. (S&G: 28)

And in 'Différance':

> Retaining at least the framework, if not the content, of this requirement formulated by Saussure, we will designate as *différance* the movement according to which language, or any code, any system of referral in general, is constituted 'historically' as a weave of differences. 'Is consti-tuted', 'is produced', 'is created', 'movement', 'historically', etc., neces-sarily being understood beyond the metaphysical language in which they are retained, along with their implications. We ought to demon-strate why concepts like *production*, constitution, and history remain in complicity with what is at stake here. But this would take me too far today – toward the theory of the representation of the 'circle' in which we appear to be enclosed. (Diff: 12)

To paraphrase: speech requires language to be established first, but language requires speech to be established first, therefore: 'one does not know where to begin'. Before any system of differences – whether between language and speech, synchrony and diachrony, or any of the terms of semiology – can be established, or accounted for, as *effects*, 'one must admit' the operation of a 'systematic production of differences', otherwise we are caught in a 'circle'. Against such a circularity, Derrida writes that: 'I have attempted to indicate a way out of the closure of this framework via the "trace"' (Diff: 12). The problem with circularity in general is that the appearance of the terms within the circle still requires an explanation; only something prior to the circle can explain its appearance and functioning.

Before attempting to deal with this challenge at its most general level, it is useful to at least note that in each case Derrida begins this citation from the *second* phrase of Saussure's sentence and paragraph. The first, omitted, phrase is: 'These two objects of study are doubtless closely linked and each presupposes the other' (*Course*: 19/37). What Derrida *once again* fails to emphasise, or wants to eliminate, is the recurring theme of reciprocity in the *Course*: between signifiers and signifieds, between differences within a system, and in this case, between language and speech. It is because of such reciprocity that the *Course* proceeds by successive reformulations, and by continually drawing different contrasts between the elements of its linguistic theory. This reflects and enacts the Saussurean shift from thinking about singular identities to thinking about relative values in a system of differences. One 'entity' defines and delineates the other, hence it is meaningless to speak about the language *first*, when it requires speech to be different from. Barthes draws attention to this when he writes that: 'each of these two terms of course achieves its full definition only in the dialectical process which unites one to the other: there is no language without speech, and no speech outside language' (Barthes 1969: 15).

More generally, the question that Derrida poses to semiology here is: where to begin? With consciousness or with differences, with language or with speech? But what Saussurean structuralism primarily questions, at all points in its discourse, is the possibility of escaping such a circle and such an intralinguistic closure. Saussure states that:

> Language at any given time involves an established system and an evolution. At any given time, it is an institution in the present and a product of the past. At first sight, it looks very easy to distinguish between the system and its history, between what it is and what it was. In reality, the connexion between the two is so close that it is hard to separate them . . . It is quite illusory to believe that where language is concerned the problem of origins is any different from the problem of permanent conditions. There is no way out of the circle. (*Course*: 9/24)

There is no way out of the circle, and the problem of the origins of language is illusory. Each term in Saussurean theory – whether it is 'sign', 'difference', or 'language user' – requires, presupposes, and delineates the others in a system of pure values, and hence each term of Saussurean linguistics is caught up within the linguistic field which it announces.

I have asked: what if the conditions of the linguistic system *did not* precede, *were not* antecedent to, the linguistic system? What would that mean? Derrida's description of the 'event' within metaphysics, of the moment 'when the structurality of structure had to begin to be thought', would seem to be apt:

> This was the moment when language invaded the universal problematic, the moment when, in the absence of a center or origin, everything became discourse – provided we can agree on this word – that is to say, a system in which the central signified, the original or transcendental signified, is never absolutely present outside a system of differences. The absence of the transcendental signified extends the domain and the play of signification infinitely. (SS&P: 280)

Such could be the progress and loosening of metaphysics that arises from Saussure's work *if* his terminology did not slip back into the logic and language of metaphysics. But for Derrida, Saussure's failure to put into question the constitution of his linguistic presuppositions indicates Saussure's failure to escape metaphysics, and he remains trapped in a circle. Let us contest the problems of this circle, and this intralinguistic closure, partially but precisely.

Following on from imagining the possibility of play in the absence of the transcendental signified, above, Derrida writes:

> But all these destructive discourses and all their analogues are trapped in a kind of circle. This circle is unique. It describes the form of the relation between the history of metaphysics and the destruction of the history of metaphysics. There is no sense in doing without the concepts of metaphysics in order to shake metaphysics. We have no language – no syntax and no lexicon – which is foreign to this history; we can pronounce not a single destructive proposition which has not already had to slip into the form, the logic, and the implicit postulations of precisely what it seeks to contest. (SS&P: 280–1)

I believe that Derrida is correct in stating that there is no sense in doing without the concepts of metaphysics in order to shake metaphysics. It is more a matter, as Derrida describes it, 'from within semiology, to transform concepts, to displace them, to turn them against their presuppositions' (S&G: 24). But we can ask: Why must such work necessarily slip into the form, the logic and the implicit postulations of what it seeks to contest? Is no progress or originality within language possible? Is all innovation within language doomed to be ineffective precisely because it remains within language? Must language be exceeded, preceded, by a transcendental function and strategy, in order to produce new configurations within language?

Conclusion

To conclude the question of this chapter: if Saussurean semiology as a theory relies on the prior existence of certain entities, then, Derrida would claim, this prior existence requires an *explanation*. If Saussurean theory cannot provide an explanation of itself, then something *other* than semiology is required. Indeed, something *prior* to semiology is required, as, to paraphrase Derrida, no semiological activity as such, however critical, can return to a point short of that familiarity (*Intro*: 35).[4] It is on this basis, by 'this solely strategic justification' (Diff: 7) that Derrida will 'admit the necessity of going through the concept of the arche-trace' (*OG*: 62). Derrida believes that such transcendental entities as 'the concept of the sign', and 'the category of the subject' are put *out of play* by Saussure, and without his own strategic intervention, become permanently inscribed within metaphysics. Such a strategy by far exceeds semiology's capacity to respond, and this analysis cannot hope or wish to overturn such a strategy in its *entirety*. However, by contesting Derrida's reading of and intervention in the *Course*, we are in a position to question the validity and necessity of Derrida's strategy in a number of ways.

First, Derrida begins his intervention in the *Course* from the presupposition that the units of Saussurean theory reproduce classical and transcendental entities. Derrida begins from the point, for example, that the concept of the sign *has always been* defined as a signifier opposed to a signified. Derrida assumes an object of study which reproduces the classical formula of *aliquid stat pro aliquo*, or a sign which takes the place of the referent in its absence; an object, also, whose identity depends upon ideality and upon repetition-as-the-same. And in reproducing such a conceptuality in the foundation of his science, Saussure reproduces all the metaphysical thinking that such an opposition carries, which is a great deal. I have argued against each of these presuppositions, and if Derrida's intervention in semiology begins from a collection of mistaken assumptions about his object of study, then much of what follows from those assumptions will also be mistaken. In this instance, to whatever degree the necessity of Derrida's transcendental strategy is based on the presupposition of working with transcendental entities, then the necessity for the strategy is undermined.

Second, everything about Saussure's critique of diachronic identity implicitly undermines the presuppositions and procedures of Derridean theory. Saussure's effort is to show that neither the 'sign' nor the 'subject' has a perfect history, which helps us to understand that it will not, cannot, have a perfect future. These would be local and contemporary terms which only have a *value* within a particular *langue* – they are social and synchronic facts. Following Saussure, there can be no 'category of the subject' or 'concept of the sign' or 'primordial difference'; these entities do not exist, and all that follows from this presupposition in Derrida's discourse is nullified. These 'entities' are not transcendental, not even provisionally so, but are only signs in the control of a language community, malleable and mortal. I do not believe that Derrida has carried through with the promise to demonstrate the transcendental existence of these entities, and I have read nothing in Derrida's work which overwhelms Saussure's detailed problematisation of diachronic identity.

Third, unlike phenomenology – which demands that we investigate the pre-linguistic and experiential origins of ideality, but leaves intact the idea itself – semiology *does* meet the demands of a semiology, *does* investigate the 'origins' of its own assumptions, and *does* measure up to semiological evidence. The elements of the semiological system mutually determine each other in a synchronic origin in the hands of a community of speakers. And this would apply to the terms of Saussurean theory as much as to the simple nouns of linguistic examples; as much to 'difference' as to 'tree'. In other words, the elements of Saussurean language theory are caught up in the system that they describe, and hence are situated as objects in that linguistic field. In such a configuration, the nostalgia for an intuitive presence that Derrida asserts is at the heart of semiological inquiry would be as irrelevant as it is impossible.

Hence we are faced with the question of choice. In Gödel's terms, it is the choice of axiomatics: of how certain truths will result from one set of axioms, and other truths from another. I repeat this quote from Gödel's editor to emphasise the point:

> If, for example, mathematics is to be founded on systems of axioms, on what basis are those systems to be chosen? The incompleteness theorems tell us that whatever system is accepted, one will need further axioms to arrive at previously unprovable truths. But which axioms, and why? (Feferman 2006: 31)

Derrida's discourse exceeds Saussure's and goes beyond semiology's capacity to respond. However, Derrida's *mastery* of Saussure is incomplete because he takes a determined *position* on the question of systematicity. When one takes the position that the constitution of a system must precede the system, then certain truths are possible; when one takes the position that the conditions of the system can be situated as objects within that system, then other truths are possible. The concluding chapter of this book will begin to sketch out the metaphysical and political implications of these two positions.

Above all, it is not a question of *whether or not* consciousness and the present ought to be kept open as questions, as Derrida would like to think. There is no doubt that the questions of 'consciousness' and the 'present' must be kept open; they must not be prescribed as determined entities for all time, as either divine creations or as originary conditions. The same applies to 'constituted', and 'produced', and 'history', and all the terms which Derrida uses under erasure in his engagement with Saussure. All of these terms must be kept open if we are to *solicit* philosophy from familiar and comfortable ground. What is at stake in Derrida's engagement with Saussure is only *how* to keep these questions from transcendental determinations. The Derridean position is that only by making a provisionally transcendental journey prior to metaphysics, before all the oppositions of metaphysics have taken hold, can we hope to loosen metaphysics. The Saussurean response indicates, on the other hand, that the questions of consciousness and the present *will* be kept open, whether we like it or not.

Notes

1. It is necessary to insert a note on a note (*'Ousia and Grammē'*) on a note (*Being and Time*). The question that interposes itself here is whether or not to expand upon and interrogate Derrida's engagement with Heidegger and the ontology of temporality. Derrida speaks of the 'vulgar concept of time' and notes that: 'I borrow this expression from Heidegger. It designates, at the end of *Being and Time*, a concept of time thought in terms of spatial movement or of the now, and dominating all philosophy from

Aristotle's *Physics* to Hegel's *Logic*' (*OG*: 72). In '*Ousia and Grammē*', Derrida describes the task assigned to *Being and Time* as the deliverance of the formulation of temporality 'from the traditional concepts that govern both everyday language and the history of ontology from Aristotle to Bergson' (31), although the canon of temporality is later rephrased as: 'From Parmenides to Husserl, the privilege of the present has never been put into question' (34). Such a gesture invites a chapter that might be called – by analogy with the first chapter of this book – 'Classical Temporality', in which some of the ancient, medieval, and modern approaches to temporality are contrasted, and the differences between philosophies allowed to be felt. However, such a task would be subject to the powerful compression of Derrida's engagement with metaphysics. For immediately *prior* to his reading of Aristotle's *Physics*, Derrida writes that: 'There is no chance that within the *thematic* of metaphysics anything might have budged, as concerns the concept of time, from Aristotle to Hegel. The founding concepts of substance and cause, along with their entire system of connected concepts, suffice by themselves – whatever their differentiation and their internal problematics – to ensure (us of) the transmission and uninterrupted continuity – however highly differentiated – of all the moments of Metaphysics, Physics, and Logic, passing through Ethics' (39). Such a statement discourages the labour involved in producing such a chapter. Instead, we could assume the result in advance: that whatever differentiation is found within the history of temporality – between subjective and objective temporality, for example – does not disturb the continuity of its metaphysical conceptuality. Hence, the project here will be more modest, that of simply allowing Saussurean systematicity to be subject to Derrida's question of primordial causality.

2. See Chapter 6, pp. 118–19.
3. Or, as David Wood puts it: 'In *Positions* and elsewhere, he writes repeatedly of the "concept" of *différance*, while in "Différance" it is neither a word nor a concept' (65).
4. Derrida's original statement is: 'No geometrizing activity as such, however critical, can return to a point short of that "familiarity"' (*Intro*: 35).

Conclusion

In his translator's introduction to *Writing and Difference*, Alan Bass notes that:

> Derrida has closed each of the essays on Jabès with the name of one of Jabès's imaginary rabbis: Rida and Derissa. In this way he alerts us to the 'latent', philosophically 'unconscious' impact of *Writing and Difference*: an expanded concept of difference through the examination of writing. Derrida's rebus-like play on his own name across this volume reminds us how unlike the Book this one is. (Bass 1978: xx)

Which helps to explain the exasperation of theorists such as Searle or Harris when all that Derrida offers might be a pun (or a lexical association, or an etymology, or a rebus-like play on his own name) in the place of sustained argument. Such wordplay, Christopher Norris suggests, will strike many Anglo-American scholars as 'a kind of sophistical doodling on the margins of serious, truth-seeking discourse' (79). In this investigation I have taken the position that Derrida's rhetorical strategy has a finite validity that is entirely rigorous, and not at all a matter of confusion or of deliberate abuse. Certain elements of Derrida's strategy, however, are difficult to refute without risking being accused of completely missing the point. I have taken on this task in the belief that making the discourses of Derrida and Saussure engage is at least partly possible, that the failures of engagement will be as illuminating as the successes, and, in the end, that a coherent resistance to the Derridean reading of Saussure can be made.

My own rhetorical strategy has been, as I announced in the introduction, to make a bridge between comprehension and contradiction; to attempt to resist Derrida's interventions, his brilliant and compelling rearrangement of meanings and relations, while at the same time making fully explicit how those interventions work. This book has three principal ambitions, which are reflected in the following three sections. The first is to gather together, from a vantage point somewhere in between Derrida and Saussure, all of Derrida's commentary and work upon the *Course in General Linguistics*. The second is to test the assumptions and procedures of this commentary against the text of the *Course* itself, and against other readings of Saussure, in order to challenge the authority of the Derridean reading. The third is to imagine the possibilities that are offered by a post-Derridean Saussure in thinking about language, signs, and truth. Having resisted the compression of Saussurean thought within a Derridean framework, I want to consider the question of *what comes next*.

What did Derrida want of Saussure?

The defining characteristic of Derrida's engagement with Saussure is that it is 'equivocal'. For if the sign is 'in systematic solidarity with stoic and medieval theology', but also facilitates the critique and displacement of that metaphysical tradition, then it represents 'a simultaneous *marking* and *loosening* of the limits of the system in which this concept was born and began to serve' (S&G: 17). Derrida finds resources in the concept of the sign to shake metaphysics from its logocentric relationship with presence. At a certain point, however, this concept will inevitably fall back into the language and logic of that which it attempts to challenge. It is useful, then, to summarise Derrida's engagement in two parts: first, the ways in which Saussurean semiology loosens metaphysics, permits the critique of metaphysics, and suggests the infinite play of difference; and second, how the concepts, presuppositions, and implications of the Western tradition re-emerge from what seems most natural and simple about the sign.

Beginning with the progress of semiology, with the loosening of metaphysics, Saussure is, according to Derrida, the thinker who instituted the field of semiology based on the arbitrary and differential character of the sign. The system of signs is arbitrary, in that meaning is not constituted in any essential and naturalistic relationship; not in their 'plenitude', as Derrida writes in 'Différance', but in 'the network of oppositions that distinguishes them, and then relates them one to another' (Diff: 10). Saussure also argues that the concrete object of linguistics is not material sound, but rather, a purely mental entity, and that language is in its essence not at all phonic. Saussure's originality within the tradition of the concept of the sign is to imagine the signifier and signified as dematerialised and differential entities. And in opening the study of language and meaning to these possibilities, 'Saussure powerfully contributed to turning against the metaphysical tradition the concept of sign that he borrowed from it' (S&G: 18).

In 'Structure, Sign, and Play', Derrida considers the 'event' of structuralism within the history of the concept of structure. Derrida writes that the concept of structure has always implied the play of differences governed and limited by a *centre*: 'a fundamental immobility and a reassuring certitude, which itself is beyond the reach of play' (SS&P: 279). However, in the moment that 'the structurality of structure had to begin to be thought' (SS&P: 280), it becomes possible to begin thinking that there was no centre, no original or transcendental signified. And if the central signified is not determined as a present thing, prior to and outside of the system of differences, then the structure is not grounded in a reassuring certitude, and thus: 'The absence of the transcendental signified extends the domain and the play of signification infinitely' (SS&P: 280). In this moment, Derrida embraces the emancipatory advance of the concept of the sign as the *possibility* of the unlimited play of difference, and of the absence of a centring, reassuring, transcendental signified.

This possibility is most forcefully applied by Derrida when he brings the play of differences to bear against Husserl's phenomenology. Throughout *Speech and Phenomena*, Derrida undermines the primordiality of phenomenological experience with a more-primordial semiological difference. According to Derrida, Husserl's phenomenological method can only function by: 'repressing difference by assigning it to the exteriority of the signifiers' (*S&P*: 82). Against this repression, Derrida's intervention proceeds: 'by reintroducing the difference involved in "signs" at the core of what is "primordial"' (*S&P*: 45–6n). Derrida's critique of Husserl's phenomenology is of a metaphysical system which aims to restore an intuitive relationship with truth, prior to any relationship with language and signs. The purpose of Derrida's intervention in the logic of the *Logical Investigations* is to bring the outside of semiological difference to the inside of phenomenological experience.

Derrida uses primordial difference against Husserl's phenomenology, and against metaphysics in general, up to the point where 'one inevitably encounters "the logocentric and ethnocentric limits" of such a model. At this point, perhaps, the concept is to be abandoned' (S&G: 17). The majority of Derrida's writing on Saussure is concerned with the ways in which the concept of the sign falls back into the language and logic of the metaphysics it seeks to contest. For if it is true that 'the difference involved in signs' helps to loosen metaphysics, then, Derrida would argue, Saussure is unable to follow through with this possibility 'in the extent to which he continued to use the concept of the sign' (S&G: 18–19). For Derrida, it is simply not possible to continue to use the classical concept of the sign 'without also bringing with it all its metaphysico-theological roots. To these roots adheres not only the distinction between the sensible and the intelligible – already a great deal – with all that it controls, namely, metaphysics in its totality' (*OG*: 13).

What the concept of the sign cannot evade, above all else, is its definition as a signifier divided from its signified; the concept of the sign has been determined by this opposition throughout its history. For Derrida, the rigorous separation of the signifier from the signified leaves in place, by rights, the possibility of thinking a signified independent of signifiers, or a transcendental signified: 'a concept simply present for thought, independent of a relationship to language' (S&G: 19). In continuing to use the concept of the sign, Saussure retains the classical opposition between an external, derivative 'signifier' (Aristotle's σύμβολον, or the Stoic *signum*) and an internal, essential 'signified' (Aristotle's παθεματα, or the Stoic *signatum*). In reproducing such categories, and in maintaining the possibility of mental experience independent of a system of signifiers, the concept of the sign slips into 'the form, the logic, and the implicit postulations of precisely what it seeks to contest' (SS&P: 280–1).

In 'Signature Event Context', Derrida shows how such a transcendental signified is implied within the classical definition of 'communication'. For if such a transcendental signified can exist independently of signifiers, that is, of language, then it can remain a pure mental essence, ready to be transported through some medium to a receiver. Communication would then be achieved by the recovery and restoration of the meaning, context, and conditions of the original utterance. Derrida apprehends a tradition of communication in which the sign functions as a 'representation of the idea which itself represented the object perceived. From that point on, communication is that which circulates a representation as an ideal content' (SEC: 6). This is the classical and logocentric structure of communication that Derrida contests throughout his engagement with signs and language.

In *Of Grammatology*, Derrida considers the role of Saussurean phonocentrism in the effort to maintain a mental experience independent of a relationship to language. Derrida argues that the exclusion of writing is not an accident of history, but rather, the necessary condition for metaphysics if it is to allow the self-present voice – or the mental, unspoken, internal voice – an immediate and pre-linguistic relationship with nature, truth, and the word of God. Saussure, in a gesture which mirrors that of Plato, Aristotle, Hegel, and Rousseau, makes writing an 'image' of speech, exterior to the natural bond between the voice and experience. In the *Course*, Saussure claims that writing is: 'not part of the internal system of the language', and that one 'must be aware of its utility, its defects and its dangers' (*Course*: 24/44). And like Aristotle, Saussure believes that: 'A language and its written form constitute two separate systems of signs. The sole reason for the existence of the latter is to represent the former' (*Course*: 24/45). In this way, Derrida is able to correlate Saussurean *phonocentrism*, or the privilege of spoken language over written language, with *logocentrism*, or the desire for a true and universal idea in the mind prior to the introduction of language. As a result, the concept of the sign: 'remains therefore within the heritage of that logocentrism which is also a phonocentrism: absolute proximity of voice and being, of voice and the meaning of being, of voice and the ideality of meaning' (*OG*: 11–12).

Within this system of classical semiology, the sign is divided between its external, derivative signifier and an internal, pre-linguistic voice, which itself has an immediate and intuitive relationship with presence. In this way, signs are utilised only when we cannot show or grasp the thing, and they hold this place until such time as this originary presence is restored. The sign is, then, both secondary and provisional, a 'detour that suspends the accomplishment or fulfilment of "desire" or "will"' (Diff: 8). The concept of the sign would then imply a deferral of presence, a deferral of the moment when the image can be rejoined to its object. In Saussurean semiology, a system of differences can be considered synchronically: as momentarily structured in their entirety. For Derrida, on the contrary, meaning does not come to rest in a structure, but continues indefinitely in a 'systematic play of differences', and he calls this *différance* (Diff: 11). In this way, *différance* economises semiological differing and referential deferral, and hence 'is incompatible with the static, synchronic, taxonomic, ahistoric motifs in the concept of *structure*' (S&G: 27).

What *différance* questions, first and foremost, is the set of presuppositions inherent in Saussurean language theory. If subject and object, synchrony and diachrony, writing and speech, are utilised by Saussure as already present entities, then what is it that created or produced them? If Saussurean semiology as a theory relies on the prior existence of these entities, then, Derrida would claim, this prior existence requires an explanation. From where have these principles arrived? Have they fallen from the sky, or are they divine, inscribed in a *topos noētos*? In a classical semiology, consciousness would be the ground or the receptacle of present intuitions, the very thing which must precede differences, as the space in which differences are distributed. For Derrida, on the contrary, the apparent unity of consciousness is only a metaphysical presupposition which depends upon a more originary potentiality. *Différance* describes the condition and possibility of the appearance of Saussure's presuppositions, which are those of the metaphysics of presence. *Différance* cannot be thought of in any terms of classical metaphysics, as it is *différance*, or the simultaneous origin and play, or cause and effect, of differences, which allows these metaphysical categories to appear.

To conclude this section we can ask, after Stanley Cavell: What did Derrida want of Saussure? Above all else, the concept of the sign provides Derrida with the notion of 'primordial difference', or a difference which precedes presence. For Derrida, the history of metaphysics is one of structures of differences thought on the basis of a reassuring presence. Derrida's deconstruction of this hierarchy begins from the proposal that presence must instead be thought on the basis of difference, and not the other way around. Such a reversal makes 'the difference involved in signs' not a derived element in the structure, but the primordially necessary condition for meaning, and for communication. In thinking 'the difference involved in signs' as prior to all the oppositions of metaphysics, and prior, even, to philosophy's founding question of 'what is', difference becomes *différance*, which is neither a word nor a concept, but the possibility of establishing such an opposition. And in upholding the principle and possibilities of primordial difference, in restoring the non-derivative character of signs, Derrida believes that: 'The concept of *différance* even develops the most legitimate principled exigencies of "structuralism"' (S&G: 28).

What if Derrida was wrong about Saussure?

Derrida's engagement with Saussure is, from the outset, focused on the delimitation of Saussurean originality. In Derrida's words, it is to investigate: 'the tradition of the concept of the sign, and . . . the originality of Saussure's contribution within this continuity' (*OG*: 324). Saussure's originality, according to Derrida, is to be found in his efforts to emphasise the dematerialised, differential, and formal characteristics of the sign. However, if the construction of the sign still allows for a signified independent of signifiers, then all that Saussure achieves is 'psychologism' (S&G: 23), or the transfer of the units of the sign from external realities to psychological entities, 'which is only to shift the problem without resolving it' (*S&P*: 47).

Against Derrida's reading, the alternative case for Saussurean originality focuses on the theory of *value*. Derrida never discusses this theory, despite every theorist in the vicinity of Derrida's engagement with Saussure – from Ortigues to Jakobson – citing this as Saussure's legitimate originality. In the place of a reading or refutation of Saussurean value, Derrida situates his criticism of the 'transcendental signified' to make such a refutation unnecessary. But even here, Derrida ignores the dozen or so passages in the *Course* which explicitly state the impossibility of thinking a signified independent of signifiers. For example, against what he identifies as a history of nomenclaturism, Saussure states that: 'Languages are not mechanisms created and organised with a view to the concepts to be expressed, although people are mistakenly inclined to think so' (*Course*: 85/122); and that 'No ideas are established in advance, and nothing is distinct, before the introduction of linguistic structure' (*Course*: 110/155).

The problem of settling the question of Saussure's originality is made more difficult by the absence of Saussure's name from Derrida's most powerful discourses upholding Saussurean theory. First, in considering the 'event' of structuralism – in which we can begin to imagine the possibility of infinite play in a structure without a reassuring centre – Derrida names only Nietzsche, Freud, and Heidegger, despite illustrating this event with 'the concept of sign' (SS&P: 280–1). Second, in *Speech and Phenomena*, in bringing 'the difference involved in signs' to bear against Husserlian phenomenology, Saussure's name is conspicuously absent, and it is left to Derrida's English translator to identify Saussure as the source of this terminology (Allison 1973: xxxviii). The possibility that Derrida either intentionally or unintentionally minimises the originality of Saussurean value is reinforced by his handling of Saussure's paper analogy, in which:

> A language might also be compared to a sheet of paper. Thought is one side of the sheet and sound the reverse side. Just as it is impossible to take a pair of scissors and cut one side of the paper without at the same time cutting the other, so it is impossible in a language to isolate sound from thought, or thought from sound. (*Course*: 111/157)

Derrida's responses to this analogy, in 'Freud and the Scene of Writing' and *Of Grammatology*, indicate that he takes the paper to stand for a single sign, and the two sides represent the simple binary exchange between a signifier and a signified. Read more closely, however, the paper represents the language system, with abstract thought on one side and abstract sound on the other. The analogy is for the action of the scissors, which mutually and reciprocally articulates the units of language. A certain imprecision, or broadness, in Derrida's reading of Saussurean value is also evident in his 'semiological' handling of Freud's dream-language. The ease with which Derrida translates Freud's 'dream-content' and 'dream-thought' into 'signifiers' and 'signifieds' confirms his willingness to understand any bipartite scheme of representation as a 'sign', specifically in the Saussurean sense.

In establishing the epoch of classical semiology and the metaphysics of presence, Derrida makes extensive use of ancient and medieval allusions. He claims, for example, that the sign is 'in systematic solidarity with stoic and medieval theology' (S&G: 17), and that the difference between signifier and signified:

> belongs in a profound and implicit way to the totality of the great epoch covered by the history of metaphysics, and in a more explicit and more systematically articulated way to the narrower epoch of Christian creationism and infinitism when these appropriate the resources of Greek conceptuality. (*OG*: 13)

In establishing such a scene, however, Derrida draws upon only three lines from *On Interpretation* and a paragraph – sometimes truncated – from Jakobson's *Essais*. Derrida gets all that he needs from these two citations by putting excessive pressure on Aristotle's statements, and by ignoring both the intention of Jakobson's paragraph, and his body of work in general. Derrida asserts that it is a question *at first* of demonstrating the solidarity of these concepts, their presuppositions, and their theology. The persistent lack of evidence for such a scene weakens the credibility of Derrida's principal contention: of the systematic, historical, and theological solidarity of the sign and the metaphysics of presence.

What Derrida mainly fails to demonstrate is the logical or linguistic co-dependence of phonocentrism and logocentrism. Derrida's conflation of phonocentrism and logocentrism proceeds on the basis of two observations. The first, in *Speech and Phenomena*, compares Husserl's *Logical Investigations*, and its privilege of a 'pre-expressive and prelinguistic stratum of sense' (*S&P*: 31), with the *Course in General Linguistics*, at the point where Saussure states that: 'Without moving either lips or tongue, we can talk to ourselves or recite silently a piece of verse' (*Course*: 66/98). The second, in *Of Grammatology*, offers a pathological profile of the linguist from Geneva, in which Saussure's ambition is of:

protecting, and even of restoring the internal system of the language in the purity of its concept against the gravest, most perfidious, most permanent contamination . . . Thus incensed, Saussure's vehement argumentation aims at more than a theoretical error, more than a moral fault: at a sort of stain and primarily at a sin. (*OG*: 34)

Derrida undoubtedly demonstrates that Saussure shares a phonocentrism with Plato, Aristotle, Hegel, and Husserl. But phonocentrism and logocentrism are very different ideas, even if they are often found together. Saussure's belief in the priority of spoken language – a belief which has some empirical legitimacy – does not necessarily confer a belief in the possibility of pure mental essences, prior to the introduction of language. Indeed, when the *Course* is compared with the *Logical Investigations* in the manner suggested by Derrida, it is quite impossible to say that Saussure would 'want to maintain' or to 'assert' that there exists 'a pre-expressive substratum of sense' (*S&P*: 80). Derrida wants Saussure to see writing, in the rupture of the natural bond between speech and thought, as a *crisis*. He cannot demonstrate this from the text of the *Course*, however, but only by assigning to Saussure the phenomenological voice, and Husserl's motivation for dividing indication from expression.

For Derrida, 'classical semiology' is essentially and irreducibly a referential semiotic, in which: 'The sign is usually said to be put in place of the thing itself, the present thing, "thing" here standing equally for meaning or referent' (Diff: 9). In response, Derrida appropriates the semiotics of Peirce, which, he says, 'goes very far in the direction that I have called the de-construction of the transcendental signified' by showing that '*The thing itself is a sign*' (*OG*: 49). For Derrida, the interpretative function in Peirce's tripartite system means that the signified is always in the position of a signifier, and hence that the difference between signifier and signified is never radical. Derrida is able to make this declaration, however, only by disregarding the *Course*'s careful attention to definitions, and by making 'signs' that stand for 'things' synonymous with the mutual articulation of 'signifiers' and 'signifieds'. As a result, Derrida's engagement with semiological structure is determined by, and contained by, the presumption of a classical relationship with presence. Or to put it another way, Derrida's understanding of semiological *structure* is determined by his view of semiological *communication*.

Finally, it is not enough to defend Saussure against what Derrida sees as the shortcomings of Saussurean theory. It is also necessary to take issue with what Derrida sees as most valid and legitimate about structuralism: the restoration of primordial difference, or, the non-derivative character of the sign. Just as Derrida neglects all of the passages of the *Course* which argue against the possibility of a transcendental signified, he similarly neglects all of Saussure's argumentation in relation to time and structure. Derrida fails to engage with Saussure's arguments that suggest, first, that the mechanism of *value* means that it is simply not possible to consider any single unit of language without considering at the same time the entire system of which it is part, and second, that the problematisation of diachronic identity is also a problematisation of historical explanation in general. Derrida never acknowledges Saussure's radical work upon the notion of linguistic identity, beyond mere psychologism; instead, he writes of 'the concept of the sign' as if it had an objective history and ideality independent from the names one might assign to it. However, such a de jure sense of the sign would be, from a Saussurean point of view, nomenclaturist, and hence from a Derridean perspective, transcendental and logocentric. Derrida's failure of engagement with Saussure's theorisation of structure is best illustrated by his claim that synchrony is 'ahistoric' (S&G: 27), and by the lengthy but finally naïve claim that differences 'have not fallen from the sky' (Diff: 11).

The fragmented, tangential, and implicit nature of Derrida's engagement with Saussure is, at times, in sharp contrast to the directness of his pro-nouncements on Saussurean theory. To reflect upon this aspect of Derrida's engagement with Saussure is, at some point, to reflect upon Derrida's decision to 'cite Saussure only at the point which interests us' (Diff: 10). According to Cavell, something similar occurs in Derrida's engagement with Austin. He asks: 'How is it that Derrida misses the extent of Austin's differ-ences from the classical and/or academic philosophers with whom Austin, as much as Derrida, is at odds? Is it that the differences at some stage stop seeming important?' (48). For Cavell, it is because Derrida 'simply hadn't read certain texts presupposed by *How To Do Things With Words*' (71), for if he had, Derrida would not have treated parasitic discourse as an 'exclusion' from Austin's theory of performatives. Cavell concludes that: 'In Derrida's case this may be particularly painful to hear because of his own loathing of being hastily and incompletely read, his being known for saying, in effect, to his detractors . . ., "Read a little more; it won't hurt you"' (71).

Beyond the Derridean Saussure

At a certain point in this analysis, I announced a shift from the argument that Derrida goes too far in incorporating Saussure within a classical semiology, to the proposal that elements of the *Course*'s originality *exceed* Derrida's capacity to contain them within his discourse of the metaphysics of presence. The imperative that follows, and which will be taken up here, is to explore what is missed, or expand what has been compressed, in Derrida's reading of Saussure. This section is not intended to outline a complete programme for the future study of Saussure and the *Course*, for that potential is as far-reaching as it has ever been: as a programme of linguistics, as a framework for the social sciences, or as a metaphysical position. What I want to expand upon here is only what has been suggested by the tension in Derrida's reading of Saussure, and to re-think and reclaim what is most legitimate about structuralism. More poetically, it is to pay attention to what the *Course* has had to tell us about itself in resisting one particular reading.

The point at which Saussure moves most sharply away from Derrida is the point at which his theory of language is at its most radical, and potentially most productive. Derrida's assumption throughout his engagement with Saussure is that linguistic identity functions through the recognition and repetition of *the same*, and that such a sameness is necessarily *ideal*. This challenges the Saussurean reader to establish the degree to which any previous notions of identity, sameness, and difference are problematised in the *Course*. For Saussure, linguistic *identity* is subject to linguistic *value*, and as such, it is difference and not sameness which is recognised by the language user. Saussure's theory of value, therefore, proposes not just to replace sameness with difference, but to replace identity with *identification*, or, the viewpoint of the language user. As Saussure states: 'Values have no other rationale than usage and general agreement' (*Course*: 112/157); 'a language never exists even for a moment except as a social fact' (*Course*: 77/112); and 'a language is not an entity, and exists only in its users' (*Course*: 5n/19n). The definitive phrasing of the priority of language users occurs at the point where it reciprocally defines and justifies the theory of synchrony:

> Synchrony has only one perspective, that of the language users; and its whole method consists of collecting evidence from them. In order to determine to what extent something is a reality, it is necessary and also sufficient to find out to what extent it exists as far as the language users are concerned. (*Course*: 89/128)

Linguistic identity, for Saussure, is not only arbitrary and differential, but rejects any recourse to extralinguistic or referential entities. All that linguistic identity requires is the viewpoint of language users. In doing so, Saussurean value breaks with all previous notions of linguistic identity and representation.

Of course, this is Derrida's complaint: that all Saussure achieves, in making the sign a bipartite relationship between sound-pattern and sense, is to transfer the units of the sign from external realities to psychological entities within a full intuitive consciousness. Derrida poses a question to Saussure which takes the form: 'From where have the elements of your theory arrived, or been produced?' Derrida's response, symmetrically, is that the explanation of what allows Saussure's categories to appear and to function must precede the system of their operation; that such a *causality* must be structurally or logically *antecedent*. But perhaps what seems most natural about this question is also what might make Saussurean structuralism so original and transforming. For what Saussurean thought offers is the possibility that the conditions and explanation of a system do not *precede* but are *caught up*, or situated as objects, within that system.

Derrida's strategy to shake metaphysics from its un-thought presuppositions is to precede metaphysics itself: to place *différance* in the role of a provisional transcendentality so that it might mark and loosen all the oppositions of metaphysics. Derrida believes that such a transcendental strategy is necessary and justified on the basis of the permanence of Saussure's categories of thought: of the self-presence of consciousness and the present. It is on the basis of 'this solely strategic justification' (Diff: 7) that Derrida will 'admit the necessity of going through the concept of the arche-trace' (*OG*: 62). Derrida believes that without this intervention, such transcendental entities as 'the concept of the sign' and 'the category of the subject' will be permanently inscribed within metaphysics. However, if the justification for Derrida's transcendental strategy is purely methodological or provisional, then one only has to take account of what Derrida says about Austin's essential distinction between serious and parasitic discourse: 'what is at stake above all is the structural impossibility and illegitimacy of such an "idealization", even one which is methodological and provisional' (LI: 67). Whatever the justification for Derrida's strategy *in general*, it obscures and neutralises what is most radical about Saussurean systematicity. For Saussure's problematisation of diachronic identity places into crisis not only historical explanation, but also the techniques and presuppositions of Derridean antecedence. Culler, for one, argues that 'attempts to theorize a perpetual self-transcendence' must fail (Culler 1975: 253), and proposes instead that: 'Rather than try to get outside ideology we must remain resolutely within it, for both the conventions to be analysed and the notions of understanding lie within. If circle there be, it is the circle of culture itself' (254).

Corresponding to this axiomatic point of divergence between Derrida and Saussure, each philosophy has what we could call, after Gödel, a *finite* legitimation. Derrida's pursuit of metaphysical presuppositions is made as a question of ethics and responsibility, and he speaks of the 'ethical-political responsibility of the theoretician' (Aft: 138). Derrida shares with Husserl a notion of the ethical responsibility to uncover hidden sediments and metaphysical roots, and to expose the naturalisation of origins. Indeed, Gasché notes that Derrida's work in the *Introduction* is: 'an enquiry into what properly makes up responsibility, that is, into responsibility's conditions' (228). Derrida explains this in relation to Husserl's phenomenological project:

> To meditate on or investigate the sense of origins is at the same time to: make oneself responsible for the sense of science and philosophy, bring this sense to the clarity of its 'fulfilment', and to put oneself in a position of *responsibility* for this sense starting from the total sense of our existence. (*Intro*: 31)

Like Husserl, Derrida believes in the ethical responsibility to *remember* origins, but at the same time, makes those origins inaccessible by placing them prior to language and to language-users. For Derrida, at least, this would have the positive value of an always-remembering, and always-loosening, of origins. However, I feel that to do precisely what Derrida forbids – to forget or disavow the beyond or before language – actually facilitates a kind of political action that has never yet been thoroughly activated.

Derrida's method proceeds first of all as an act of remembering, or un-forgetting, of sedimented sense. Such a method allows us to expose the meta-physical system that supports and legitimises a word such as 'consciousness'. Derrida's position is that only by making a provisionally transcendental journey prior to metaphysics can we hope to *solicit* these questions from tran-scendental determinations. The Saussurean response indicates, on the other hand, that the questions of consciousness and the present *will* be kept open, whether we like it or not. As Harris says:

> We are dealing with a model which assigns to the individual vis-à-vis *la langue* a role which matches exactly the socio-political role assigned to the individual vis-à-vis the institutions of the modern nation state. As a member, the individual can do no more than what the commu-nity, through its institutions, makes it possible for an individual to do. (Harris 1987: 216)

In this kind of inquiry, *responsibility* lies within a democratic theme rather than with metaphysical-philosophical history. Arguably, the grounding of Derrida's politics in metaphysical history encourages us to *too easily* demon-strate how cultural forms become naturalised and uncritical. Such a legitima-tion and method places itself beyond or prior to 'the circle of culture', able to reveal to us what the culture users themselves cannot see. In moving beyond or prior to the 'forgetfulness' of culture users, it effectively denies the view-point of the culture user, that is, of a text that is both synchronic and social. For David Wood, it is clear that:

> Derrida believes in making, at least with one foot, the 'step beyond' – beyond 'metaphysics', 'beyond man and humanism', beyond presence, beyond security, beyond the language of Being. . . . I am not objecting to this in principle. What I am questioning is Derrida's self-understand-ing – his understanding of the possibility of a discourse *other than* that of 'metaphysics'. (68)

A post-Saussurean philosophy would begin by questioning the very possibil-ity of *either* the word *or* the concept of 'consciousness' surviving through time, and instead reaffirm, as Culler writes, that: 'The question the analyst constantly asks is what are the differences which have meaning for members

of the speech community' (Culler 1986: 51). Saussure proposes that the only
legitimation in language is the social, and that 'only by suppressing the past
can he enter into the state of mind of the language user. The intervention
of history can only distort his judgement' (*Course*: 81/117). In such a social
and synchronic engagement with language, and with language communi-
ties, it is necessary and also sufficient to critically engage with the point of
view of language users, and not take recourse to a sediment of sense or to
forgotten origins in classical texts. What that challenges us to do is to find
it *more difficult* to criticise the popular. It forces us to work harder to shake
the position of the naturalised and uncritical, and forces us to engage more
thoroughly (and responsibly) with those thoughts and beliefs that we find
problematical.

The most controversial and divisive development lies in the way Saussurean
theory points towards linguistic relativism. At the very least, the removal of
'referents' from linguistic consideration provides what Sturrock calls: 'The
remarkable degree of autonomy which language enjoys in respect of reality'
(19). Going further, Saussure states that the viewpoint of language users
constitutes the *only* legitimate reality in language: that, for example, the
only test of the proposition 'a dog is an animal' is to collect evidence from
language users. But how far are we to follow through with this suggestion?
The proposition at stake in Derrida's engagement with Saussure is whether or
not the conditions and rules of a linguistic system can be situated as objects
within that linguistic system. Let us test the proposition with the following
aphorism:

> Language does not have the capacity to reflect the truth; it has only the
> capacity to reflect a social agreement.

The problem for such a statement *ought* to be that it breaks its own rule.
Because a statement, according to nomenclaturist linguistics, or referential
semiotics, *ought* to be verifiable. In being verifiable, we infer that it has a referential relationship with some reality, and hence can be proven, at least the-
oretically, to be true or false. However, when the statement itself is adhered
to, the statement is not in conflict with itself. It is, in other words, only in
ratifying the statement that the statement can be realised. For as a statement,
it rethinks the value of 'statements', as finite social agreements, rather than
infinite truths. If, at some point in time, in English, the statement is no longer
ratified, perhaps because the meanings of the key terms have mutated too far,
then the statement will no longer be 'true'.

The weak theorem of relativism arising from the *Course* might be that: 'In
order to determine to what extent something is a reality, it is necessary and
also sufficient to find out to what extent it exists as far as the language users
are concerned.' In this case, the primacy of language users in determining
reality is a *truth* for all people and all time. The problem with such a state-

ment of linguistic relativism is, of course, that it refers to an extralinguistic truth. Or, as Derrida phrases it: 'relativism, like all its derivatives, remains a philosophical position in contradiction with itself' (Aft: 137). However, Saussurean systematicity indicates that even the basic statements asserting relativism would be wholly subject to time, place, and language. That is, that Saussurean theory contains no transcendental or temporarily transcendental elements. Such a formation is not *prior* to the question of 'what is', but among it, co-dependent with it, and forever in differential articulation with it. The aphorism in question is perpetually circular, and can never ground itself in anything but the play of differences. The statement economises, in Derridean terms, its own *différance*: its constitution of itself and its difference from itself.

Conclusion

We have previously asked: What did Derrida want of Saussure? But perhaps Bennington phrases it better when he asks: 'What has Derrida done to Saussure?' (2004: 200). In other words, how much is the image of Saussure today a product of the Derridean reading? Culler considers this question, and is struck by:

> how frequently theorists draw upon Saussurean insights in order to contest what they take to be the principles of structuralism. . . . [This] shows that reading Saussure can help one question the facile distinction between structuralism and post-structuralism, which may caricature structuralism and transfer to post-structuralism what is most interest-ing in structuralist writings. (Culler 1986: 6)

If Derrida's reading of Saussure is today the dominant reading, then what would be Derrida's role in this caricature? Is it in determining that Saussure's only originality is psychologism? Or in uncovering Saussure's passion against the sin of writing? Or by inferring that in making differences synchronic, Saussure forgets that differences have not fallen from the sky?

I have made the case in this book that Derrida's reading of Saussure is not always attentive to the text of the *Course*, nor does it always appear to be in good faith. But Derrida's object of criticism was not primarily the text of 1916, but the structuralism of 1966: the structuralism of Lévi-Strauss, Lacan, Barthes, Benveniste, and Martinet; the phonology of Jakobson and the glossematics of Hjelmslev. This was a structuralism that was not rigor-ously Saussurean; perhaps even less so than Derrida's radical reappraisal. Bouissac's review of structuralist activity shows that:

> Saussure's insights were put to work in a great variety of intellectual contexts. At the same time, Saussurism underwent some kind of

hybridising and creolisation ... For the semiotic generation of the 1960s, the interface with Saussure's ideas was not in the form of textual erudition and exegesis. (Bouissac 2004: 246–7)

As a result, Peuch asks: 'Could this diluted approximation to Saussure's ideas be one of the reasons for the fate of his teaching in France?' (132). And Harris repeatedly demonstrates, in *Saussure and his Interpreters*, how infrequently close attention was paid to this subtle text, even in the structuralism which purported to uphold it.

This is why I am able to say that 'structuralism', circa 1966, *needed* the radical reappraisal that Derrida's intervention provides. Derrida's intervention in the questions of communication and structure comprehensively and immediately changed the way Saussure was read: from an argument about the abstract components and rules of language to a question about the construction of truth. In this way, Derrida's radical reappraisal has been profoundly enabling. Through the opening(s) that Derrida's work provides, new kinds of inquiry into language and society have become possible. However, an alternative reappraisal of Saussure, and other kinds of inquiry into language and society, is both possible and necessary. To borrow from Cavell: 'to imagine these revolutionaries asking, What Is To Be Undone? is to imagine them answering, Everything' (Cavell 1995: 68).

List of Works by Derrida and Saussure

Works by Jacques Derrida

'Différance', in *Speech and Phenomena, and Other Essays on Husserl's Theory of Signs*, trans. David Allison, Evanston, IL: Northwestern University Press, 1973, pp. 129–60. Originally published as 'La Différance' simultaneously in the *Bulletin de la Société française de philosophie*, 62 (3), 1968; and in *Théorie d'ensemble*, Paris: Éditions du Seuil, 1968.

Speech and Phenomena, and Other Essays on Husserl's Theory of Signs, trans. David Allison, Evanston, IL: Northwestern University Press, 1973. Originally published as *La Voix et le Phénomène*, Paris: Presses Universitaires de France, 1967.

Of Grammatology, trans. Gayatri Chakravorty Spivak, Baltimore, MD: Johns Hopkins University Press, 1976. Originally published as *De la grammatologie*, Paris: Éditions de Minuit, 1967.

'Freud and the scene of writing', in *Writing and Difference*, trans. Alan Bass, Chicago: University of Chicago Press, 1978, pp. 196–231. Originally published as 'Freud et la scène de l'écriture' in *Tel Quel*, 26, summer 1966.

'"Genesis and structure" and phenomenology', in *Writing and Difference*, trans. Alan Bass, Chicago, IL: University of Chicago Press, 1978, pp. 154–68. Originally published as *Genèse et structure*, ed. M. de Gandillac, L. Goldmann and J. Piaget, The Hague: Mouton, 1964.

'Structure, sign, and play in the discourse of the human sciences', in *Writing and Difference*, trans. Alan Bass, Chicago, IL: University of Chicago Press, 1978, pp. 278–93. Originally published as 'La structure, le signe et le jeu dans le discours des sciences humaines' in *L'Écriture et la différence*, Paris: Éditions du Seuil, 1967.

'Implications: interview with Henri Ronse', in *Positions*, trans. Alan Bass, Chicago, IL: University of Chicago Press, 1981, pp. 1–14. Originally published as 'Implications. Entretien avec Henri Ronse' in *Lettres françaises*, 1211, 6–12 December 1967.

'Semiology and grammatology: interview with Julia Kristeva', in *Positions*, trans. Alan Bass, Chicago, IL: University of Chicago Press, 1981, pp. 15–36. Originally published as 'Sémiologie et grammatologie. Entretien avec Julia Kristeva', in *Information sur les sciences sociales*, 7, 3 June 1968.

'Différance', in *Margins of Philosophy*, trans. Alan Bass, Chicago, IL: University of Chicago Press, 1982, pp. 1–27. Originally published as 'La différance' simultaneously in the *Bulletin de la Société française de philosophie*, 62 (3), 1968; and in *Théorie d'ensemble*, Paris: Éditions du Seuil, 1968.

'*Ousia* and *Grammē*: note on a note from *Being and Time*', in *Margins of Philosophy*, trans. Alan Bass, Chicago, IL: University of Chicago Press, 1982, pp. 29–67. Originally published in *L'Endurance de la pensée. Pour saluer Jean Beaufret*, Paris: Plon, 1968.

Glas, trans. John P. Leavey Jr. and Richard Rand, Lincoln, NE: University of Nebraska Press, 1986. Originally published as *Glas*, Paris: Éditions Galilée, 1974.

'Afterword: towards an ethic of discussion', in Gerald Graff (ed.), *Limited Inc*, trans. Samuel Weber, Evanston, IL: Northwestern University Press, 1988, pp. 111–60.

'Limited inc a b c . . .', in Gerald Graff (ed.), *Limited Inc.* trans. Samuel Weber, Evanston, IL: Northwestern University Press, 1988, pp. 29–110. Originally published as a supplement to *Glyph*, 2, 1977.

'The Original Discussion of "Différance"', in David Wood and Robert Bernasconi (eds), *Derrida and Différance*, Evanston, IL: Northwestern University Press, 1988, pp. 83–95. Originally published in the *Bulletin de la Société française de philosophie*, 62 (3), 1968.

'Signature Event Context', in Gerald Graff (ed.), *Limited Inc.* trans. Samuel Weber, Evanston, IL: Northwestern University Press, 1988, pp. 1–23. Originally published as 'Signature événement contexte' in *Marges de la philosophie*, Paris: Éditions de Minuit, 1972.

Edmund Husserl's Origin of Geometry: An Introduction, trans. John P. Leavey, Lincoln, NE: University of Nebraska Press, 1989. Originally published as *Edmund Husserl's L'Origine de la géométrie*, traduction et introduction par Jacques Derrida, 2nd edn, Paris: Presses Universitaires de France, 1974.

Works by Ferdinand de Saussure

Cours de linguistique générale, ed. Charles Bally and Albert Sechehaye with the collaboration of Albert Riedlinger, 2nd edn, Paris and Lausanne: Payot, 1922.

'Notes inédites de F. de Saussure', *Cahiers Ferdinand de Saussure*, 12, 1954.

Course in General Linguistics, ed. Charles Bally and Albert Sechehaye with the collaboration of Albert Riedlinger, trans. Wade Baskin, New York: Philosophical Library, 1959.

'Lettres de F. de Saussure à Antoine Meillet', *Cahiers Ferdinand de Saussure*, no. 21, 1964.

Course in General Linguistics, ed. Charles Bally and Albert Sechehaye with the collaboration of Albert Riedlinger, trans. Roy Harris, London: Duckworth, 1983.

References

Allison, David (1973), 'Translator's introduction', in Jacques Derrida, *Speech and Phenomena and Other Essays on Husserl's Theory of Signs*, Evanston, IL: Northwestern University Press, pp. xxxi–xlii.

Arens, Hans (1984), *Aristotle's Theory of Language and its Tradition: Texts from 500 to 1750*, Amsterdam and Philadelphia, PA: John Benjamins.

Aristotle (n.d.), *On Interpretation*, trans. E. M. Edghill, <http://classics.mit.edu/Aristotle/interpretation.html>.

Aubenque, Pierre (1962), *Le problème de l'être chez Aristotle: essai sur la problématique aristotélicienne*, Paris: Presses Universitaires de France.

Barthes, Roland (1969), *Elements of Semiology*, trans. Annette Lavers and Colin Smith, London: Jonathan Cape.

Barthes, Roland (1977), *Image Music Text*, trans. Stephen Heath, London: Fontana.

Bass, Alan (1978), 'Translator's introduction', in Jacques Derrida, *Writing and Difference*, Chicago, IL: University of Chicago Press, pp. ix–xx.

Bennington, Geoffrey and Jacques Derrida (1993), *Jacques Derrida*, trans. Geoffrey Bennington, Chicago, IL: University of Chicago Press.

Bennington, Geoffrey (2004), 'Saussure and Derrida', in Carol Sanders (ed.), *The Cambridge Companion to Saussure*, Cambridge: Cambridge University Press, pp. 186–202.

Bouissac, Paul (2004), 'Saussure's legacy in semiotics' in Carol Sanders (ed.), *The Cambridge Companion to Saussure*, Cambridge: Cambridge University Press, pp. 240–60.

Cavell, Stanley (1995), *Philosophical Passages: Wittgenstein, Emerson, Austin, Derrida*, Cambridge, MA and Oxford: Blackwell.

Chandler, Daniel (2001), *Semiotics for Beginners*, University of Aberdeen, 24 Sept. 2001 <http://aber.ac.uk/media/Documents/S4B/sem01.html>.

Condillac, Etienne Bonnot de (2001), *Essay on the Origin of Human Knowledge*, trans. Hans Aarsleff, Cambridge: Cambridge University Press.

Critchley, Simon (1992), *The Ethics of Deconstruction: Derrida and Levinas*, Oxford: Blackwell.

Culler, Jonathan (1975), *Structuralist Poetics: Structuralism, Linguistics and the Study of Literature*, Ithaca, NY: Cornell University Press.

Culler, Jonathan (1982), *On Deconstruction: Theory and Criticism after Structuralism*, London: Routledge.

Culler, Jonathan (1986), *Saussure*, revised edn, London: Fontana.

Culler, Jonathan (1988), *Framing the Sign*, Norman, OK: University of Oklahoma Press.

Culler, Jonathan (2003), 'L'essentiel de l'arbitraire', *Cahiers de l'Herne*, 76: 52–61. A revised version of this essay appears as 'The Sign: Saussure and Derrida on arbitrariness' in Jonathan Culler (2007), *The Literary in Theory*, Stanford, CA: Stanford University Press, pp. 117–36.

Deely, John (1990), *Basics of Semiotics*, Bloomington, IL: Indiana University Press.

Eco, Umberto (1976), *A Theory of Semiotics*, Bloomington, IL: Indiana University Press.

Eco, Umberto (1984), *Semiotics and the Philosophy of Language*, Basingstoke: Macmillan.

Eco, Umberto (1989), 'Denotation', in Umberto Eco and Constantino Marmo (eds), *On the Medieval Theory of Signs*, Amsterdam and Philadelphia, PA: John Benjamins, pp. 43–77.

Eco, Umberto, Roberto Lambertini, Constantino Marmo and Andrea Tabarroni (1989), 'On animal language in the medieval classification of signs', in Umberto Eco and Constantino Marmo (eds), *On the Medieval Theory of Signs*, Amsterdam and Philadelphia, PA: John Benjamins, pp. 3–41.

Feferman, Solomon (2006), Review of *Incompleteness: The Proof and Paradox of Kurt Gödel* by Rebecca Goldstein, *London Review of Books*, 28 (3): 30–2.

Freud, Sigmund (1953–75), *The Standard Edition of the Complete Psychological Works of Sigmund Freud*, ed. and trans. James Strachey, London: Hogarth Press, vols 1, 4 and 19.

Gadet, Françoise (1989), *Saussure and Contemporary Culture*, trans. Gregory Elliott, London: Hutchinson Radius.

Garver, Newton (1973), 'Preface', in Jacques Derrida, *Speech and Phenomena and Other Essays on Husserl's Theory of Signs*, Evanston, IL: Northwestern University Press, pp. ix–xxix.

Gasché, Rodolphe (1994), *Inventions of Difference: on Jacques Derrida*, Cambridge, MA: Harvard University Press.

Guiraud, Pierre (1975), *Semiology*, trans. George Gross, London: Routledge.

Harman, Gilbert (1998), 'Semiotics and the cinema: Metz and Wollen', in Leo Braudy and Marshall Cohen (eds), *Film Theory and Criticism: Introductory Readings*, 5th edn, Oxford: Oxford University Press, pp. 90–8.

Harris, Roy (1987), *Reading Saussure*, La Salle, IL: Open Court.

Harris, Roy (1995), *Signs of Writing*, London: Routledge.

Harris, Roy (2001), *Saussure and his Interpreters*, Edinburgh: Edinburgh University Press.

Husserl, Edmund (1970), *Logical Investigations*, trans. J. N. Findlay, London: Routledge, vol. 1.

Jakobson, Roman (1949), 'The phonemic and grammatical aspects of language in their interrelations', in *Proceedings of the Sixth International Congress of Linguists*, Paris: Librairie C. Klincksiek, pp. 5–18.

Jakobson, Roman (1963), *Essais de linguistique générale*, Paris: Éditions de Minuit, vol. 1.

Jakobson, Roman (1973), *Essais de linguistique générale*, Paris: Éditions de Minuit, vol. 2.

Macksey, Richard (1972), 'Concluding remarks', in Richard Macksey and Eugenio Donato (eds), *The Structuralist Controversy: The Languages of Criticism and the Sciences of Man*, Baltimore, MD and London: Johns Hopkins University Press, pp. 319–22.

Macksey, Richard and Eugenio Donato (1972a), 'Preface', in Richard Macksey and Eugenio Donato (eds), *The Structuralist Controversy: The Languages of Criticism and the Sciences of Man*, Baltimore, MD and London: Johns Hopkins University Press, pp. xv–xix.

Macksey, Richard and Eugenio Donato (1972b), 'The space between – 1971', in Richard Macksey and Eugenio Donato (eds), *The Structuralist Controversy: The Languages of Criticism and the Sciences of Man*, Baltimore, MD and London: Johns Hopkins University Press, pp. ix–xiii.

Manetti, Giovanni (1993), *Theories of the Sign in Classical Antiquity*, trans. Christine Richardson, Bloomington and Indianapolis, IN: Indiana University Press.

Maras, Steven (2002), 'A semiotics of the proxy', *Social Semiotics*, 12 (1): 115–29.

Meier-Oeser, Stephan (2003), 'Medieval semiotics', in Edward N. Zalta (ed.), *The Stanford Encyclopedia of Philosophy*, Winter 2003 edn, <http://plato.stanford.edu/archives/win2003/entries/semiotics-medieval>.

Normand, Claudine (2004), 'System, arbitrariness, value', in Carol Sanders (ed.), *The Cambridge Companion to Saussure*, Cambridge: Cambridge University Press, pp. 88–104.

Norris, Christopher (1987), *Derrida*, London: Fontana.

Ogden, C. K. and I. A. Richards (1927), *The Meaning of Meaning: A Study of the Influence of Language upon Thought and of the Science of Symbolism*, London: Kegan Paul, Trench, Trubner; New York: Harcourt, Brace.

Ortigues, Edmond (1962), *Le Discours et le symbole*, Paris: Aubier.

Peirce, Charles Sanders (1965), *Collected Papers*, ed. Charles Hartshorne and Paul Weiss, Cambridge, MA: Belknap Press of Harvard University Press.

Peuch, Christian (2004), 'Saussure and structuralist linguistics in Europe', in Carol Sanders (ed.), *The Cambridge Companion to Saussure*, Cambridge: Cambridge University Press, pp. 124–38.

Plato (2002), *Phaedrus*, trans. Robin Waterfield, Oxford: Oxford University Press.

Searle, John R. (1977), 'Reiterating the differences', *Glyph*, 1: 198–208.

Sebeok, Thomas A. (2001), *Signs: An Introduction to Semiotics*, 2nd edn, Toronto: University of Toronto Press.

Sless, David (1986), *In Search of Semiotics*, Beckenham, Kent: Croom Helm.

'Space' (1989), *Oxford English Dictionary*, 2nd edn, Oxford: Oxford University Press.

Spivak, Gayatri Chakravorty (1974), 'Translator's preface', in Jacques Derrida, *Of Grammatology*, trans. Gayatri Chakravorty Spivak, Baltimore, MD: Johns Hopkins University Press, pp. ix–lxxxvii.

Sturrock, John (1993), *Structuralism*, 2nd edn, London: Fontana.

Tabarroni, Andrea (1989), 'Mental signs and the theory of representation in Ockham', in Umberto Eco and Constantino Marmo (eds), *On the Medieval Theory of Signs*, Amsterdam and Philadelphia, PA: John Benjamins, pp. 195–224.

Tallis, Raymond (1995), *Not Saussure: A Critique of Post-Saussurean Literary Theory*, 2nd edn, Houndmills and London: Macmillan.

Weber, Samuel (1976), 'Saussure and the apparition of language: the critical perspective', *Modern Language Notes*, 91: 913–38.

Weber, Samuel (1978), 'It', *Glyph*, 4: 1–31.

Weber, Samuel (1991), *Return to Freud*, trans. Michael Levine, Cambridge: Cambridge University Press.

Wood, David and Robert Bernasconi (eds) (1988), 'The original discussion of "Différance"', in *Derrida and Différance*, Evanston, IL: Northwestern University Press, pp. 83–95.

Young, Robert (1981), *Untying the Text: A Post-Structuralist Reader*, London: Routledge and Kegan Paul.

Index

absence, 8, 13–15, 19, 27, 51, 55, 64–5, 89–91, 95–6, 105, 110, 123–8, 133–7, 145, 154–8, 163–9, 174
aliquid stat pro aliquo, 23, 30, 36, 86–93, 95–6, 164, 169
Allison, D., 35, 89, 177
  air and water, 105–7
  analogy, 46–9, 139
  chess game, 46, 139–41, 146
  fallen from the sky, 12, 130, 135–47, 159–60, 176, 180, 185
  Geneva-to-Paris train, 120–1
  sheet of paper, 46–9, 105, 177–8
antecedence, 47, 65, 135, 144, 150–70, 176, 181–2; *see also* priority
arbitrariness, 6, 25, 35, 38–40, 79–84, 92, 100–6, 117, 122, 132–42, 155, 173, 181
Arens, H., 28–9
Aristotle, 4–6, 11, 20–42, 53–4, 61, 64, 68–70, 96–8, 107, 137, 141, 145, 170, 175–9
articulation, 25, 40, 47–9, 67, 77–84, 98–100, 104–7, 116, 179, 185
Aubenque, P., 28–9
Augustine, St, 29–33, 53, 61
Austin, J. L., 2, 16, 180, 182
axiomatics, 17, 135, 145, 148, 152, 159–65, 170

Barthes, R., 1, 47, 99–100, 166–7, 185
Being, 5, 8, 19–22, 33, 64, 67, 112–13, 135, 149, 152–8, 162, 175, 183
Bennington, G., 62, 76–7, 89, 185

bipartition, 23–5, 37, 90, 94–7, 100, 106, 116, 178, 181
Bloomfield, L., 122–3

causality, 92, 134, 140–3, 148, 159, 171, 181
Cavell, S., 16, 176, 180, 186
classical metaphysics, 5–6, 10, 19–24, 32–3, 48–9, 57–68, 108, 112–13, 128, 134–5, 148–52, 161, 176
classical semiology, 1, 6, 9, 14, 17, 19–37, 40–4, 53, 61, 69, 71, 86, 93–100, 107–8, 130, 137, 143–5, 169, 174–80
communication, 9–14, 17, 35, 41, 44, 60, 64–9, 83, 86, 90–3, 99–100, 109–14, 123–30, 138, 175–6, 179, 186
  communication as transport, 10–13, 17, 21–2, 31, 44, 51, 57, 63–6, 84, 109–10, 126, 130, 175
community, 3, 60, 70–1, 88, 103, 113, 122, 126, 143, 150, 163, 169, 183–4
Condillac, E. B. de, 64–5, 84, 124, 136
consciousness, 4, 10, 14–15, 30, 35, 56, 67–9, 83, 96, 101–3, 112, 118–28, 147–58, 163–7, 170, 176, 181–3
context, 13–14, 104, 109–15, 121–8, 175
conventional signification, 5, 20–2, 28–9, 40, 79, 82, 91–2, 95, 100, 106
Culler, J., 84, 93, 102–3, 108, 119–21, 142–6, 182–5

deconstruction, 17, 48, 53, 59–61, 101–2, 106–7, 112, 128, 176, 179